TRANSFORMING TWISTED THINKING

Straight Thinkers Accept Responsibility

Jerry Price, MA

2BRealMen Publishers

2BRealMen Publishers
www.2BRealMen.com

© 2012 Jerry Price, MA. All rights reserved.

No part of this book may be reproduced, stored in a retrieval system, or transmitted by any means without the written permission of the author.

Unless otherwise indicated, Scripture quotations are from
The Holy Bible, New International Version (NIV)
© 1973, 1984 by International Bible Society, used by permission of Zondervan Publishing House

Other Scripture Quotations are from:

The Holy Bible, King James Version (KJV)

Holy Bible, New Living Translation (NLT)
© 1996. Used by permission of Tyndale House Publishers, Inc. All rights reserved.

Library of Congress Control Number: 2012909600

Printed in the United States of America

This book is printed on acid-free paper.

Certain stock imagery © Thinkstock.
Any people depicted in stock imagery provided by Thinkstock are models, and such images are being used for illustrative purposes only.

Because of the dynamic nature of the Internet, any web addresses or links contained in this book may have changed since publication and may no longer be valid.

What Others Are Saying

I find we all have a bit of twisted thinking within us. Some more than others. Jerry Price has hit the nail on the head with Transforming Twisted Thinking.

KEN RUETTGERS
Author of *Homefield Advantage* and former Green Bay Packer

Jerry Price has an uncanny ability to understand where and how we have walked away from God. From inmates to housewives to pro athletes Jerry has the ability to go to the core of one's thinking. TTT details how our individual thinking patterns drive our emotions and behaviors. Get ready to understand how you think and why you do what you do. This book has the potential to rock your world!

TOM ROY
Author of *Release* and President/Founder of UPI Inc.

When I sat down to read Twisted Thinking I thought I could better understand certain people and try to help them. What I found instead is that I am a Twisted Thinker! The good news is this book helped me to recognize how I could change my thought patterns to help straighten me out. I highly recommend this book, but let me warn you, get ready to take a good hard look at yourself!

TED BARRETT
Major League Umpire #65

Jerry Price gives his readers an opportunity to come face to face with who they are on the inside Reflection is a primary gift from Jerry as he entertains the reader through a wonderful process of learning.

JOE URCAVICH, PhD
Former Chaplain for the Green Bay Packers

I have relished the friendship of Jerry Price for virtually his entire adult life in Christian ministry. His is an uncompromising faith in Jesus Christ. His gifts include skilled bible teaching, human compassion, and inspired insight into human nature. Transforming Twisted Thinking is a distinctive, indispensible contribution to Christian and secular thought; skillfully written, thought provoking and like changing.

GORDON KELLY
Retired United Airline Pilot and National Senior Racquetball Champion

I loved the book. Transforming Twisted Thinking is helping me to become like the overcomer of Revelation 3:21

TERRY PRICE
Jerry's twin Brother, Chattanooga, Tennessee

Inevitably and rightly, the substance of a book of this nature is amenable to authentication. We can attest to the validity of what the author is teaching here. Our dear, wonderful, precious, talented and unconditionally loved son is the "Brian" mentioned in this book.

ANONYMOUS

CONTENTS

Foreword ix

Introduction xi

Chapter 1: The Same Mud 1
    Stirring It up and Sorting It Out

Chapter 2: Becoming a STAR 13
    A Straight Thinker Accepting Responsibility

Chapter 3: The Transformation Process 34
    Dealing with First Principles

Chapter 4: Closed Thinking 44
    The Invisible Man

Chapter 5: Martyred Thinking 64
    "I Blame You"

Chapter 6: Inflated Thinking 79
    Defining Good/Being Realistic

Chapter 7: Stubborn Thinking 95
    "I won't"

Chapter 8: Reckless Thinking 113
    "What's in it For Me?"

Chapter 9: Impatient Thinking 129
    Assumptions

Chapter 10: Fearful Thinking 145
    Being Balanced

Chapter 11: Manipulative Thinking 167
    Power Without Being Powerful

Chapter 12: Arrogant Thinking 185
    Blessed Are the Humble

Chapter 13: Possessive Thinking 200
    "I Own You"

Chapter 14: From Darkness to Dawn... 220
    Becoming a STAR Is Possible

Appendix A: Twisted Thinking Definitions 229

Appendix B: Going for the Big E!... 231

Appendix C: Pulling Everything Together 232

Appendix D: Discussion Study Guide 236

Appendix E: STAR Energizer Evaluation 243

Dedication

To Judy, my wife and faithful friend,

to our children
Jana, Nathan, and Melinda,

and to all who know what it is to live
with a man who is transforming
his twisted thinking.

FOREWORD

Restored. Rejuvenated. Renewed.

Each of these words communicates the possibility of a brand new start. And yet the challenge of restoring health and balance to a human life sometimes seems insurmountable. It's one thing to talk about restoring an antique dresser, or renewing the shine of an old car, but what about rejuvenating a living person?

Deeply entrenched patterns of behavior can be almost immune to change. Long-established habits can seem utterly impossible to transform, even when they can destroy the people we care about the most.

That's the dilemma faced by twisted thinkers. The longing for healthy relationships is motivating and real, but the risk involved in abandoning familiar ways of thinking is often scarier still. That's why we literally paralyze ourselves, unable to bring about a future any different from *what we've grown accustomed to*. The ruts get deeper and the promise of renewal becomes more fleeting every day.

Yet it doesn't have to be that way. This book is about hope. It echoes the message that the Apostle Paul communicated to his friends in Romans 12:2, when he told them that true transformation comes through the renewal of the mind.

The pages ahead will help you explore a whole new way of thinking about the world and the people you share that world with. Better still, the material in this book is proven and practical. Every principle has been carefully processed in the "life laboratory" of the author. That gives his words an integrity you will vastly appreciate as you immerse yourself in these radical but deeply rooted principles. They have all been tested, verified, and successfully applied in the real world. I encourage you to accept them as a gift.

And by the way . . . when you read a book like this it's easy to make all kinds of third-person applications. "My husband could sure use a dose of this." "There's the pattern I see in my son; now I understand him." "I never realized how twisted my mom's thinking really was."

You are certainly encouraged to use this material to understand more fully the behaviors of the people around you, but don't put this book down until you've honestly examined some of the patterns in your own life. Twisted thinking is a universal reality. Every one of us is touched by the curse of sin, and it often expresses itself in the way we think. That means there's something in these pages for every reader.

Straightened thinking means strengthened relationships. I know you'll benefit from finding that connection in this book.

Marv Penner, D.Phil
National Director of Youth Specialties, Canada
Associate Staff Member, Center for Parent/Youth Understanding

INTRODUCTION

In forty-four years of ministry and counseling I've seen communities, marriages, and families disconnected and devastated by what I call *twisted thinking*. It's a style of thinking that takes many forms, all of which share one common trait.

They all desperately need transformation. Genuine hope for the kind of clarity and contentment that God intends for us to have in our relationships isn't possible without transforming our thinking patterns.

That's why I wrote this book—to help readers recognize and correct the missteps in their lives that arise from twisted thinking and the chaos it creates.

Let me show you how insidious twisted thinking can be. At a picnic, a man saw a wasp eating jam on his plate and decided to cut him in half. What he did was actually quite cruel, but the wasp paid no attention and continued with his feast. Only when he tried to fly away did he have to deal with what had happened.

Now, I'm not trying to be gruesome but people involved in twisted thinking can be like that disengaged wasp. We focus on our own agendas and become so insensitive to the world around us that we almost seem to be living in self-created cocoons. Only when we try to "fly away" to the next feast do we realize that we've become disconnected from other people, from our own humanity, and from the Creator Himself.

And almost no one escapes. We've all been affected by events brought about by twisted thinking. Often they provide blatant, mind-boggling examples of how self-indulgent people disconnect from their basic responsibilities as caring human beings. They also catalog the loss of one of the most valued character traits necessary for building solid and secure communities. It's called *conscience*.

The Apostle Paul challenged a young man named Timothy to understand how that can happen. He talked about individuals who abandoned their faith to embrace deceiving spirits and things taught by demons. Getting what they wanted mattered more than almost anything else and they were being encouraged to think that way by some of the people they respected most!

Paul said that such teachings come from hypocritical liars whose consciences have been seared, "as with a hot iron" (1 Timothy 4:2). This book explains how the modern conscience can be seared as well, and how that can be overcome.

Sadly, we also communicate our own twisted thinking to our children. We don't have to teach them to do what's wrong because they'll do that by default. Instead, we need to educate our children on how to live positively, *on purpose*, by having respect for themselves and for others.

In his letter to the Ephesians, Paul talks about mankind's mind being naturally bent in understanding. That's how we separate ourselves from the responsible way of living, and from heaven's way of loving. The biblical passage below refers to this as the *futility of thinking*, because humanity has a darkened mind without Christ.

> From him the whole body, joined and held together by every supporting ligament, grows and builds itself up in love, as each part does its work. So I tell you this, and insist on it in the Lord, that you must no longer live as the Gentiles do, *in the futility of their thinking*. They are darkened in their understanding and separated from the life of God because of the ignorance that is in them due to the hardening of their hearts. (Ephesians 4:16-18, emphasis added)

As the last two verses in the above passage demonstrate, habitual irresponsibility is a real possibility for all of us. Yet verse 16 clearly tells us how our relationships with others should work!

However, unless we understand the thinking behind our own choices to be irresponsible—and the choices that others also make—we'll remain confused, controlled, and unable to free ourselves from the futility that Paul mentioned.

In this book I want to challenge you to examine *ten twisted thinking patterns* that are almost always behind the typical behaviors of people who hurt others. Can conscience be recovered? Can relationships be restored? Can we be open and honest with each other? The answer is yes, but only if we know *how, where,* and *why* the disconnections occur.

Otherwise, our society will continue to be like the jam on which twisted thinkers will feed, even as they remain unaware of their own brokenness.

Jerry Price, M.A.

Chapter One

THE SAME MUD

Stirring It up and Sorting It Out

As he climbed into a basement window of the Varsity Club in downtown Indianapolis, the would-be burglar knew he couldn't miss. He knew the night watchman had been fired. The squad car had just made its hourly patrol and the coast was clear. This robbery would be a lead-pipe cinch.

Unfortunately, as he was about make a six-foot drop onto the floor, a newly hired night watchman blinded him with a powerful flashlight and shouted, "Stop dead in your tracks, buddy, or I'll let you have it right where you are!"

Caught off guard, the burglar shouted back, "You and who else?" Then, as he turned back toward the window he suddenly heard a whip-like cracking sound. Instantly he felt a sharp pain in his side and fell all the way to the floor below.

The bullet missed his heart by an eighth of an inch, collapsed one lung, and came to rest on top of his spine. When he arrived at the hospital the doctors gave him only four hours to live.

On November 2, 1946, the night this happened, the man should have been home celebrating his wedding anniversary. But the next day, an early morning newspaper screamed out the headline: "Father of Thirty-Day-Old Twins Shot Down on the North Side." As one of those twins I had no idea that this headline would herald the beginning of my own spiritual journey.

A Beginning Point

Eleven blood transfusions later, after my father recovered, the judge sentenced him to one year of hard labor at the Indiana State Prison Farm. While he was there a miracle happened. During a prison chapel service, while a blind girl sang "No One Ever Cared for Me Like Jesus," my father stumbled down the aisle, praying all the way.

"O God, swim, sink, or die, it's all the way with you!" From that moment on, the passion of my father's life involved sharing the Good News and giving hope to anyone who had ears to hear. Dad told his story thousands of times and continually worked on renewing his mind, dismayed and disgusted by the pain he had caused others through a prior life of crime.

The irresistible force of God's love changed him. Released from prison and coming home as a forgiven man, he found himself freed him from the enslavement of an irresponsible lifestyle. From then on he no longer embraced the kind of the twisted thinking that almost destroyed him in the past. He recovered his conscience and made things right.

But even though my father's life turned completely around, the same sad process by which he once controlled his relationships to achieve immediate satisfaction is no less common today. The same twisted ways of thinking reinforce unloving, irresponsible, and often illegal behaviors just as much as ever.

Yet it doesn't have to be that way for you. I want to show you how transforming twisted thinking must play a major part in the redemption and restoration of every twisted thinker. Without transformation it's impossible to become a STAR—A Straight Thinker Accepting Responsibility. Let me begin by explaining how I've come to understand the whole dynamic.

A Personal Reflection

My father's fresh beginning helped our family embark in a new direction, much like a lighthouse does for ships in distress.

Granted, in leaving his past behind he faced a lot of struggles that created pain within our family. He wasn't perfect, but then—neither were we. Some of the same thinking that can bruise or damage any family was just as much a part of mine during those growing up years. Yet the power of God's love held our family together in spite of the storms.

Meanwhile, I faced my own conflicts as a youth. Although ours became a Christian home, I made choices by using the same poor reasoning my father had employed in his pre-Christian days. At times I consciously developed bad habits in attempts to twist or manipulate relationships. Most people saw my behavior as a part of growing up, but my thinking errors were becoming ingrained in all their subtlety.

I remember playing in a little league baseball game with my twin brother. He was the pitcher and I was the catcher. The field didn't have lights and darkness was falling. In the last inning, the umpire threw in a brand new baseball for my brother to pitch to the next batter. Our team was ahead but the game was on the line. So, when I caught Terry's next pitch I purposely dropped the ball and rubbed it in the dirt. Because a dirty ball would be harder to see, I hoped that slick move would give us an edge.

The umpire caught me and reprimanded me in front of everyone, including my mother. Did I consider what my teammates might think? No! Did I think about how the batter could be seriously injured? No! Did I care? No! Did I think I would get caught breaking the rules? Absolutely Not!

And beyond all that, did I think about how my actions might humiliate my mother? No, I didn't. The only thing on my mind was winning the game, any way I could. In hindsight, if I'd known what I know now about the pain my thinking and my actions caused others, I believe it could have been averted.

Caught By Surprise

By the time I hit little-league age I was already becoming a twisted thinker, but I concealed it by being funny and nice—at least on the outside. I became comfortable at hiding the real me. One way I could hide was to bask in the limelight of my father's testimony. It was a love-hate thing. I didn't like being known as a preacher's kid but I loved the moment in the story in which he'd talk about his twin boys.

Looking back, I realize that I basked in the attention because I longed to feel important. But much of that also happened because I wanted a better relationship with my father, who was gone a great deal as an evangelist. Yet another part of me used the attention to "manage" what other people thought of me.

Many times I'd go with dad to prisons, jails, or churches and hear him preach about Christ's love for everyone. The family also spent a lot of time at rescue missions, where he was the superintendent. God used many of those occasions to touch my heart with a desire to know His Son. But He was also beginning a process whereby He would catch me in my own twisted thought patterns—a process of which I was blissfully unaware.

After high school I attended the Grand Rapids School of the Bible and Music in Michigan. My agenda was to play basketball and study the Bible, pretty much in that order. Frankly, I enjoyed being on a championship team during the four years I competed (no bragging here, eh!).

I remember finding ways to beat the system without being caught by the referees. I also had an unspoken rule that it was okay to use psyche jobs whether I talked trash to opposing players, or incensed them with other methods. Since then it has become more and more clear to me that my twisted thinking patterns were truly deep-seated. Even though I didn't realize how they were affecting my life, they followed me into my marriage.

Judy and I had three children by the time I began studies for a Masters of Biblical Counseling at Grace Seminary in Winona Lake, Indiana. On May 17, 1985, while at the seminary, I got a devastating call from my mother.

Losing My Father

My father had died. He was only fifty-nine. I was stunned. My dreams of joining in ministry with him were shattered. It was especially difficult to move beyond the loss because I was angry with God for taking him. What I didn't realize was how my anger further compounded issues that were already tangling up my marriage.

In seminary, so much was uncovered about my failure to love Judy and the kids. That year became a life-changing experience for all of us. I found myself trying to figure out what it meant to be a man, at age 38.

After graduation I still had a longing to be "re-fathered" but kept the thought private, wondering how God could do it. Judy seemed to enjoy the new tone I was setting in our home. After Grace we headed to Wisconsin, where it became apparent that God, like the good father he is, was preparing me for something I had never even dreamed about.

One day, while reading the employment ads I saw a job opening at the Social Services Department in Sheboygan, Wisconsin. It involved treating the county's criminal population by addressing errors in the thinking behind their criminal activities. One of my first thoughts was: "I have a pretty good grasp on how criminals and alcoholics think, simply because I've heard my father's story over and over. I understand them."

Do you get any sense of my arrogance at that point in my life, via the "I understand them" remark?

I also believed being around relatives who had legal problems and struggled with alcoholism qualified me. I also thought being a rescue mission director's kid further prepared me. I'd seen plenty of individuals burdened by drinking and the criminal life style. And finally, by participating with my father in prison ministries I'd developed a certain comfort zone about being where men were locked up. With all the above in mind I applied for the position.

And Then They Hired Me!

For an office I was given an interrogation room at the jail. My supervisor thought this workspace was ideal for identifying with the inmates and gaining the jailor's respect. I felt like Jonah because being in that room felt like being inside a whale. Even though I could leave whenever I wanted, when the jailors locked me in the six-by-eight-foot room I could get out only by entering the cellblock on that side of the jail, after pushing a button to call a guard to come and get me.

Nonetheless, during the next three months I spent my in-whale time designing a program for treating the inmate's thinking errors. I studied writings on the criminal mind by Drs. Stanton E. Samenow and Sam Yochelson, which helped me immensely. For additional training, Social Services would also send me to observe programs for other prison populations in Wisconsin, even though those programs weren't designed for a county jail having inmates with shorter sentences.

Meanwhile, I soon began to realize why I knew the minds of these inmates so well. It had nothing to do with the reasons I've already mentioned. On a deeper level, God revealed to me that I had an attitude like theirs. I demanded absolute control over my world, and look out if you tried to challenge me!

When this attitude hooks up with twisted thinking it always leads to irresponsible decision-making, habitually irresponsible behaviors, and a loss of conscience. Although that thinking hadn't been a part of my daily life I'd occasionally binge on it, leaving others in pain. As I mentioned before, I was hiding my ugliness behind the veneer of a nice Christian guy.

But that veneer really wasn't very thick, and soon a deepening sense of disgust at the thought of hurting God and other people began to weigh heavily on me. I was also surprised by the root problem in my own thinking—one that I had never fully recognized even though my personal growth at Grace Seminary had been significant.

I wasn't a menace to society. I wasn't thinking about breaking the law, and I wasn't abusing drugs. But I *was* involved in avoidance. When certain comfort levels were disrupted I found ways to avoid being a responsible husband and father. When this happens it doesn't matter whether there's criminal behavior or not, because the need for transforming twisted thinking is just as real. Damage is damage whenever it keeps anyone from being open, honest, and connected to God and others.

So, in the privacy of the office I was caught in my own searchlight. Studying the material and setting up the program at the jail exposed many of my own strategies for avoiding responsibility. Those strategies amounted to nothing more than a game of "deflection," or what my father called "lickety-split" in his prison ministries.

Lickety-Split

My father used the term *lickety-split* to explain a prison inmate's avoidance strategies. It describes how a rabbit takes a hunter on a wild chase. The game then involves running in circles until the hunter eventually loses his ability to track the rabbit and ends up with nothing.

Inmates typically play the game when people try to hold them accountable. They'll keep you going in circles until the rabbit/inmate wins! Staying in control of forbidden agendas is the prize, while remaining unaccountable is the method by which they win it—and also a secondary part of the main prize itself. Either way, the circles they run to avoid detection can be intellectual, verbal, emotional, psychological, or even spiritual lickety-splits.

When he was talking to inmates my dad would often expose their games before they even had time to run. I was amazed at how quickly he'd figure out what the prisoner was really saying. This usually happened when he spoke about their need to have a personal relationship with Jesus Christ. They'd try to run him in circles to avoid the subject, but they rarely won.

On one occasion I heard an inmate say to my father, "I've got a lot of rabbit in me. I don't need this Jesus stuff."

At the time it seemed like they were talking in some jailhouse code, but it soon became clear that dad was trying to convince the man not to make a prison break. Maybe the inmate thought my dad was just some preacher who wouldn't understand the way he used the term "rabbit." But my father knew because he had also been planning to make a prison break on the very day the miracle happened for him.

After all those years the prison vocabulary hadn't changed. Lickety-split can be played many ways, and even though I first heard the term via my father's prison ministry, the game can be played by anyone—not just inmates but by all of us, young and old alike.

A Granddaughter's Game

Graciana is our granddaughter. Some years ago, at age three, she decided to play with my laptop computer. The screen saver on the computer was a cyber cat named Felix, who appeared as I worked. This cat would look at me in a variety of ways, but most often he'd act curious and cute. I'd almost want to reach out and touch him but resisted the impulse, because the computer screen was made with liquid gel and was very expensive to replace.

On the day all this happened, when I walked into the room I noticed that Graciana acted surprised. I didn't realize that I'd almost caught her at something because she smiled at me and batted those big brown eyes.

"Graci, you can sit there and look at Felix as long as you don't touch the screen."

"OK, Papa."

It all sounded innocent, but later in the day I realized that Graci had been playing her own game of lickety-split. On the screen were circles drawn by a blue ballpoint pen, as if something had been traced. Graci was busted! She had chased Felix with a pen and had followed him all over my computer screen.

I figured out the caper had already been committed when I warned her not to touch the screen. Hence, the surprised look on her face as I entered the room.

Immediately I yelled for Graci. I then told her how disappointed I was to see her artwork all over my computer screen. She immediately dropped her head, said she was sorry, and asked me to forgive her.

Yes, a three-year-old put that concept together! However, I chose to go deeper and stated my real disappointment.

"Graciana, you didn't tell Papa what you had done after I told you not to touch the screen." I realize we're talking about a three-year-old, but I thought, "Why not go there; she's a bright child."

Then it happened! Graci began playing another game of lickety-split. She batted her eyes just like she had when I caught her the first time. She began making funny faces and I had a hard time not laughing. Clearly, my granddaughter was uncomfortable and was trying to direct the conversation elsewhere. The rabbit was loose!

Remember, according to the game, if I chase the rabbit I lose the ability to track and catch him. No way would I fall for those big brown eyes the second time! Melting in front of her and letting things go would have encouraged her to escape accountability.

"Graci, I can see that you don't like what I'm saying. I think you are batting your eyes and making faces at me so you don't have to feel sad. You don't want to hear how keeping the truth from me hurt your Papa." Graci shook her head up and down in agreement.

This was scary stuff. If I had fallen for Graci's seduction, although Graci didn't know it as that, I would have endorsed the masking of her true thoughts when she batted her eyes and made faces. She was feeling bad about lying, but somehow she knew that if she could keep those bad feelings a secret she could play the same game of avoiding responsibility that I used to play.

If I had ignored the game and humored my granddaughter, I believe our relationship would have broken down. It might not have looked that way on the outside but it would on the inside, subtle as the change might have been.

After I held Graci accountable she took ownership of her behavior. It felt great to be real with each other, again.

I'm telling you this story because I want you to know that transforming twisted thinking is not just about irresponsible people making wrong choices. It's about how any person can subtly demand control of their world, to keep their sins hidden. And, how they twist relationships in the process. Even our children can do this.

Lickety-split is the same game some of the Pharisees played in Jesus' day, but they played it in an overt and sometimes violent manner. They were guilty of murdering Him relationally, and then literally giving orders to crucify Him. They hid behind their masks of religiosity.

Their mindset originated in a dark place, and it's a place where all of us have been at some point. Or will be. And once we've entered, the only way to get out and stay out is to get right with God and right with man.

Masks

Have you ever played lickety-split while concealing your motives with a mask? I remember a time in the mid-sixties when one of my masks fell away and exposed me.

Before we were married, Judy and I were students at the Grand Rapids School of the Bible and Music. One day we were sitting together on a staircase in front of the cafeteria doors. I remember feeling pretty good about myself for getting someone else—mostly in secret—to do major parts of a project for one of my classes. Then pride took over, my mask fell away, and I told Judy what a cool thing I had done (although I doubt that I used the word "cool" because it hadn't been invented yet).

Instantly she voiced her disapproval, at which point I got up from that step, stomped over to the wall, and punched it so hard I cracked it. Meanwhile, the message I sent to Judy was, "You have no right to hold me accountable or disapprove of anything I do!"

At the same time I justified my thinking by feeling hurt, which is another avoidance strategy common to the lickety-split game.

That decision also put a crack in our relationship, which wasn't addressed until long after we were married. In fact, our relationship was broken the moment I hit the wall, literally, but I didn't think about that. This episode taught Judy to be afraid of me—"Don't disapprove or I'll hit you next." That wasn't my actual thought, but when I look back I see that as the actual message.

The memory of that time still haunts me. I had gone to a dark place in my soul, and in the process I seared my own conscience. Judy has since forgiven me but that still doesn't diminish the damage I was responsible for.

Change for me resides in remembering that truth. It keeps me from being trapped by thinking that a change in behavior is all a person needs to get on in life. Unfortunately, you don't fix the house you just burned down by throwing away the match.

In contrast, I've found that most people focus on overt behaviors to determine if changes in their lives have taken place. At one time I also operated under the same assumption—"If it looks like someone has changed, they have." But as I worked with inmates the truth of an old cliché became extremely real to me.

"It takes one to know one."

I Was No Different

Working with the inmates made me look in the mirror and realize that I was made of the same mud. I was trapped by my own awareness, and I had to address the hardness in my own soul just like the inmates had to do. In the process I finally confronted the fundamental, bedrock truth on which all my personal progress, all my counseling sessions, and all my efforts to communicate what God has revealed to me have rested ever since.

Genuine transformation begins with our relationship to God. It starts when we change our thinking about Him, recognize who He truly is, accept His forgiveness, and commit ourselves to a life of fellowship and obedience.

But notice the sequence. *We have to change our thinking first!* We can't enter into a genuine relationship with God until we give up our false notions, abandon our false motives, drop all our false pretenses, and initiate a straight-across connection in which no pretense of any kind whatsoever is allowed. No more static on the lines!

But what so many of us don't seem to realize is that the bedrock dynamic for static-free interactions with other people starts in exactly the same way. Again—␣we *have to transform our thinking first.*

The only difference is how we have to do it largely on our own when our "relationship partner" is another person. God often provides incredible insights and powerful supports along the way, but we have to be willing to examine ourselves on a human level first. Only then can we truly "own" the changes in our thinking patterns that then allow us to develop static-free relationships with other people.

At least from our own perspective, for we must never expect other people to be completely godlike in their reactions to us!

Strangely, the time I spent in that Sheboygan jail became one of the most creative, soul-changing periods in my own life, and in my family as well. We all began to face one another openly and honestly. We became real people—"our own persons"—instead of wearing masks.

A few years later, a phrase from a novel called *The Enquiry*, by Dick Francis, began jumping out at me. A man falling in love with a woman who was struggling to become her own person said, "Fetters of the mind are iron bars in the soul."

The context of that novel wasn't twisted thinking, but it did reveal what I was discovering about twisted thinking. It truly is a fetter of the mind. It's what every human being suffers from. Joy is available, but first we have to take off our masks and come out from behind our own iron bars.

I Know About Hope

In Ezekiel 18:23, God says:

> "Do I take any pleasure in the death of the wicked," declares the Sovereign LORD. Rather, am I not pleased when they turn from their ways and live?"

There's hope. I know, because my father turned from his forbidden ways. As he put it, he "took a leap into the light." God was pleased and so was society. No longer would he cost the state of Indiana big money.

Something marvelous happens when twisted thinkers leap into the light.

Chapter Two

BECOMING A STAR

A Straight Thinker Accepting Responsibility

In *Dangerous Wonder: The Adventure of Childlike Faith* by Michael Yaconelli, the author shared his desire for the reader to feel a stirring of childlike qualities within himself: realness, curiosity, abandon, passion, and wonder. Such qualities are the source of life itself.

The author wanted the fire of Jesus' presence to fill every one of the reader's waking moments with passion and adventure. He offered story after story of children demonstrating the natural, profound joy of asking questions, not necessarily to get answers but to have relationships.

The author moved my heart toward being childlike with God, yet I feel sadness for what's going on in the hearts of some children today. Childhood innocence is disappearing. People are dying because some youngsters have lost their consciences and act on irresponsible fantasies. Meanwhile, society spends billions of dollars trying to find answers. I applaud the efforts but I believe we are missing the mark in many cases.

Something is seriously wrong! It seems that we are spending more time trying to get kids to *change* their behavior rather than trying to understand the thinking *behind* that behavior and *dealing proactively* with *that*. On the contrary, we seem to believe if we work with kids from an intellectual perspective and "teach" them *via their minds* how to behave, they will automatically do so.

But that doesn't change the hearts and souls of kids who are not STARs. It doesn't work with anyone, unless something has changed on the inside first. Twisted thinkers won't ask questions so they can build responsible relationships. They're not interested in building responsible patterns of behavior and becoming what we used to call "good, responsible citizens."

Instead, they ask questions for one reason only: to get the answers that serve their own particular desires. So . . . how can a *twisted thinker* become a STAR? To find the answers, let's begin by going back to where it all started.

In Paradise

Chapter 3 of the book of Genesis, in the story of Adam and Eve's fall, gives an account of good people gone bad. The whole idea behind Satan's success in tempting them was getting them both to believe that God is a liar. And they did!

There's a part of me that wants to say what young people say when adults don't get it. "Well, duh! Adam, you had it made! How come you didn't get that?" However, I'm not trying to point a finger at Adam but I'm certainly feeling a profound sadness over what he did, because we're all made of the same mud.

One of Adam's tasks involved leadership. All good leaders take responsibility for their decisions, as Adam did when he named the animals. After completing that job he took a nap. Then he woke up and met the woman God had created for him.

Up to that point, although Adam's work was good it couldn't provide the deeper joy and satisfaction that God wanted him to have. That could only develop out of a two-way relationship with someone who could complete him even as he completed her. Even so, the original God/Adam/Eve relationship gave us an even more beautiful picture of how most of mankind can only be fully complete via three-way relationships, with God in the first position.

Lucifer began by convincing Adam and Eve that God had cheated them both. Then, in his secret thoughts, Adam chose to let Eve test the fruit. Scripture doesn't record his saying anything to stop or to protect her.

What seems so diabolical about this story, apart from man's rebellion against a loving, compassionate God, is how Adam, was willing to twist and waste his wife. The stakes were high: death. Eve never saw it coming until she heard her man say to God, "It's the woman you gave me" (Adam's game of lickety-split).

Only then was she able to make sense out of what he had done. I can imagine the questions racing through Eve's mind. Over the years, I've heard similar ones in marriage counseling.

"Adam, did you decide God was a liar before I took the fruit? Did you then decide to sacrifice me to a sure death? How could you abandon me for your own advantage? Where was your conscience?"

Notice that this all happened suddenly. There's no place outside of Adam's heart and mind to determine the cause for this. It's the most mind-boggling moment in history. I mean, until that moment they were in paradise!

THE FIRST MANIPULATOR

Eve heard Adam deny responsibility, minimize his own behavior, and then blame both her and God for his actions. She was created to help Adam, and now he breaks her heart. How could she trust him anymore? Eve was left out on a limb to take the fall.

We can only imagine what she was thinking at that point. "There's no way to feel safe or be secure with this jerk! He's the only man on the planet and I'm stuck with him." Therefore, the question Eve would eventually have to answer would be: "How can I stop being vulnerable to this man so I can feel secure?"

Adam's twisting of Eve and God, to gain personal advantage and satisfaction, became a full-blown relational catastrophe. He was responsible for embracing an unwritten rule that has plagued mankind ever since: *It's perfectly natural and acceptable to manipulate relationships for personal survival without being accountable to God or anyone else.* Thus "By one man sin entered into the world, and death by sin; and so death passed upon all men, for all have sinned" (Romans 5:12, KJV).

If Eve had been living by that rule then she alone would have been responsible for choosing how she would respond, and not Adam. But sin had first entered the world already, through the mind of Adam. Technically Eve was still in the sinless position.

However, the words "for all have sinned" (Romans 3:23) indicate that Eve decided to play by Adam's rule (see above), and the devastation of family structure began. As they say in law enforcement, three out of the first four family members in Genesis "had a record." Indeed, once Cain killed Abel that effectively winnowed the family back down to the guilty ones only!

I'm troubled when I read the Bible describing how the first broken relationship on the planet started—in the secrecy of a person's mind and in the privacy of his home. Maybe it bothers me because I'm reminded that we're all made of the same mud. Or, maybe it's because I'm reminded what I see isn't necessarily what I get, and that can be scary.

Can conscience really be recovered? Can twisted thinking really be transformed? Where's the hope in restoring this mess? Those are the questions that pushed and pushed at me until I began to find the answers I've included in this book.

WE NEED A TOOLBOX

Technology helps us find core problems that affect our physical bodies. We now have X-ray machines, telescopic surgeries, computer programs, and many other sophisticated resources that enable the medical experts to diagnose most of our illnesses and identify potential cures.

But what about the *soul* issues that twist and turn inside our heads, thereby ruining individuals, marriages, and whole families? Unfortunately, the tools I want to suggest, for becoming a STAR, tend to trouble our culture—maybe even our Christian culture. Why? Because they call for commitment to a struggle most people shy away from.

Even Christians have a tendency to act independently of God, by relying only on what can be seen or measured. We're used to observing things as solid as the ground we walk on, until we feel ourselves sinking into quicksand. Then, before anyone can help, we go under even as we continue to grab for what is visible. Finally, with one hand above the surface and the quicksand pressing all around, we feel a stick being pushed into our fingers and we hold on for dear life. Only when we are pulled out do we then understand that being independent and relying only on what we can see could have killed us.

We all struggle with depending on a God who can't be brought into view via the human eye. Choosing to be dependent on what we can see or feel is much easier. And yet, in our modern society, most people are helpless to control another thing that is also very difficult to see—sometimes even more so than the actual "hand" of God.

I'm talking about the *intent of another person's heart*. And in either case, like it or not we are forced to deal with the unseen for what it is—something very real.

How often have we heard of tragedies in which people have taken other lives arbitrarily—even murderers who are children? Again and again we say, "We never saw it coming." Then what are some available tools for helping twisted thinkers become STARs so they can be humanly connected; so broken relationships can be restored; so children aren't perpetrating horrible tragedies?

Using sheer self-discipline won't get the job done. There are very disciplined people out there, many of whom are Christians, and they can't seem to stay on track. Even praying more and behaving better won't get the job done.

Nonetheless, I believe there's hope. However, before sharing what I believe are the most basic tools, I first want to offer two assets that God provides to encourage success in changing twisted thinking. To use a well understood but decidedly non-academic term, these will help us "get our heads on straight."

The first asset is *confidence* and the second asset is *wisdom*.

A Sense of Confidence

No major undertaking in life can be accomplished without a sense of confidence backing up the effort. In 2 Chronicles 32, an Assyrian King laid siege to Jerusalem. The Israelite king, Hezekiah, consulted with his officials and his military staff about a strategy for resisting the Assyrians. Water was blocked off from springs outside the city and diverted inside through underground tunnels. Broken sections of the wall were repaired, towers were built, and more weapons were made.

Hezekiah also appointed military officials to encourage the people to be strong, courageous, and unafraid even though they were outnumbered by the enemy. His message was relentlessly positive. Here is how verses 7 and 8 put it:

He appointed military officers over the people and assembled them before him in the square at the city gate and encouraged them with these words: "Be strong and courageous. Do not be afraid or discouraged because of the king of Assyria and the vast army with him, for there is a greater power with us than with him. With him is only the arm of flesh, but with us is the LORD our God to help us and to fight our battles." And the people gained confidence from what Hezekiah the king of Judah said.

Verse 21 then tells us how all this ended:

And the LORD sent an angel, who annihilated all the fighting men and the commanders and officers in the camp of the Assyrian king.

None of that could have happened if Hezekiah and the people of Israel had not had limitless confidence in God. As Proverbs 3:26 states, "For the Lord will be your confidence and will keep your foot from being snared."

Where Does It Come From?

The confidence of which I speak comes not only from knowing the dynamics behind twisted thinking, but also in knowing that God can straighten them out. Throughout Scripture, God gives confidence to individuals who walk upright and trust Him. Therefore, if we're going to deal with the darkness of twisted thinking, and if we're going to try to help bring about changes in the twisted thinker—or even in our own lives—we'll need a sense of confidence that can only come from being on the right track.

Ultimately, God's involvement will reveal the unseen world of the twisted thinker's heart and soul, and will give us understanding of how we can help. I believe that's why Jesus talks about the unseen world in the deeper parts of man, which He called the heart's intent. He was showing the way to the transformation that provides the second asset to encourage success in changing twisted thinking.

To Know the Intent Of the Heart

In Matthew 22:15-22, the Lord confirms that it's humanly possible to know the intent of people's hearts. Hear Him cutting to the chase with a group of Pharisees.

> Then the Pharisees went out and laid plans to trap him in his words. They sent their disciples to him along with the Herodians. "Teacher," they said, "we know that you are a man of integrity and that you teach the way of God in accordance with the truth. You aren't swayed by others, because you pay no attention to who they are. Tell us then, what is your opinion? Is it right to pay the imperial tax to Caesar or not?" But Jesus, *knowing their evil intent*, said, "You hypocrites, why are you trying to trap me? Show me the coin used for paying the tax." They brought him a denarius, and he asked them, "Whose image is this? And whose inscription?" "Caesar's," they replied. Then he said to them, "So give back to Caesar what is Caesar's, and to God what is God's." When they heard this, they were amazed. So they left him and went away. (emphasis added)

Jesus saw their evil intent by looking at the agenda behind their questions. He saw their depravity. He went below, into their personal infrastructure, and knew where they were heading. No one escapes God's ability to see the unseen. Adam didn't escape. These Pharisees didn't escape. I can't escape, and neither can you!

Now, some of you might be saying, "But Jesus is Jesus. We're not like him. He's God. He knows what we don't know." All this is true, yet God has given us information in the Bible so that we can know and discern the evil intents of a twisted thinker.

This is very important to grasp. *There is no hope for a deep, lasting transformation of twisted thinking—no hope for a recovering of conscience—unless the point of entry is into the dark, private place where we all struggle—the intents of the heart.*

Jesus was confident about that, and we can be too. Any tool used for changing twisted thinking means nothing unless we can get all the way there. The good news is that we can, because the light of life leads the way. That's why there's hope even though this part of the journey can take us into unfamiliar territory.

One Of These Days

As a kid, I remember watching a television show called *The Honeymooners*. Jackie Gleason played a big, loud, arrogant bus driver named Ralph, who tried to dominate his marriage with Alice. The bantering seemed funny, yet in hindsight it was actually abusive.

During the 1953 Christmas special, Ralph got into a typical noisy battle with Alice about going to the store and getting some potato salad. (He certainly didn't have a servant's heart.) Finally Ralph gave in, and while he ran the errand his friend Norton brought people to Ralph's apartment to entertain Alice and his wife.

It was a happy time. Alice said it was the best Christmas she ever had. Norton's genuineness kept coming through—he was a man willing to care for others. He was also my favorite personality on the show because his unpretentious relational style had a redemptive quality.

Norton's job of going into sewer tunnels and making repairs is a good picture of the work involved with transforming twisted thinking. It calls for someone to go down a spiritual and relational manhole to encounter a tunnel system in a person's heart—the places where relationships break.

Discovering what's down there is disturbing because we begin the journey by going into the heart of every child—a place almost no one would think to look. I'm not diminishing the idea of our children's innocence or the joy of raising them, but there is a need to reflect upon the "dark window" in every soul.

Signs of Life

Bob Lenz, the director of Life Promotions in Appleton, Wisconsin, once sent me a newsletter called "Signs of Life." In it he talked about all the awesome things going on in his ministry as a speaker for public school assemblies. A portion of his letter supported the idea of looking into the dark window of every child's soul. Listen as Bob shared what a school principal said about reaching troubled kids.

> I begin to replay the principal's words in my mind from the last school assembly.
>
> "Bob, I don't know if I can do this anymore. It's too hard. I had to call the police three times in the last two weeks. A student threatened a teacher, students are coming to school drunk, and sexual abuse, misconduct, and verbal atrocities all threaten our school. Teachers are quitting. Morale is so low. Parents are crying out, saying, 'We can't control our kids!'"
>
> Heaviness comes over me now because the school I'm speaking of was an elementary school, grades third through eighth. This was in rural Wisconsin, not inner city Detroit.

The above reminds me of a story in the media about a six-year-old boy in Michigan who shot and killed a classmate. Legally he couldn't be charged for it because he was too young.

Where can we go to understand how that could happen? Again, I believe we have to go below the street, into the tunnels of twisted thinking even though going there, in a strange way, feels twisted itself. Yet we need more proverbial Nortons to enter the deep parts—not the infrastructure of the city, but of a person's thinking and motives.

Why I Go There

I want to tell you why I do this—why I share what I've learned about restoring twisted thinkers and their broken relationships. In 1 Chronicles 28:9, just before he gives him plans for building the temple, King David gives a message to Solomon, his son, on how to live and rule as king. "The Lord searches every heart and understands every *motive* behind the *thoughts*. If you seek him, he will be found by you" (emphasis added).

I don't believe we can understand every motive behind all the thoughts of another person. Only God can do that. But when it comes to twisted thinkers and the directions their motivations take them in, we can. This is not about making assumptions; it's about observing what they are saying and doing, which is how they reveal where they are going. Therefore, even though God instantly understands every motive behind our thoughts—and we can't—His statement should still inspire us.

With confidence and wisdom, multiplied by experience, we *can* look at the infrastructure of every twisted thinker (including ourselves) and every broken relationship (including our own) that we encounter. The view begins in God's darkroom, as we learn to develop a photo I call the "mug shot." Without this picture, which allows no touch-ups to hide flaws, it's impossible to break through to the place where conscience can be recovered and the twisted thinker can become a STAR

A Word Of Caution

Before we look at the photograph I want to caution parents of young children at risk. Many things are being discovered today about children suffering from *Attention Deficit Disorder*, or a more recent finding called *Attachment Disorder*.

Families can be in agony over children diagnosed with these disorders, who seem to be without conscience. Almost out of nowhere they sometimes become aggressive. Much work is being done to treat these disorders, using methods that include medication or socialization, such as holding the child to help them connect.

By no means would I attempt to minimize any of those approaches, but one thing still seems very clear. *Responsibility for changing ultimately belongs to the child.* Therefore, I believe it would be wise to consider that one reason some children may or may not respond to treatment could be due to habits of twisted thinking.

The Mug Shot

While working at the jail I once saw the jail's captain do something impressive. Typically, as he led groups of adolescents through the facility he demonstrated how inmates are booked. At the guard window, students had to check in just like regular inmates would. Then the captain directed small groups into a room where offenders got fingerprinted and had their mug shots taken. The security was tight and the atmosphere was tense. The kids couldn't step past designated yellow lines on the floor, just like inmates couldn't. There was only one difference between the tour groups and regular prisoners. The youths weren't handcuffed.

After one group left I went into the room and stood where the pictures were taken. I turned so I was facing the camera. Then I turned to the side. I felt a bit sheepish because I was doing this without guards in the room. Maybe I was trying to see what my father went through when he was processed into a prison system. I'm not quite sure why I did it, but I definitely experienced something that felt a lot like shame while pretending that my image was being captured and put into the system. I finally got out of there and went back to my office, but not without a huge sense of relief.

When we go to Scripture, there is no way to escape the moment of shame or the sudden sense of horror when the Bible reflects a man's mug shot. We all turn into centipedes when it happens. Imagine yourself as a centipede being discovered under a plate in a dark cupboard. After being exposed, what feeling of comfort would you have?

That centipede likes darkness. It doesn't sit there and say, "Take a picture of me while I pose for you because I've got a hundred legs! And oh, by the way, sorry you caught me in your cupboard." That little creature finds the fastest path to another dark place. What a sense of emergency when it's exposed! So the centipede plays lickety-split and gets out of there, pronto!

A man in Scripture tells us what he felt when God took his mug shot. The difference is that God chose not to step on him. But more important, even though he could not escape feelings of shame and horror, the exposure was redemptive. It came while Isaiah was being commissioned by God as a prophet.

"Woe to me!" I cried. "I am ruined! For I am a man of unclean lips, and I live among a people of unclean lips, and my eyes have seen the King, the Lord Almighty." (Isaiah 6:5)

As an adult exposed by the Almighty, Isaiah's own dark side overwhelmed him. Yet God provides a mug shot of every man or woman's heart before each one becomes an adult, and it's available for the seeing by anyone who knows what to watch for. The exposure puts us all behind yellow lines, caught and handcuffed.

In my youth, I loved watching Superman on TV. Sometimes I wondered if anyone could actually see through walls—and if they couldn't, what a neat thing it would be one day if they could. Now, modern technology has developed night scopes that let us see people in total darkness.

Yet the biblical camera goes farther. It's better than Superman's X-ray vision or today's most advanced technology. It takes a picture of humanity's soul, exposing the spiritual darkness within. This camera is so quick and powerful that it traces the thoughts and intents of the heart from birth. Once we see them we can then track where the twisted thinker is going. Let's begin with the front view of a typical picture.

THE FRONT VIEW

The writer in Proverbs 22:15 said, "Folly is bound up in the heart of a child." Why do parents have to teach children to do right, and *not* to do what's wrong? The answer is that doing wrong comes naturally for children. God calls it "folly," and kids are bound up with it. And I didn't come up with this idea on my own; it's also found in Psalm 58:3-5.

> Even from birth the wicked go astray; from the womb they are wayward and speak lies. Their venom is like the venom of a snake, like that of a cobra that has stopped its ears, that will not heed the tune of the charmer, however skillful the enchanter may be.

The front view of the mug shot is shocking. God teaches that kids are responsible for their choices. As a good father of his children, God is clear about making that point in Isaiah 1:15-17.

> When you spread out your hands in prayer, I will hide my eyes from you; even if you offer many prayers I will not listen. Your hands are full of blood; wash and make yourselves clean. Take your evil deeds out of my sight! Stop doing wrong, learn to do right! Seek justice encourage the oppressed. Defend the cause of the fatherless, plead the case of the widow.

While developing the treatment program for inmates in Sheboygan County, I found lots of support for this front view in my research. In *Before It's Too Late*, Dr. Stanton E. Samenow says that children who choose to practice the criminal mindset start down that path between the ages of three and five.

Does that shock you? I wish I could say it shocks me but it doesn't anymore. If you were to sit in my office you'd hear parents of very young offenders pour out their pain over what their sons or daughters do. They have no problem with the front view of this mug shot because they're living with the evidence through their children. I'm talking about good parents whose kids are making bad choices.

Where does that come from? The Bible says, "Folly is bound up in the heart of the child." Meanwhile I can almost hear the usual questions, especially the ones that followed the Jonesboro and Columbine tragedies. "What about the parents? What's *their* responsibility for what's happening today?"

Society wants to blame someone, so there's been a wave of parent blaming. Again, I'm not ignoring parental influences but our world has a hard time understanding that children can go that far on their own, even with good parenting behind them. They can.

A Family Member's Front View

My wife Judy and I went through a nightmare when our youngest daughter, at age seventeen, appeared in court for committing a crime. I remember one of the guards at the jail talking to me about his confusion about why so many young people were being incarcerated at the jail. What confused him? They were coming from good homes with responsible parents, and that broke all the stereotypes.

I remember thinking, at the time, that he was right because our home certainly wasn't a training ground for criminal behavior in spite of my own struggles with twisted thinking. Meanwhile, everybody in our house was hurting. Court dates were set for Mindy and we began to prepare for the worst. We could only do what parents do at a time like that—pray for help and endure the shame.

I realized that some of my concerns for Mindy might have been tainted by the desire to find a way of escaping the shame, rather than helping her. Although understandable, that was unacceptable. My responsibility was to love her unconditionally. So Judy and I embraced the shame, completely.

We entered the courtroom to find the judge supporting us. In fact, for accountability purposes he paroled Mindy to me; she'd pay the fine or do the time. It seemed like another one of those poetic God moments. I don't know if being the developer of the jail's treatment program helped me when the judge made his decision, but Judy and I were grateful for the ruling.

We had issues just like any other parents, but one thing was clear. Mindy made choices. She was responsible for her own behavior. Through a long and painful time, Judy and I determined it would be worth the effort to see our daughter restored. We were humbled, because many parents in similar situations never see their children change.

It took five years for Mindy to become a STAR. We progressed from having the court involved to creating a family contract she had to sign in order to live with us. We were able to enforce the contract because the court backed us. I did everything I could to teach her about twisted thinking, which became a starting point for growth. Judy was a tower of strength throughout the process. God also brought other people and events into Mindy's life to reinforce his love. We weren't alone.

To her credit, our daughter came out of this dark time and started to grow. A great, heart-swelling, lump-in-the-throat moment came when she left for Ravencrest Chalet, a Bible Institute in Estes Park, Colorado. What joy! She was developing into a wonderful, caring woman who delighted in pursuing God.

Through it all we learned that Proverbs 20:11 is true: "Even a child is known by his actions, by whether his conduct is pure right." Mindy's responsible behaviors became more consistent and her twisted thinking became transformed. Our family embarked on the road to relational harmony, and we are still enjoying the journey to this day.

One reason for this is that every member of our family accepts the reality of a person's mug shot, in all its detail, as taken by the biblical camera. Let's look now at the side view.

THE SIDE VIEW

In April of 1994, Joe Stommel, the administrator of alcohol and drug services for the Colorado Department of Corrections, was giving a seminar organized by two Sheboygan mothers. The Sheboygan Press quoted some interesting things he said about the causes behind criminal behavior or substance abuse. Joe stated:

> Broken homes don't lead to lives of crime. Neither do drugs, alcohol, or peer pressure. The message of people being responsible for their own behavior is one parents and society doesn't often hear. We're a parent-blaming society in particular. We want to find out what causes breaking rules, regulations, norms, and values on almost a continual basis. Criminal behavior is linked to no specific mental illness. Some mentally ill people commit crimes, but there is no direct link between the two.

> Peer pressure doesn't draw children into criminal activity. Quite the opposite, they go looking for the kinds of groups that act out their type of behavior. Poor families and economically depressed neighborhoods don't produce crime. People of all backgrounds grow up to be either responsible or irresponsible adults. People usually commit their first crimes before they become drug and alcohol abusers. But when you combine drugs and crime, there's a combination that's

potentially lethal. In order to commit criminal acts, there has to be an established thinking process going on. Changing that has got to be the first priority.

Again, as I've pointed out twice before, in Proverbs 15 the Bible says that "Folly is bound up in the heart of a child." It's an internal issue well before any "folly" ever becomes visible in a child's behavior. Regardless of how hard parents are working—or "however skillful the enchanter may be" according to Psalm 58—when a child chooses foolishness he will not heed the tune of the charmer (the parent).

We don't like this idea. It's scary, but nevertheless it's a fact. How else do we explain how and why Adam and Eve, created pure and without sin, still chose to sin? God knew it was coming but that doesn't make Him a bad parent just because He knew. He fulfilled his responsibility to set boundaries. In His goodness, He gave them a choice and was strong enough to allow them to make that choice, even if they broke His heart in the process.

God doesn't violate our capacity to make choices. The first adults on the planet chose to do the wrong thing, and they didn't come from a dysfunctional family. That choice resulted in the loss of a human connection with each other, and with God. God knows what parents feel like when they see their young children go astray. He saw fully—and completely understood—the twisted thinking behind Adam's choices in the Garden.

Twisted Beliefs Attached to the Mug Shot

In his *Confessions*, Saint Augustine said something about living as a thief in the days of his youth. I appreciated his openness and honesty.

> I willed to commit the theft. I was not driven to it by any need. It was rather to enjoy the actual theft and the sin of theft. Foul was the evil and I loved it.

If we updated the language, although what Augustine wrote was excellent, I think he would give you the perspective of a twisted thinker. He might have written something like this:

My own style of living is exciting, secretive, illegal, and harmful to others. I don't care how they feel because I'm superior. I'm proud of my arrogance. As far as I'm concerned, life is a one-way street; my way. I trust only people I can manipulate or use to maintain an edge over them. I believe in lying because it's easy. I don't need to be concerned with facts, nor am I concerned about wanting truth, if truth and facts interfere with my intentions. If I think something is a certain way then that's the way it is. My responsibility is to please me. I believe in living only for the moment, so I'll decide what's right for you and me at the time.

What a sewer of beliefs, but any twisted thinker could say in all honesty after having been restored, "Foul was the evil and I loved it."

Going for the Big E!

The above beliefs are all supported by irresponsible fantasy worlds and are reinforced by the twisted thinking errors I'll expand on in other chapters. But first, right here I want to insert something that I consider even more important.

> The ultimate goal of any twisted thinker's irresponsible fantasy is to pursue an unadulterated *"Big E"*—the *Excitement of the Forbidden*.

This term came out of Drs. Samenow and Yochelson's work with the criminal population in America. They discovered that every criminal they interviewed had the same goal of pursuing any brand of excitement that was forbidden. It's the proverbial drug of choice because forbidden excitement can be achieved anytime and anywhere. It's a rush! Their studies support what Augustine had already stated in *Confessions*.

I believe both examples support what the Bible calls "the cravings of sinful man, the lust of his eyes and the boasting of what he has and does" (I John 2:16). So, whether it's criminal behavior, an addictive issue, or being habitually irresponsible, excitement of the forbidden is the pursuit and that's why it's called the *Big E*.

At the same time there's nothing wrong with legitimate forms of excitement. Since moving to Wisconsin in 1987 I've become a Green Bay Packers fan. (Sorry, Detroit!) In Sturgeon Bay, Wisconsin, there's a man in the church I once pastored who loves the Chicago Bears. Between us there's a lot of excitement when the Bears and Packers meet—it's about enjoying competition between friends. No one is trying to control the other, but there is excitement.

Yet the *Big E*'s promise of power and control is illegitimate because it always hurts someone or something. When someone chases it they will twist the relationship, even when other people are ignorant of what they're doing.

Something sick happens to a person when irresponsible fantasies are indulged. The Bible calls it a "searing of mind" in which tunnel vision keeps the person from thinking about what the consequences might be. Unfortunately, in searching for explanations, well-meaning people often ask questions that could alter the mug shot and hinder healing. Typical questions imply that low self-esteem or family dysfunctions are behind the twisted thinker's irresponsible behavior.

So, Is It Low Self Esteem?

Not in this mug shot. Seven common antisocial behavior patterns in problem children indicate just the opposite. In fact, antisocial children tend to have such high self-esteem that it's often unhealthy. Take a look at the commonality of the following patterns.

1. They believe that life is a one-way street.
2. They disregard injury to others.
3. They have unrealistic expectations and pretensions.
4. They take the easy way.
5. They lie as a way of life.
6. They refuse to be held accountable.
7. They are islands unto themselves.

Doesn't all of the above sound like what John said in his first letter to believers when he talked about the "lust of the flesh, the lust of the eyes, the pride (*or braggadocio*) of life" (1 John 2:16, KJV)? And it all starts when a child makes wrong and often secret choices no one knows about, until suddenly the results of those choices appear, shocking parents, families, and communities. Low self-esteem isn't the issue when that happens.

For Christians in Rome, low self-esteem wasn't a concern either. In the light of the Cross of Christ, the apostle Paul encouraged believers to be transformed by the renewing of their minds.

> For by the grace given me I say to every one of you: Do not think of yourself more highly than you ought, but rather think of yourself with sober judgment, in accordance with the measure of faith God has given you. (Romans 12:3)

The problem with twisted thinkers is not low self-esteem. We should be much more concerned about the opposite—unhealthy high self-esteem. If Paul could warn the Roman Christians of his day against that, the same problem is just as likely to affect a twisted thinker here in the modern age.

Listen as Paul describes a spiritually dark place that many of the Gentiles lived in before they came to know the Savior. It's below-the-street thinking that resulted in destructive above-the-street behaviors. And it wasn't due to low self-esteem but, rather, to a chosen ignorance that hardened their hearts, which is another way of saying they had no empathy for anyone.

> So I tell you this, and insist on it in the Lord, that you must no longer live as the Gentiles do, in the futility of their thinking. They are darkened in their understanding and separated from the life of God because of the ignorance that is in them due to the *hardening of their hearts*. Having lost all sensitivity, they have given themselves over to sensuality so as to indulge in every kind of impurity, with a continual lust for more. (Ephesians 4:16-17, emphasis added)

In Matthew 6:21-23, Jesus also made it clear about where it starts when people choose to go bad.

For where your treasure is, there your heart will be also. The eye is the lamp of the body. If your eyes are good, your whole body will be full of light. But if your eyes are bad, your whole body will be full of darkness. If then the light within you is darkness, how great is that darkness!

Jesus also said:

No good tree bears bad fruit, nor does a bad tree bear good fruit. Each tree is recognized by its own fruit. People do not pick figs from thorn bushes, or grapes from briers. The good man brings good things out of the good stored up in his heart, and the evil man brings evil things out of the evil stored up in his heart. For out of the overflow of his heart his mouth speaks. (Luke 6:43-45)

The cause behind the sewer sludge in our souls is not society, parents, churches, corporate America, too little education, or low self-esteem. The Light of the world just took a mug shot of man—of you and me. The details are all there and it's sobering, especially when we see what starts so early in the developmental stages of youth.

The twisted thinker's relationship is usually broken because of an unhealthy high self-esteem. Sin in the heart, and the choice to act out that sin, is every person's own responsibility. For God to redeem us and continue reshaping our families, marriages, and communities, this awful picture must be revealed and recognized for what it truly is.

Yet, there is wonderful, refreshing hope for transforming twisted thinking and restoring broken relationships. Primarily, it's because of our Lord's willingness to connect with humanity by entering the dark window of every soul. He wasn't afraid to go there and take the mug shot. What love!

Becoming a STAR

A number of years ago, a friend of mine asked if I'd visit his son. It was urgent. Brian was an alcoholic and had made self-destructive choices over a long stretch of time. He was aware of his own failures and realized that hope was fading fast for any sort of decent life. So he agreed to see me.

This young man came from a good family. His parents loved and walked with God. He understood the gospel of Christ. So, I took a plane to see him and have a talk. This may seem flimsy, but I had hope simply because Brian was still alive and God was in control. Solomon's statement in Ecclesiastes 9:4 became my encouragement: "Anyone who is among the living has hope—even a live dog is better off than a dead lion."

However, when I speak of my hope for Brian it actually reflected my desire that he would understand how he'd become a twisted thinker, because he already knew Christ as his savior. He believed he was going to heaven. He had some knowledge of the Bible. But he also knew he was an alcoholic, and he understood that he'd almost become his own god by demanding that everything go his own way.

I spent three days working with Brian, identifying his thinking errors and helping develop a plan for stopping his drinking. God was invited to be a major part of the transformation, and Brian finally got desperate enough to make the commitment. Meanwhile, I felt privileged to be part of his healing process and wasn't judgmental, condemnatory, or condescending in any way.

For Brian, realizing that he'd become a twisted thinker was everything. He went into the sewer of his thoughts and discovered that God still loved him. He found out how to untangle the mess his life had become. And, as he turned away from twisted thinking the longings of his heart for genuine relationships began to re-emerge and come alive.

The rest is history. Over a period of time Brian changed in deep and meaningful ways. Today he is on another track. He took a wonderful leap into the light. He no longer hides from himself or from others, although he also understands that restoring ourselves and healing or preventing broken relationships will always be an on-going process.

Eventually Brian moved back to his home city, met a beautiful woman who loves the Lord, married her, and started a family. In other words, he became a STAR after being caught in his own sin and trapped by God's love.

What a combination!

Chapter Three

THE TRANSFORMATION PROCESS

Dealing with First Principles

What did Judy look for in me, to see if trust could be rebuilt? What did we look for, as parents, to determine whether our daughter was really changing? What did I look for in Brian, to see if his commitment was real? What should society look for to know whether lawbreakers have truly been rehabilitated?

Beyond all that, what should we look for in young children, like our granddaughter, who was developing her own folly at the age of three? What can you look for as you attempt to untangle yourself from twisted thinking?

To answer those questions I will now introduce the STAR Toolbox, to help twisted thinkers become Straight Thinkers Accepting Responsibility.

THE SOUL MAP

The first tool in the box is a soul map. As you look at the soul map, think of it like a roundabout when you're driving. Even though it all starts with understanding the thinking errors, entry points aren't necessarily laid out in any particular sequence. Thus entry points one through four might open up at different intervals, during the process of understanding each thinking error mentioned in the book.

Overall, I've been amazed at how some people can go through the first four entry points and still decide to quit, in favor of pursuing another *Big E*. But on this particular roundabout it can happen. Even so, the following soul map will provide sufficient direction for change—a genuine repentance process.

Entry point one: We need to understand any twisted thinking patterns because they all reinforce irresponsible fantasies used in pursuing *Big Es*. No deep or consistent change is possible until these thinking patterns are acknowledged and understood.

Entry point two: We must determine whether twisted thinkers have genuine self-disgust for hurting others. Expressing words of sorrow won't be enough, because self-disgust involves the twisted thinker's ability to consider who might get hurt by their actions before they make an irresponsible decision. Granted, some change may be going on if they're troubled even by the thought of hurting another person. Yet only when they purposely avoid making decisions that damage other people is the twisted thinker definitely moving toward self-disgust. Doing it right once doesn't mean that real change has happened, even though the twisted thinker might like us to believe it has.

Entry point three: Does the twisted thinker have a profound sense of empathy for the victims of their behavior? If they can't tell you what others feel as a result of their actions, whatever changes seem to be happening are only "above the street." You should probably keep excitement about any behavioral changes to a minimum, until the twisted thinker consistently demonstrates legitimate empathy for others.

Entry point four: Here we look for deep remorse, powerful enough to motivate the twisted thinker to do whatever it takes to provide restitution for his victims. In fact, at this point they won't have to be told to do this. Out of respect for victims, and from a desire to rebuild relationships, they'll offer it on their own.

Unfortunately, this step often "goes missing" in the twisted thinker's restoration process, which is why there's often no sense of resolution for anyone. The apostle Paul understood this when he called himself the "chief of sinners" in 1 Timothy 1:15 (KJV). In another place he said:

> I am obligated both to Greeks and non-Greeks, both to the wise and the foolish. That is why I am so eager to preach the gospel also to you who are at Rome. (Romans 1:14-15)

He didn't owe a debt to God because God took care of that through his son, Jesus Christ. But Paul had a deep sense of debt to the human race.

The Transformation Process

After his conversion he spent his whole life paying it back, by preaching the gospel.

The last entry point: I believe that twisted thinkers arrive at the most important benchmark when they genuinely become God-fearing people. A changing twisted thinker could appear to become consistently responsible, but without movement toward a relationship with God, transforming the mind, he always falls short. I believe the tendency to be self-absorbed and self-centered begins to change when there's a passion to know God and obey what He says in the Bible.

> Although a wicked man commits a hundred crimes and still lives a long time, I know that it will go better with God-fearing men, who are reverent before God. (Ecclesiastes 8:12)

Both King David and King Solomon got tangled up in their own twisted thinking, and its consequences. They had serious problems as both ordinary men and kings. But along the way we see them pursuing God and being willing to struggle in the process. Their lives clearly demonstrate that becoming a STAR is the most responsible, reasonable journey any twisted thinker can take.

STAR Evaluation

Let's begin with a clear definition of twisted thinking.

> *Twisted thinking is a network of thinking errors used in decision making by people who have been irresponsible.*

All of us occasionally struggle with twisted thinking. That's what I mean by being made of the same mud. But real twisted thinkers are committed to irresponsible lifestyles in which pursuing the *Big E* truly becomes their way of life. A total transformation in their thinking is critical for them, because every "twisted" pattern we will discuss in this book reinforces that lifestyle.

So, the next tool in the STAR toolbox is an evaluation that will help you identify any twisted thinking errors in your own life that need to be corrected.

If you take the evaluation, think of what you believe at the time you're taking it, then determine your score by using the table at the end of this chapter. That score will expose two things: (1) what errors in your thinking need transforming, and (2) what level of difficulty you might experience in your struggle for change.

At that point you might also have some immediate concern regarding a particular error in thinking, and you might be tempted to jump ahead in this book. But before you do that, let me give you a word of caution. Rather than focusing on only one critical error, read the whole book first to understand the *whole change process*. You'll need to know how all twisted thinking patterns are networked and connected.

You can then use your current evaluation to chart your progress periodically, perhaps once every three months. It may be used for ages ten and up. And it is not a psychological evaluation but it can give you a clear picture of the twisted thinking battles going on right now.

I have also used the evaluation tool to help family members evaluate each other. My hope is to encourage new beginning points that can help you redefine and rebuild all your relationships with other people.

The List of Twisted Thinking Patterns

Another tool in the box is a record of each twisted thinking error, coupled with its definition. Each succeeding chapter will then build on those definitions, providing greater understanding on how to begin correcting each error. However, once again I recommend that you take the evaluation before you study the list to avoid distorting the evaluation itself.

Bookend Principles

The last tool in the STAR toolbox will help you recognize the thinking patterns of twisted thinkers, what their next steps might be, how their decisions are supported, and what they can do to change. It provides a bird's-eye view for anyone in conflict with them. I call it *The Bookend Principles*, which reveals all ten twisted thinking errors and shows whether repentance is truly happening.

				The Bookend Principles *Twisted Thinking Patterns*					
1	2	3	4	5	6	7	8	9	10
C	M	I	S	R	I	Z	M	A	P
L	A	N	T	E	M	E	A	R	O
O	R	F	U	C	P	R	N	R	S
S	T	L	B	K	A	O	I	O	S
E	Y	A	B	L	T		P	G	E
D	R	T	O	E	I		U	A	S
	E	E	R	S	E		L	N	S
	D	D	N	S	N		A	T	I
					T		T		V
							I		E
							V		
							E		

First Principle
i.e., Patterns 1 & 6 etc.
<---------------------------->

Second Principle
i.e., Patterns 1 & 5-6-7 etc.
--->

Third Principle
i.e., Patterns 1 through 10
-->

First Principle: "Closed Thinking" always joins another twisted thinking pattern or cluster of patterns. No one pattern or cluster of patterns will ever stand apart from closed thinking. So, at a minimum, two patterns will be active at one time (i.e., patterns 1 & 6; 1 & 3; 1 & 8 etc.).

Second Principle: Each pattern, when dominant (e.g., like the one for impatient thinking) will be joined by the less dominant thinking patterns on each side of it, making a cluster. Closed thinking will always be a part of that cluster because of the first principle (i.e., patterns 1 & 5-6-7).

Third Principle: Possessive Thinking, when dominant, includes all other twisted thinking patterns as the cluster (i.e., patterns 1 through 10).

APPLICATION OF PRINCIPLES

How can the bookend principles help hold accountable a person who is struggling with any of these thinking errors? It allows those who are doing the confronting the freedom to address a lesser dominant pattern. There's certainly nothing wrong in addressing the dominant thinking pattern, but they can also start with the less dominant patterns that are a part of the cluster before eventually addressing the dominant thinking pattern.

There's no pressure to be absolutely right by guaranteeing that you won't make a mistake in holding the twisted thinker accountable. These principles show how they've developed their irresponsible decision/behavior patterns. It can also show where they are headed, by identifying the less dominant patterns as well. If addressing a dominant or less dominant pattern receives greater resistance in the moment of accountability, then closed thinking can be addressed as the dominant pattern because it is always present.

Evaluation of Twisted Thinking Patterns

Place the letter of a response in the space provided for each numbered statement you believe to be most descriptive of your thinking.

Scale

A—Most of the time
B—A good part of the time
C—Some of the time
D—A little of the time
E—None or almost none of the time

_____ 1. I think about making responsible changes in my life.
_____ 2. I blame other people and situations when I find myself having problems.
_____ 3. I feel terrible and have a sense of deep remorse when I know I've hurt others.
_____ 4. I avoid doing things that are boring or disagreeable.
_____ 5. I'll do whatever it takes to practice responsible behavior and honor my commitments.
_____ 6. I think about consequences and who gets hurt before I make decisions.
_____ 7. I avoid dangerous situations.
_____ 8. I need to have things go my way.
_____ 9. I think of myself as better than others.
_____10. When I see something I want, if I think I can get away with it I'll take it.

_____11. I like to make the rules and follow them.
_____12. I like keeping others informed about what I'm going to do.
_____13. I do what I can with others so that everyone will be a winner.
_____14. I'm not afraid to accept or admit that I have fears about any given thing.
_____15. I like to set goals and work hard to reach them.
_____16. I will respond to most things if I think I can get something out of it.
_____17. When I don't want to do something I will make excuses so I can avoid it.
_____18. I don't like it when people won't listen to me when I say, "I didn't intend to hurt you."
_____19. I resent and resist others who try to wreck my fun when I think I deserve it.
_____20. I'm my own best critic.

Use the Twisted Thinking Errors Score Sheet on the next page to find your score.

Twisted Thinking Errors Score Sheet

Place the numerical value of the letter used for each selection in the space provided. Then add the score for each selection, referring to the same thinking error to arrive at a combined score. Next, total the combined scores to arrive at the scoring index. That scoring index indicates the level of your present struggle with twisted thinking errors, and measures their potential impact on your behaviors.

Scoring Example:

1. A.0 B.1 C.2 D.3 E.4 3 Closed Thinking + 20. A.4 B.3 C.2 D.1 E.0 3 = 6

Challenge: If the combined score for a particular thinking error is above 4, that error in thinking may need more immediate attention than those that don't.

Combined Scores

1. A.0 B.1 C.2 D.3 E.4 ____ Closed Thinking + 20.   A.4 B.3 C.2 D.1 E.0 ___ = ___
2. A.4 B.3 C.2 D.1 E.0 ____ Martyred Thinking + 19.   A.4 B.3 C.2 D.1 E.0 ___ = ___
3. A.0 B.1 C.2 D.3 E.4 ____ Inflated Thinking + 18.   A.4 B.3 C.2 D.1 E.0 ___ = ___
4. A.4 B.3 C.2 D.1 E.0 ____ Stubborn Thinking + 17.   A.4 B.3 C.2 D.1 E.0 ___ = ___
5. A.0 B.1 C.2 D.3 E.4 ____ Reckless Thinking + 16.   A.4 B.3 C.2 D.1 E.0 ___ = ___
6. A.0 B.1 C.2 D.3 E.4 ____ Impatient Thinking + 15.   A.0 B.1 C.2 D.3 E.4 ___ = ___
7. A.0 B.1 C.2 D.3 E.4 ____ Fearful Thinking + 14.   A.0 B.1 C.2 D.3 E.4 ___ = ___
8. A.4 B.3 C.2 D.1 E.0 ____ Manipulative Thinking + 13. A.0 B.1 C.2 D.3 E.4 ___ = ___
9. A.4 B.3 C.2 D.1 E.0 ____ Arrogant Thinking +12.   A.0 B.1 C.2 D.3 E.4 ___ = ___
10. A.4 B.3 C.2 D.1 E.0 ____ Possessive Thinking +11.   A.4 B.3 C.2 D.1 E.0 ___ = ___

Scoring Index: Total _____

Scoring Index

- **1-18—Mostly Responsible Thinker**—Some thinking errors: behaviors consistently responsible
- **19-38—Somewhat Responsible Thinker**—Many thinking errors: behaviors occasionally irresponsible but in danger of becoming frequently irresponsible (behaviors more hidden from others)
- **39-58—Moderate Twisted Thinker**—At risk/all thinking errors: intact and operative: irresponsible behaviors more frequent (behaviors not hidden from others)
- **59+—Extreme Twisted Thinker**—All thinking errors intact and operative: practices habitually irresponsible behaviors/addictive or illegal

TWISTED THINKING PATTERNS & DEFINITIONS LEADING TO HABITUALLY IRRESPONSIBLE BEHAVIORS

1. Closed Thinking
a. I am not receptive (tunnel vision—the only way is how I see things)
b. I am not self critical (emotionally vacant—I don't care how I hurt others)
c. I am not disclosing information (deliberately vague—I won't give details)
d. I'm good at pointing out and talking about the faults of others e. I lie by omission

The Transformation Process

2. **Martyred Thinking**
   a. I view myself as a victim when I'm held accountable.
   b. I blame social conditions, my family, the past, and other people for what I do.

3. **Inflated Thinking**
   a. I view myself only as a good person to avoid responsibility for offenses.
   b. I fail to acknowledge my own destructive behavior.
   c. I build myself up at the expense of others.

4. **Stubborn Thinking**
   a. I won't make any effort to do things I find boring or disagreeable.
   b. When I say "I can't" I'm really saying "I won't."

5. **Reckless Thinking**
   a. I think living in a responsible way is unexciting and unsatisfying.
   b. I have no sense of obligation but I'll get you to obligate yourself to me.
   c. I'm not interested in being responsible unless I get an immediate payoff.

6. **Impatient Thinking**
   a. I do not use the past as a learning tool when it gets in the way of my plans.
   b. I expect others to act immediately when I demand it.
   c. I make decisions based on assumptions, not the facts.

7. **Fearful Thinking**
   a. I have irrational fears but refuse to admit them.
   b. I have a fundamental fear of injury or death when I'm not in control.
   c. I have a profound fear of being put down.
   d. When I'm held accountable I feel lousy and experience a "Zero State."

8. **Manipulative Thinking**
   a. I have a compelling need to be in control of others and every situation.
   b. I use manipulation and deceit to get into and take control of situations.
   c. I refuse to be a dependent person unless I can take advantage of it.

9. **Arrogant Thinking**
   a. I think I'm different and better than others.
   b. I expect out of others what I fail to deliver. **(JP)**
   c. I'm super-optimistic because it cuts my fear of failure.
   d. I will quit at the first sign of what I consider failure.

10. **Possessive Thinking**
    a. I perceive all things and people as objects that belong to me.
    b. I have no concept of the "ownership rights" of others.
    c. I will use sex for power and control and not intimacy.

Chapter Four

CLOSED THINKING

The Invisible Man

I am not receptive (tunnel vision—the only way is how I see things). I am not self critical (emotionally vacant—I don't care how I hurt others). I am not disclosing information (deliberately vague—I won't give details). I'm good at pointing out and talking about the faults of others. I lie by omission

In a song called "Let the Walls Fall Down," written by John and Anne Barbour and Bill Batstone from Maranatha Music, one verse finishes by saying, "One in Him, we'll live forever; Strangers He has reconciled." The chorus ends with "By His love, let the walls fall down."

It goes without saying that when the walls are up there's no problem remaining a stranger to anyone. The message of "His love" speaks about God appearing to mankind through Jesus Christ, for redemptive purposes. In spite of our foolishness, disobedience, deceit, and enslavement to all kinds of passions and pleasures, God commits Himself to be involved with us over the long haul. In fact, eternity is the view.

When we have hope in His redemptive love, rather than remaining unwilling to be open and vulnerable to Him we can then see walls coming down. In other words, we stop being strangers to God, our spouses, our families, and our communities. His love encourages us to develop a healthy sense of boundaries *within* relationships rather than putting up walls to keep others *out*.

Boundaries And Walls

At a family meal with our oldest daughter, son-in-law, and granddaughter, a boundary issue demonstrated how walls were coming down. We were all having fun, eating one of Judy's fabulous home-cooked meals, when suddenly our three-year-old granddaughter, Graci, stood on her chair and leaned into her daddy's eating space. Craig was startled but handled it with wisdom. While continuing to eat he began moving his arm up and down to create an imaginary boundary. Graci cocked her head back and sat down, somewhat troubled. Still using his arm movement as a visual aid, Craig said, "Graci, this is my eating space and that is your eating space." It was all done without emotion, in a matter-of-fact way.

What I liked about Craig's approach was how he continued to offer relationship to Graci. He didn't set up an imaginary boundary to keep her away from him or stop her from having fun. Instead she got a lesson in respecting the space of others, and as a result the joy of having Graci at the table increased.

In my view, this was one of those prime moments in which teaching was crucial. If Graci had been allowed to think it was okay to invade the space of others without asking, their relationship could have slowly broken down. This would be especially true if Craig really thought her behavior was inappropriate. Instead, he got involved in a small but profound way, and in that moment the level of intimacy within our family grew. Because she understood the family wasn't shutting her out, Graci came out of her confusion, quit pouting, and started having fun, because acknowledging boundaries will build and support relationships.

I remember posting a cartoon in my office at the jail that demonstrated the same boundary issue. It was one of those *Hagar the Horrible* moments, reflecting Hagar's habit of crossing personal boundaries with people who aren't ready for his stuff. Hagar is sitting at the table with his spouse, drinking coffee. Suddenly, he looks at her and says, "Y'know, in Ireland if you embarrass someone it's considered a CRIME!"

Hagar's wife turns with a cup in one hand and a saucer in the other, saying, "It's good we don't live there; we'd never get you out of the SLAMMER!"

In contrast, I'm reminded of how God initially chose to present Himself to a lost and dying world. He did not intimidate, push, control, or violate our choices when calling us to relationship. In a loving way, God established a boundary to which man could relate. He became flesh! He came to this earth as a baby, was tempted as a man yet remained without sin, endured the cross and its shame, and finally became our high priest able to sympathize with our weaknesses, all done without violating our personal boundaries. Yet what He established through all the above was a boundary line that mankind is not to cross.

In other words, the redemptive boundary line for man became Jesus Christ, God's son. However, He's not interested in building walls to keep us away from Him, even though He knows that we don't really have the capacity to absorb the greatness of His supernatural light and love. Yet He does make it available if we respect His precondition.

The Bible says, "Whosoever will may come." It's like He moves His arm up and down and says, "This is my space and that is yours," and if we cross His boundary line it's because we've accepted his invitation to come via the Cross.

Again, God doesn't embarrass or violate anyone. That would twist the relationship and He won't let that happen. Personal walls, on the other hand, are used to isolate us from others. They block our ability to progress to deeper levels of intimacy.

If this happens, discovering what *closed thinking* is, and what it looks like, will be an immense help in restoring broken relationships.

Closed Thinking Defined

Closed thinking is what results when we choose to be non-receptive to others. It's characterized by an unwillingness to hear, listen, or consider other people while maintaining personal agendas that promote the *Big E*. The only way to see things is how the closed thinker sees them. No one else is even supposed to have a mind.

There's also an unwillingness to be self critical about any irresponsible thinking or behavior. In fact, this attitude comes from an emotionally vacant person who really doesn't care how they hurt others. It results in decisions to withhold information by not telling the whole story, because exposure would mean full accountability.

When talking to a twisted thinker who has been caught being irresponsible, you can tell that decision has been made because you'll find them speaking with a deliberate vagueness, and you are left making assumptions to fill in the blanks. When that happens you've just been hooked.

The thinking goes something like this: If I'm held accountable because you know all the facts, then I can't pursue my *Big E*. Closed thinkers try to make themselves invisible by pointing out other people's fault. That way they don't have to talk about their own plans. At the same time they avoid vulnerability.

If we're not wise to what they're doing we'll be misdirected by chasing the rabbit I talked about in chapter one. Closed thinking promotes a life of pretense and is the first wall to tear down with twisted thinkers.

God warns of the consequences of this thinking error in the following passage:

> How long will you simple ones love your simple ways? How long will mockers delight in mockery and fools hate knowledge? Since they hated knowledge and did not choose to fear the Lord, since *they would not accept my advice and spurned my rebuke*, they will eat the fruit of their ways and be filled with the fruit of their schemes. For the waywardness of the simple will kill them, and the complacency of fools will destroy them; but whoever listens to me will live in safety and be at ease, without fear of harm. (Proverbs 1:22, 29-33, emphasis added)

God also speaks to Isaiah about the same thinking patterns in many of the Israelites:

> They know nothing, they understand nothing; their eyes are plastered over so they cannot see, and *their minds closed so they cannot understand*. No one stops to think, no one has the knowledge or understanding to say, "Half of it I used for fuel; I even baked bread over its coals, I roasted meat and I ate. Shall I make a detestable thing

from what is left? Shall I bow down to a block of wood?" (Isaiah 44:18-19, emphasis added)

TO A BLOCK OF WOOD

"Shall I bow down to a block of wood?" has always struck me as one of the Bible's most bizarre passages. Time and again, Israel chose a block of wood over Him! They had His presence and He fought for them. He fed them in the wilderness. He was faithful. He revealed His plan for their lives and honored them as His children. But they still bowed down to blocks of wood!

God begins to untangle this mess by calling their blocks of wood what they really were—"fuel for fire." His disgust was the only appropriate response. The Israelites' idolatry represented the ultimate disconnect, and there was no evidence that they had any conscience about it. Now, that's closed thinking!

The twisted thinker uses closed thinking as a metaphorical block of wood to shape his fantasy world and stay in control. It's the material he uses in fabricating his idol, the *Big E*. What's so revolting is how this same person actually *turns into and becomes* the block of wood being worshiped. He thinks the world revolves around him. The ultimate message coming through is "I'm God and He's not."

That's why God said that the Israelites hadn't stopped and thought about what they were doing or where they were heading. They started out as children created to enjoy a loving relationship with Him, but they turned themselves into blockheads. As I've said before, closed thinking results in the ultimate disconnect. And it comes with consequences.

I'm reminded of the passage in Isaiah 14, which describes Lucifer as fallen and explains how he will be judged in his final moment before God, as a result of his closed thinking.

> But you are brought down to the grave, to the depths of the pit. Those who see you stare at you, they ponder your fate: "Is this the man who shook the earth and made kingdoms tremble, the man who made the world a desert, who overthrew its cities and would not let his captives go home?" (Isaiah 14:15-17)

Pretty pathetic! In this passage, God refers to Lucifer as a supernatural being rendered impotent on judgment day. Because that's so it's even more disgusting and pathetic for man, a natural being, to think he's worth being worshiped by the creator! And it gets worse when God's children take that line of thought even though they should know better. Clearly, God wanted his people to see their own closed thinking patterns when He asked, "Shall I bow down to a block of wood?"

In the *TIME* magazine article entitled "Man of Israel" (November 13, 1995), I believe the author supports the call for restoring broken relationships by using the perfect Hebrew word.

> For Israelis of Yitzhak Rabin's generation, perhaps the single most valued quality an individual can have is summed up by the word *dugri*. It refers to a manner of behavior that is simple, direct, and honest. It conveys the idea of placing substance before style, of stripping away layers of subterfuge, of making no attempt at pretense or deception.

But closed thinking characterizes a life full of pretense and not the *dugri* of Yitzhak Rabin's generation. Closed thinking is a wall that must come down in before the charades can be stopped—a wall that won't come down unless we recognize what those walls are.

The Non-Receptive Charade

We've all heard comments like these: "That's stupid." "You don't know what you're talking about." "I already know that." "I only trust others after I get to know them." And even, "Let's pray about that." All of these statements can be used as tactics to avoid being open and receptive to others.

When my family moved to Winona Lake, Indiana, and I entered Grace Seminary, I went with the wrong attitude. My goal: Get the facts and the degree to make me a better preacher and counselor. I later discovered that the arms of my heart were folded in a defensive posture. Looking back, I was closed in my thinking and wouldn't genuinely participate during the first semester.

The instructors of the program put students into lab groups. I was troubled by the possibility of being vulnerable to other group members. I wondered why getting this degree couldn't be just an academic process. Why not focus on what is intellectual instead of exploring my relational style? After all, things are either black or white and you call it the way you see it.

I couldn't figure out how everyone else but me knew I was cold, calloused, and closed. I thought, "If they don't have chapter and verse from the Bible for what they want out of me in this group, I ain't listening." Of course, I didn't say that out loud. I kept that thinking and my feelings a secret because I wanted my Master's degree. No dugri in this attitude, was there?

I hid behind the Bible like some kid holding on to his mama's dress. Then, quite suddenly I was faced with a crisis involving one of our children. After handling it in a disgustingly miserable manner, I knew I was in trouble with myself for the first time in my life. I felt paralyzed and numb. Yet when I went into the lab the next day I was still hiding behind my walls.

Then it happened. I took my turn as the client needing to be counseled. When the lab instructor came into the room, I turned away from him to hide my weakness. In hindsight I now know what really happened—I was holding this man in contempt. But when I responded to the group as a client, something took place I hope I never forget.

The instructor looked at me while he was weeping, and with a combination of anger, compassion, and courage, stunned me with these words: "You are the most arrogant man I have ever met in my life."

I have this picture in my mind of being an armadillo: an ugly little arrogant creature, scooting around under a load of armor that nothing can penetrate. I used this image as a bluff for self-protection, a charade of non-receptivity. I didn't want anyone to see what was really underneath. But when the armadillo gets turned over on its back his soft and vulnerable belly gets exposed.

Well, God used that dear brother to roll me over on my back. He had the courage to tell me what no one else ever had. Or, if they had tried I had never listened. But this time I heard him and immediately understood that I was a broken man. By choosing to be open and honest I finally encountered the truth of Proverbs 28:13: "He who conceals his sins does not prosper, but whoever confesses and renounces them finds mercy."

From that point onward that lab group became a major part of the restorative and healing process for me, my marriage, and my family. My charade of non-receptivity was ripped away and I started to grow as a man.

The Nondisclosure Charade

Closed thinking is also secretive and self-righteous. However, twisted thinkers lie more often by omission than commission. Via that method they hide most of the clues that might reveal their hidden agendas. Other people are often exhausted by the charade, but the twisted thinker gets pumped up by the chase. Because, in many cases, the *Big E* is nothing more substantial than being secretive for its own sake!

Sadly, many kids come to believe that keeping secrets is the only way to survive. Many adults have told me that when they were feeling controlled and overwhelmed by a parent they survived by keeping secrets. Sometimes they made a conscious decision to be two different people. They learned to lie about who they were to their parents, believing that disclosures brought shame followed by punishment—but the shaming would feel worse than the punishment.

Sadly, for many, the above was true. Plus, even though keeping secrets is understandable, when a youngster uses secrets to escape being shamed he's developing a habit that will eventually lead to twisted thinking.

One such man related how his father once humiliated him with a spanking during his early teen years. He got caught in a predicament that prevented him from coming home under the curfew. After the spanking, he concluded that being honest would only get him in more trouble with his father. This man now realizes that he was once an emotional latchkey kid. No one was there to listen. It was easier to act like a good kid and lie than to face "parent shaming."

In the beginning, sprinting from one lie to the next seemed to work. But it all caught up to him after he got married. Whenever he felt controlled or overwhelmed by his wife he would leave the scene by emotionally shutting down all levels of intimacy with her.

To compensate he substituted pornography, satisfying himself sexually. Of course, his wife didn't know any of this before the marriage, which helped him take the easy way out whenever he struggled with her. Then she caught him surfing the Internet for pornography, at which point his "no disclosure" charade was finally exposed.

What began as an effort to handle the abusive moment he experienced at the hands of his father gradually morphed into the nightmare of closed thinking. The man was still handling the pressures in his life by "escaping the spanking" he never should have received as a teenager. Only now, the victim had become the victimizer.

With his disclosure, he learned his wife was willing to struggle through the pain he caused and work on forgiving him. He understood just the opposite of what had been taught to him by his parents during those early teen years. Since then it's been a long haul, but the marriage truly is being restored, and disclosing secrets has been pivotal to the process.

He's becoming a man of strength who can also be vulnerable. Yet even so, part of his healing involved facing the next closed thinking charade as well.

The Denial/No Self-Criticism Charade

From the comics section of the newspaper comes a *Marmaduke* strip, by Brad Anderson, that shows how important it is not to keep secrets. We see Marmaduke sitting in a big soft chair with a forlorn look on his face. Meanwhile, his master stands before him, holding up a mirror while he says, "See? You *are* a dog!"

It's like the secret is now out and the charade is over. No matter how hard Marmaduke tried he couldn't fool anyone . . . except, perhaps, himself. He really was a dog.

In the real world there's truly something redemptive about becoming open enough to face ourselves in the mirror. Conversely, the charade of denial causes damage in relationships because it allows the twisted thinker to be indifferent to other people, even after hurting them.

While watching a movie called *The Nuremberg Trial*, I was chilled to hear what the actor, playing the psychologist responsible for interviewing Nazi officers on trial for war crimes, had to say. When asked why he thought they exterminated six million Jewish people during WWII, he said, "The absence of empathy is the essence of evil."

That absence, matched with propaganda framing the Jewish people as nothing more than rats needing to be exterminated, provided the Nazis with permission to murder them. They chose to ignore their consciences.

Without empathy for the victims of twisted thinking there will be no deep, lasting changes for twisted thinkers, and no hope of restoring them to humanity. This was graphically demonstrated during the trials. Those responsible for the Holocaust had no empathy for their victims, no ability to figure out how unfair they had been, and no awareness of what those victims had felt. Not a single one even said, "I'm sorry."

So how do we put all this together to build our own awareness of closed thinking? How do we determine if, in fact, our own charades are continuing or stopping?

Three developments have to occur before a closed thinker can be open to reality and can deal with the world "straight up."

1. He has to move from non-receptivity to *receptivity*.
2. He has to move from no self-criticism to *disgust for being irresponsible*.
3. He has to move from no disclosure to *telling the truth and nothing but*.

When one of these developments has not truly occurred, we'll eventually know that a person closed in their thinking has lied to us. Let me illustrate these three realities in several ways, because it's imperative to grasp this point.

Sitting on the Outside; Standing on the Inside

Travel back a few years prior to seatbelt laws and imagine a three-year-old boy standing up on the backseat. He's ordered to sit down three times. The father is concerned for the son's safety. The boy still continues to stand. Ever been there?

With one hand on the stirring wheel, the father reaches back with the other, grabs the boy, and forces him to sit down. This three-year-old is smiling, and most likely thinking, "Okay, Dad, you're bigger and stronger. I'm sitting down on the outside, but on the inside I'm still standing up."

He's acting receptive but he's not disclosing his real thoughts, which is actually an old story. In the passage below, God speaks of Lucifer as the morning star and son of the dawn.

> Then, Lucifer said in his heart 'I will ascend to heaven, I will raise my throne above the stars of God . . . I will make myself like the Most High.' (Isaiah 14:12-14)

Was Lucifer being self critical and receptive to God? Would it be fair to say I doubt it? He might have acted that way, but he didn't disclose what was in his heart and mind. Now let me ask you a question about yourself. Do you think it's possible to be an honest person but not an open person?

I've sat in prisons, jails, churches, restaurants, and counseling offices listening to people disclose. Some of the most honest people I've ever met are sitting behind bars—seriously! They tell you the story and it's the truth. I've talked to many an inmate who'll say they rate honesty at the top of their values list, and they mean it.

I've also watched parents get really excited when their kids say the right things after they've been caught being irresponsible. And if you ask the young person if they're telling you the truth, they'll say, "Yes!"

I've especially seen this happen when they admit to using drugs. It's amazing how many parents believe that their child is changing just because they speak the truth *in that one instance!* I don't blame them because they are in pain. However, the same parents don't seem to realize how the twisted thinking in their children can break the family apart. It's subtle and below the street at first, until it keeps happening above the street even after their kids tell the truth.

So, it's possible to be honest about disclosing data but not open for transforming twisted thinking. If you believe change is happening just because you got the right facts from a twisted thinker, get ready for more surprises.

We've all heard the cliché, "Honesty is the best policy." I'd like to amend that cliché by going deeper. "Honesty with an open heart for change is a better policy." Don't get too excited about their honesty—or raise your hopes too quickly—if their heart hasn't truly opened up.

False Remorse

What about the twisted thinker who seems to be self critical, in the sense that he has some remorse for hurting others? Does that mean change is happening? Not necessarily. Stay with me, now, because I know this could be tough to hear, but the Bible shows us a man who was that way. Let's see what happened as we check for any genuine changes within the man himself. The account occurs in Matthew 27:3-5.

> When Judas, who had betrayed him, saw that Jesus was condemned, he was seized with remorse and returned the thirty silver coins to the chief priests and the elders. "I have sinned," he said, "for I have betrayed innocent blood." "What is that to us?" they replied. "That's your responsibility." So Judas threw the money into the temple and left. Then he went away and hanged himself.

No doubt Judas was self-critical in this passage, but let's proceed into the sewer of his closed thinking. Something is missing. It seems that Judas did all the right things to demonstrate change. He was seized with remorse and he disclosed his sin, yet he was not receptive to change.

To understand what I'm saying, look at the direction of Judas' behavior. Why did Judas go only to the chief priest and elders? Did he think his confession would motivate them to change their minds? Did he misunderstand their agenda and think that all he had to do was say they got the wrong guy?

Even if Judas really felt seized with remorse, it still seems that he was not a broken man who was willing to face the guys who had walked with him for three years. I think the chief priests and elders got it right when they said the betrayal was the responsibility of Judas himself.

Then, in the one last act of control in his narcissistic life went out and hung himself. I believe he was self-critical but not open to change. He went out of this world with a closed mind, all the way to the biggest eternal sewer ever made.

In my mind I can hear someone asking, "Did Judas refuse to change, or was he simply overcome with so much shame that he couldn't get beyond it? Would he have changed if he hadn't preempted the process by ending it? Was he really depressed beyond help or did he just *think* he was?" These are good and honest questions. For additional details we have to go to Matthew 26:21-25.

I Tell You the Truth . . .

At the last supper Jesus told the twelve, "I tell you the truth, one of you will betray me." Saddened by what He'd said, everyone began to respond with, "Surely not I, Lord." Everyone, that is, except Judas. His answer was different, although at first it may seem insignificant. He asked, "Surely not I, Rabbi?" In verse 25, Jesus answered, "Yes, it is you."

Rabbi but not *Lord*—therein lays the closed thinking Jesus knew was going on in the mind of Judas from day one when he joined the group. He was willing to give Jesus the rank of a teacher and a religious leader, but he did not call him Lord. And that would be his downfall.

Now, even if the implications of that thought might seem like a stretch for some readers, I think it's also interesting that, when Jesus fingered Judas He didn't say Judas was going to be depressed, or that he'd be overcome with shame and then kill himself. Jesus only said, "It would be better for him if he had not been born." The choices being made by Judas would have dire consequences both *in* and *on* his life.

Luke 22:3, 4 tells us, "Then Satan entered Judas, called Iscariot, one of the twelve. And Judas went to the chief priests and the officers of the temple guard and discussed with them how he might betray Jesus." There was no indication that Judas was moving toward depression when all that was going on.

Might I suggest that, given Judas' mindset, in spite of what he saw throughout the ministry of Jesus it wasn't like Satan wasn't invited. Judas was there when the physically sick—and those overcome with their sins—were healed. He saw people make Jesus their Lord and then live responsibly. That's why I believe that having a closed door in his mind, to the Son of God, led to an open door that let in the prince of darkness instead.

On that slippery slope, Judas had refused to change. He chose not to get beyond the shame. To ask, "Would he have changed if he hadn't given into the temptation of ending it?" is to invite an uncertain answer. I know some twisted thinkers who haven't changed, even after they've decided against suicide.

Again, what I'm illustrating with this account is that it's possible to be self-critical and disclose the truth, but if the twisted thinker is not *receptive* to change there really *is* no change. After that the "con" is a charade, or the *Big E*, and it can end in the worst imaginable scenario.

Here's another example. All of the above emerged from the evidence when Jeffrey Dahmer went on trial for murder in Milwaukee. To the psychologist, Dahmer reported feeling remorse after his first murder. He felt so bad after getting rid of the body that he went north to live with a relative in West Allis, Wisconsin. Dahmer mentioned reading the Bible and going to church, but eventually the force came upon him again, and he believed it was his destiny to kill. So, he became a serial killer.

Do you hear Dahmer being self-critical? It may sound like he is but only in the sense that he said he felt remorse. What's missing? Well, if he felt so bad about the first murder, why didn't he turn himself in to the police? Why not get some help?

In reality, he might have felt bad after the first murder but Jeffrey Dahmer was not really receptive to deep personal change. The papers even reported that one detective said Dahmer took pleasure in knowing he had a private world of his own that no one else knew about. That doesn't sound like being self-critical to me. It's possible that he changed once he was in prison, but at the time he made the other statements Jeffrey Dahmer was closed in his thinking.

I don't believe I can say the following strongly or often enough. It's the key for going deeper into the dark places of twisted thinking. For a twisted thinker, the elements for being open are (1) *receptivity to change*, (2) *legitimate self-criticism,* and (3) *disclosure*. If one of those elements is missing the other two can't make up the difference, any more than a three-legged stool can stand up and be secure on just two of its legs.

The Foundation for All Thinking Errors

I have another important reason for believing that understanding this principle is critical. Closed thinking is the foundation for networking every thinking error I mention in this book. Those errors aren't committed unless the person's thinking is already closed. Closed thinking always works in concert with at least one other thinking error, although they often come in multiples.

Given all that, there is no way to transform twisted thinking, recover the conscience, or repair broken relationships unless we "unclose" our thinking first. If we don't we'll wind up chasing a rabbit—or maybe an entire colony!

Sometimes closed thinking isn't exposed until the damage has already been done. This became evident in a church in crisis. A man attending the church was exposed for sexually harassing several women in the fellowship. The church tried to do the right thing, but they weren't aware of the twisted thinking patterns of the perpetrator. It didn't take long for news to get out, so the leaders called a congregational meeting to allow this man to publicly confess and ask forgiveness. After all, in front of them the man had wept and expressed sorrow for his behavior.

But another storm was developing at the same time. Some of the people had problems with how the crisis was handled. Something seemed missing, and then it became apparent. The leadership had called the meeting without consulting the victims and without assessing the damage to them or their families. They lost their focus on the bigger picture while trying to follow the discipline procedure that Matthew 18:15-29 encourages.

So, while the perpetrator agreed to the congregational meeting the victims didn't attend. Apparently no one realized that this meeting might put them in compromising positions in which they would look bad for not cooperating and helping restore a perpetrator. Conflicting emotions began to swell up in the congregation, even as the pain of the victims increased.

Unwittingly, the leaders traumatized these victims by not going slower and putting this man to a greater test before scheduling a meeting. They didn't find out if he was receptive to a long-term accountability commitment in which his counseling needs would be met. They also didn't find out if he'd help pay the victim's counseling bills. And, they didn't find out if the man really had any legitimate empathy for the damage he'd caused to these women and their marriages.

Finally, they didn't check to see if this man's behavior might have been illegal, to avoid being sued as accomplices for not reporting it. All they had was a man who got caught, who wept, and who said he was sorry. That was it!

Sadly, in order to rebuild from the devastation this crisis brought to the church, the leadership needed to own the impact of their failures, even if they hadn't intended to do harm. They had to start there to clean up the mess so that people could trust again.

It grieves me to know that similar scenarios are being played out in churches across our country, in which well-meaning leaders, easily persuaded by the tears of perpetrators, believe repentance has happened when it hasn't. If they understood the concept of twisted thinking they would know better. But because many don't, the victims often have to pick up the pieces on their own while the perpetrators find themselves lifted up, often to places of honor, without any accountability beyond mere words. When that kind of thing happens, every twisted thinker will take advantage of good, loving, forgiving but ignorant people wanting to make everything all right.

I believe with all my heart that we need to more fully assess the true prerequisites for deeper change and repentance, to see what each new situation really looks like "under God's own microscope." Unless there's understanding of foundational, "below the street" twisted thinking patterns, we will rush naively into weak "Christian" applications that inadvertently support the very thinking God wants transformed.

Remember, Jesus put the emphasis on our hearts and minds as the places where change comes first. Listen to how he criticized the religious leaders of his day for accepting and even closing their eyes to conditions in people who actually needed a good "internal scouring." He wanted the leaders of that day to be real people, vulnerable to him but not too easily swayed by the people they served.

> "Woe to you, teachers of the law and Pharisees, you hypocrites! You clean the outside of the cup and dish, but inside they are full of greed and self-indulgence. Blind Pharisee! First clean the inside of the cup and dish, and then the outside also will be clean." (Matthew 23:25)

Becoming Vulnerable

Before revealing how the twisted thinker can be held accountable for closed thinking, I want to address the subject of vulnerability—of being open. Talking to others about this has familiarized me with some questions that need our attention. For example, is refusing to be open the same as being closed thinkers? And how do we deal with the fear of appearing weak when we become open?

I don't believe refusing to be open versus being closed in thinking always involves the same dynamics. It's possible to set boundaries, as Israel did with twelve gates in the walls around Jerusalem. Only one gate was used to allow Gentiles into the city for visits and trade. If they tried going through other gates they could have been arrested and jailed. If they stayed past sunset and failed to leave through the proper gate at the designated time, they could be arrested.

Boundaries are important, although the neat thing about gates is that they offer some level of relationship, whereas walls just keeps people out. Yet it's entirely possible that both can be present in a relationship even though the person is still "open."

For instance, if someone says to me, "I'm closed about that subject now," or "I'm not ready to discuss that subject now," that's not necessarily closed thinking. If they express the desire to let me know when they're ready to talk, I have to respect that one gate even if it's temporarily closed. At least they are open about it, even though that gate might feel like a wall between us at a given moment.

But closed thinking always leads to protecting good ole number one, just so some irresponsible behavior or fantasy can be entertained and/or indulged. It can be hard to identify closed thinking within some people, but remember that closed thinking will always network its way to irresponsible behavior. If closed thinking is going on, stand still long enough and, in time, the rabbit will circle back.

What about appearing weak when we are vulnerable or open? I understand that we all have moments when appearing weak can be embarrassing, and we don't want anyone to see it. As a senior in a high school speech class, I gave an informative talk on photography—a subject I knew nothing about. It was a five minute speech during which the whole class, teacher included, laughed uproariously. I remember thinking, while I was giving it, that maybe my fly was unzipped, but was I going to look? I couldn't figure out why they were laughing but I held my form anyway. And, at the end of the speech they gave me a standing ovation.

After I sat down another student, still laughing, said, "That was the funniest thing I have ever seen or heard, Jerry. I couldn't believe you said what you did while you kept such a straight face." I didn't have the slightest idea what he was talking about but I finally asked him, at which point he convulsed all over again.

"It was the way you were saying the word photography. That was wild man!" Evidently, I was pronouncing it as "Photo-Graphy." Without hearing what I said you might not get how this sounded, but it came off like I was one of the Beverly Hillbillies. And, I think I must have mispronounced it at least twenty times in the speech.

But, do you think I was going to let on that I didn't know what I was doing? No way! Instead of appearing weak or embarrassed I acted confident, as if I'd known exactly what I was saying. And quite frankly, that's exactly the strategy many closed thinkers will use, consciously or otherwise.

Becoming vulnerable is tough no matter how we look at it, but without vulnerability for the twisted thinker, transforming their thinking isn't possible. So, how can we help them correct this thinking error so they can become the STARs that chapter two mentions?

When approaching twisted thinkers on any twisted thinking issues, we need to do so out of love and respect for their dignity. If that is our posture we can then be firm and flexible at the same time.

It's worth bringing them to new beginning points in the transformation process, but in going below the street we will sometimes come away with a stench, and we'll wonder why we ever went there in the first place. But keep the faith! Remember God's mercy and his counsel for us.

> Therefore, since through God's mercy we have this ministry, we do not lose heart. Rather, *we have renounced secret and shameful ways*; we do not use deception, nor do we distort the word of God. On the contrary, by setting forth the truth plainly we commend ourselves to every man's conscience in the sight of God. (II Corinthians 4:1-2, emphasis added)

To overcome closed thinking the twisted thinker needs to develop Paul's attitude. If we're challenging them we need to listen for their evasiveness even as we seek additional information, while doing so in a matter-of-fact way. Be patient in getting the whole story or you will come across as judgmental. Get more facts and go for full disclosure!

The bottom line in closed thinking is how secrets are kept to guarantee pursuit of the *Big E*. But Paul encouraged believers to enjoy their freedom in Christ. In II Corinthians 3:17 he said, "And where the Spirit of the Lord is, there is freedom." Nothing can be left hidden while the person pursues *Big E*s.

True excitement resides in a relationship with Christ and the joy of heaven. Paul expressed this thought, too, when he said, "For to me to live is Christ" (Philippians 1:21). Yet even if a twisted thinker doesn't have a relationship with Christ, the principle of hiding nothing to pursue the *Big E*s is still what promotes the freedom to be a STAR.

No Secrets Allowed

With twisted thinkers who enter counseling, the one thing I contract for is *no secrets*. Their unveiling then involves helping them look at their irresponsible behavior while thinking through what they did wrong, or thinking about what they could have done better. This takes time but the process needs to be repeated whenever they're caught, until it becomes a habit for them.

The twisted thinker needs to understand what we are saying, if we're going to hold them accountable. If they aren't listening, you'll know. Don't argue but be open to bringing things up later. You can get plenty of mileage by asking, "Are you open for discussion?" That gives them a choice, and they also know that they are then responsible for it.

They also need to be reminded that repentance and change take time. This is hard for the twisted thinker to hear because they are all sprinters. Remember, they love the game of lickety-split and they're constantly looking for shortcuts while avoiding responsible thinking. They need to hear that change is a process, not a shortcut, and being self-critical is what responsible people do.

David's Guilt Forgiven

The process is difficult but worthwhile. An example of this can be seen in King David's life, when he finally became vulnerable and was transformed by a change in thinking, which led to God's forgiveness.

> Blessed is he whose transgressions are forgiven, whose sins are covered. Blessed is the man whose sin the LORD does not count against him and in whose spirit is no deceit. When I kept silent, my bones wasted away through my groaning all day long. For day and night your hand was heavy upon me; my strength was sapped as in the heat of summer. Then I acknowledged my sin to you and did not cover up my iniquity. I said, "I will confess my transgressions to the LORD"—and you forgave the guilt of my sin. (Psalm 32:1-5)

David's transformation involved daily and sometimes moment-by-moment choices.

Becoming Vulnerable to Become Visible

Before we move into the next chapter, allow me to emphasize one more time how understanding closed thinking can provide a fundamental breakthrough in the twisted thinker's transformation. When that person refuses to remain open, will not be disgusted at what they do to hurt others, and remains unwilling to keep the facts straight on a consistent level, the walls are still up. It's paramount to discovering if they're becoming a STAR

> I will instruct you and teach you in the way you should go; I will counsel you and watch over you. Do not be like the horse or the mule, which have no understanding but must be controlled by bit and bridle or they will not come to you. Many are the woes of the wicked, but the LORD'S unfailing love surrounds the man who trusts in him. (Psalm 32:8-10)

Chapter Five

MARTYRED THINKING

"I Blame You"

I view myself as a victim when I'm held accountable. I blame social conditions, my family, the past, and other people for what I do.

A married couple decided to attend the Community Church in Sturgeon Bay, Wisconsin, where I was the pastor. Both John and Diana had a great sense of humor. Diana, especially, liked to laugh. She was also a very perceptive woman.

I noticed for several weeks, during sermons, how she was smiling at me. After one Sunday service Diana approached me, wearing that same smile, and then said, "Jerry, you can't preach a message without giving a sports illustration." The comment felt a bit unsettling, as if she had something on me, and I had the following thought: "Just because I showed a six-minute clip from *Hoosiers*, one of the best sports movies ever made, she comes up with a crack like that."

Seriously, I know Diana as the good-natured lady she is, and rather than indulge in any of the martyred thinking this chapter will focus on I let the comment go. Still, I was a bit irritated, and over the next few Sundays I paid attention to see if she was right. As I've said before, she is a very perceptive woman. So, here comes my six-minute sports story about martyred thinking; the sequential, twisted thinking pattern that leads to closed thinking, which equates to being invisible and invulnerable.

A Six-Minute Sports Story

For a number of years I've coached small college and high school basketball. In one high school, while I was coaching the junior varsity, one of the athletes had problems fitting into our team's mix. Even though David was a freshman he thought he should play varsity ball. All the coaches agreed, but one thing was missing in his character—humility.

As the JV coach it was my job to get David ready to play varsity ball at mid-season, something he didn't even know about. Did I think he'd interpret staying on the JV squad as a putdown? Not really. Humility was an issue with him, but I didn't know how much until I caught him playing the martyr and disrupting the team.

One of his offensive assignments as a point guard was driving to the basket and breaking down the defense. On the way to the hoop, he was to look for a pass to our low post-position. Most coaches would love having a player who could penetrate the lane to make that pass, and David could do it.

Unfortunately, during games his passes were often difficult to handle, making the post player look like a clumsy oaf. And typically he would screw up his face and give the teammate a painful look, communicating to the crowd and to me that the post player was at fault. I'd call time-outs telling David to soften up on his passes. It never seemed to happen and I was a bit confused, because the problem hadn't been showing up in practices.

A Coaching Insight

Finally, I began watching him more closely during actual games. Meanwhile, the team continued to struggle until it dawned on me that David's actions were deliberate. I had a hunch that he'd already made up his mind, before the season started, that playing varsity ball was a given. Being held accountable to a coaching staff that was thwarting this decision upset him. So his response was to play well in practice but not in games.

I can't say the actual thought that "You guys are going to pay for keeping me off the varsity!" was traveling through David's mind. Yet he had a prepared tactic for resisting every order I gave him to soften up on his passes under

Martyred Thinking

the basket. If my suspicions were accurate his martyred thinking could have worked like this: "Make myself look like the victim of an inferior JV team and it will force the coaches to move me up to the varsity."

His behavior seemed to escalate after time-outs were called, and sure enough it soon happened again during one particular game when I specifically said, "David, you need to think of other players and soften up on the passes. Your job is to make them better." He nodded, as if in agreement.

After that time-out this skilled athlete still continued to embarrass the team in the same manner. At that point I made the decision to take him off the floor. I knew something drastic had to be done. The team was discouraged and some players felt like quitting. When the game was over I walked into the locker room and announced, "David, you are suspended until further notice."

It was a tense moment. His mouth dropped in shock, as did everyone else's. The look on his face seemed to say, "You can't do this to the star of the team!" Meanwhile, the rest of the team hadn't figured out his tactics; they thought the problem was their fault for not being able to play at his level, so it looked like I was being unjustly hard on David. Nevertheless, I was willing to risk it.

In a private meeting, I then gave this troubled athlete only one requirement for coming back. He would have to look each teammate in the eye and ask, "Will you forgive me for being a jerk?" I said, "David, you have purposely made this team look bad in every game you've played in. Each teammate—and me too—will be asked that question before you ever step back into a game for this school again. That's the deal!"

To his credit, David took responsibility and humbled himself. In the same team meeting he did exactly what was required. Every athlete forgave him and our walls fell down. Then, he looked at me and asked the question, "Coach, will you forgive me?" As a coach, it was one of the most powerful moments I've ever experienced. My response was "Yes, welcome back," and the team bonded.

Now, you might be wondering whether he fulfilled my requirement because he was disgusted by the harm he'd created or because he simply wanted back on the team. I can't say for sure but the fact is, he did do it. It was a difficult time for all of us, but I believe everyone came to terms by taking responsibility for their part, in being the forgiver or the forgiven.

What about the rest of the story? Well, David softened up on his passes and we started winning. At mid-season, the coaching staff believed he was ready to move up to the varsity, and start—but not because his basketball skills had improved. There'd been no question about those from the beginning. Now, the coaches based their decision on the improvement in his character. Instead of playing the victim he chose to think of other teammates and brought their level of play up as well.

A Powerful Moment

It seems to me, as a first response to hurting others, most people don't think about saying the words, "Will you forgive me?" If we say anything at all we tend to go with "I'm sorry" and let that be enough.

As a counselor I've seen many victims of domestic abuse settle for this proverbial crumb. I think that victims accept meager apologies for many different reasons, one of which might result from the longing for a human connection. When the abuser offers some slight expression indicating that maybe, just maybe he "owns" his own twisted behavior, victims then think it's better than nothing at all.

How sad! The one request I hear over and over from wives of abusive husbands is, "Will you just take responsibility for what you've done and stop blaming me?" When the husband complies, many wives begin to believe that their spouse will start the change process—and that he will stop being rigid and distant to avoid the responsibility involved in loving them without artificial restraints.

But, there's more to this hope of rebuilding a relationship. It's about understanding relational power. When the words "Will you forgive me?" are genuinely said, because the speaker understands the impact their destructive thinking and antagonistic behavior has had on others, I've found that it gives the appropriate relational power back to the victim. Conversely, unless this power is given back, no real resolution and no healing occurs because the twisted thinker is changing only on the surface.

When that question is asked, accompanied by a willingness on the part of the victim to forgive, something happens that is strange, wonderful, healthy, and yet mysterious all at the same time. The victim stops being the victim! They have been fully authorized by the victimizer to become the forgiver. This is a powerful moment in any relational context, because people start becoming alive to each other whenever it happens.

God's relationship with fallen man involves the same dynamic. Although he's willing to forgive, God can't and doesn't until authorized by the sinner. His whole dialogue with Israel about sin offerings, in Leviticus 4 and 5, teaches how important it is to give relational power back to the offended. Love is unconditional but forgiveness isn't. When appropriate sin offerings were brought to the Lord, in the right way, He forgave those who brought them—but not until then. That's how God operates in relationship with fallen man.

Why should it be any different between twisted thinkers and the people they hurt? We don't do sin offerings as Israel did but the principle of asking for forgiveness is similar. By refusing to ask, the twisted thinker preserves his own martyred thinking; he's ready to blame someone else for his own irresponsibility. Victims aren't allowed to forgive even if they wanted to.

However, when victims are authorized to forgive, that becomes a powerful moment. That's a major reason why I believe that raising consciousness about twisted thinking is so important. That's how the door for applying genuine forgiveness can be opened.

Raising Our Consciousness

In the apostle Paul's day, some beliefs taught in his society were constructed to pacify people's guilt when they disconnected from each other. These beliefs covered up their twisted thinking patterns, prohibiting anyone from adequately identifying them, which is also what's happening in our culture today.

A few centuries later a group of Epicureans generated a different belief system, promoting a universal anesthesia for all troubling emotions: "Eat, drink, and be merry." With all that good feeling stuff going around, who would care about damage being done to others when a person could sooth their guilt with whatever temporary happiness they could produce? Every twisted thinker buys that idea.

I believe the need to start talking about patterns of twisted thinking is absolutely crucial because it relates to real guilt from irresponsible actions. That small window in time and space for David and the basketball team became a practical opportunity for speaking directly to this issue. In hindsight, one of my hopes for the team members was recovering what has generally been lost in our society, a *consciousness of the diagnosis of sin, exposed by every twisted thinking pattern this book addresses*. Those patterns keep people from transforming their minds, from building up true self-respect, and from encouraging authentic relationships.

There are times, even in the family of God, when people have ignored the sin found in these patterns. Listen with me as God talks to the weeping prophet of Israel about that:

> From the least to the greatest, all are greedy for gain; prophets and priests alike, all practice deceit. They dress the wound of my people as though it were not serious. "Peace, peace," they say, when there is no peace.
>
> Are they ashamed of their loathsome conduct? No, they have no shame at all; they do not even know how to blush . . . This is what the LORD says: "Stand at the crossroads and look; ask for the ancient paths, ask where the good way is, and walk in it, and you will find rest for your souls. But you said, 'We will not walk in it.' I appointed watchmen over you and said, 'Listen to the sound of the trumpet!' But you said, 'We will not listen.'" (Jeremiah 6:13-17)

God said his people deliberately decided to close their ears to Him. They would not listen because they were closed in their thinking. We can see it in their behavior and attitudes.

> Will you steal and murder, commit adultery and perjury, burn incense to Baal and follow other gods you have not known, and then come and stand before me in this house, which bears my Name, and

say, "We are safe"—safe to do all these detestable things? Has this house, which bears my Name, become a den of robbers to you? But I have been watching! Declares the LORD. (Jeremiah 7:9-11)

My prayer is for God to strengthen churches in this world via people who know how to weep over serious wounds coming from sin, particularly from the practice of twisted thinking. What happened in Jeremiah's day can also happen with God's people of today—to think otherwise is naïve. We need servants who will stand at the crossroads and point others to the ancient paths and the good way, and then walk with them in it.

The Springboard to Irresponsible Behavior

Throughout the Bible we see sin cycling over and over. Yet, in the cycling of these same sin patterns we also see God doing His part to raise our consciousness. As He does, His desire to redeem people from those patterns is repeatedly seen in the mercy He shows twisted thinkers of biblical times.

I believe that by providing us with the Bible—His spiritual laboratory—God extends His mercy. Between those covers, sin patterns are accurately recorded so we can get a grasp on the dynamics behind them. This is important because clues are also given that point the reader toward salvation and transformation. We know that learning from history can help, but God wants a lot more for us.

The same principle is essential for understanding twisted thinking. Cycles and patterns provide clues to anyone practicing them, showing how serious heading in the wrong direction really is. Because others have gone through the cycle, we have history to learn from. And, these patterns are familiar regardless of the age we live in. With that in mind, let's look more closely at the sequential error following closed thinking so we can begin to pick up on cycles of twisted thinking.

The twisted thinker will naturally go from closed thinking to martyred thinking simply because it maintains the drive for another *Big E*. Acting like a victim when they aren't functions like a springboard into irresponsible behavior.

If they are closed in thinking, they will already have a prepared accountability tactic in their toolbox for use in escaping the moment. The martyred thinker would rather pretend to feel put down than to reveal a conscious, deliberate strategy to avoid being responsible. They will aggressively blame social conditions, their family, their past, or you for what they do.

WHERE THE CYCLE STARTED

As I've noted before, the twisting of man's broken relationship started in Genesis when Adam said to God, "It was the woman you put here with me. She gave fruit from the tree and I ate it." Do you see the closed thinking, followed by martyred thinking? Look at the twist in Adam's mind.

Most of what Adam said was true. God did put the woman in the garden, she did hand him fruit from the tree, and he did eat it. And yet, everything Adam pointed at was an external reality. He disclosed above-the-street behaviors and used them as the foundation for his below-the-street "truth." The blame game is a pretty good con, isn't it? Adam thought so, but God didn't buy it.

Why didn't he protect his wife? Why did he choose to disobey the God who loved and created him? Let me cut to the chase. Adam bought into the fantasy the serpent gave him ("You will be like God, knowing good and evil"). His sin originated in his heart before it became an action of his body. The body was only the facilitator of choices made in the soul. No one but God knew Adam had already fallen into the dark place of twisted thinking.

His closed and martyred thoughts, suddenly yet finally, came out as if he were a sewer rat cornered in the darkness of night by someone walking down his sidewalk, near his sewer lid. Then, he attacked. It didn't take long for the ripple effect of Adam's sin to endorse relational chaos. In one irresponsible fantasy, nurtured by twisted thinking, Adam ruined the world he lived in.

Adam's world is now our world. In spite of all the exciting things happening in technology and science, mankind is still plagued by deep, personal, uncomfortable, insecure feelings of being lost. We see it more recently in questions being asked by many who are searching for reasons behind today's horrible crimes, especially those committed by young people.

But the true answers seem beyond society's grasp as we rush about looking for explanations.

Adam's sin originated in the unseen world of his heart and mind. I believe we must go to that world for answers.

Watching the Cycle

Years ago, while reading the *Muskegon Chronicle* in Muskegon, Michigan, I came across a story describing the consequences and outrage of martyred thinking. A tragic headline, "Dad faces charges after using gun to discipline kids," caught my attention.

The four children, ages three to seven, were not hit by gunfire. However, a neighbor heard their screams and called the police. After being arraigned, the thirty two-year-old father told a Muskegon County Sheriff's detective: "Those damn kids will not listen to anything I say. I got tired of yelling, so I pulled out the gun and shot holes in the wall. I thought maybe they would listen to that. I'm just about ready to call Protective Services and have them take these kids out of here."

I hope they did! Do you see the martyred thinking of this man? He saw himself as a victim of his own children and responded by shooting his gun to keep them from inconveniencing him.

The father fired the first shots coming up the stairway to the second floor, where two bedrooms were located. Several bullets went through the open door of one bedroom and lodged in the wall. The children were all "huddled in the corner" of the other bedroom. The bullets missed the children by a few feet. According to the detective, "The father was looking and yelling at them when he fired."

This man's choice to disconnect from his children and behave like a victim resulted from a classic combination of closed and martyred thinking. Although his behavior was an extreme example, the direction of his actions was the same as David's in my six-minute sports story. It doesn't matter if irresponsible behavior is extreme or not, because martyred thinking permits a person to disconnect from people on *any level*, purely for the sake of convenience.

That doesn't mean all twisted thinkers will ultimately descend into a life of crime. But the person who practices *any twisted thinking patterns at all*, whether they are aware of the direction of their thoughts or not, will always act out in some irresponsible manner. They will act out in ways that violate others, and then will blame them for their own behavior. They willfully and knowingly deny being responsible for their own actions.

The writer in the book of Proverbs put his finger on it. He writes about twisted thinkers who are clean in their own eyes yet choose to see themselves as victims, rather than looking at the evil they are doing.

> "There are those who curse their fathers and do not bless their mothers; *those who are pure in their own eyes* and yet are not cleansed of their filth; those whose eyes are ever so haughty, whose glances are so disdainful; those whose teeth are swords and whose jaws are set with knives to devour the poor from the earth, the needy from among mankind." (Proverbs 30:11-14, emphasis added)

There's a song by the Pretenders, released by Sire Records Company, called "Criminal." It reflects the above passage from Proverbs 30. The song talks about a man blaming his girlfriend for being a criminal after believing he got burned by her. He thinks that because he loved her he had a right to be an outlaw when she dumped him. The man is obsessed! He pleads for her to fix him or else. You hear the martyred thinking throughout the whole song.

But, "The devil made me do it!" or even "My girl friend made me do it!" doesn't cut it with responsible people. It won't cut it with God, either, when all humanity stands before the Throne of Glory someday. He will go straight to the intent of any twisted thinker's heart. No one will escape by assuming the role of a martyr.

Even so, this sort of thinking still seems to be emerging as the norm in our culture. What's worse, people actually seem to believe their own lies. I can almost hear someone saying, "Jerry, you're only talking about the skid row people, the down and outers, the addicts, the culturally challenged . . . right?" My answer, of course, is no.

Candidly, my first thought is we're all made of the same mud. I know I've played the blame game by deliberately acting like a victim when I wasn't. I've been left with egg on the face more times than I care to admit. Having a wife who has the gift of mercy is a marvelous thing. And meanwhile, we'd rather keep on struggling and growing than live in denial of personal responsibility, like the man in the following story did when he told me he was nothing more than a ricochet.

The Ricochet

"What I did as a kid was nothing more than being a ricochet. Somebody else always started it. I was the projectile, not the one who pulled the trigger. I didn't have choices."

It's amazing how a person can fall into the trap of martyred thinking, even when they are cultured, educated, and religiously inclined, as this guy was. During his youth, the *Big E* for him was finding a house to run through—in the front and out the back without getting caught. He did this in broad daylight with people at home. He also claimed that there were no choices in his life, then or now. This allowed him to practice several addictions. Can you imagine being married to this self-made martyr with a self-proclaimed impulse disorder?

Dr. Stanton E. Samenow included a chapter in his book, *The Criminal Personality*, on "Getting Over On Shrinks." He deals with the subject of impulse disorders as it relates to criminal behaviors like kleptomania (stealing) and pyromania (setting fires). It was clear from his study that such people are as much in control of their behavior as the bank robber. They simply do what they do out of some twisted joy in the result.

It's great to know that there are professionals in our country who aren't conned by the so-called "ricochet" behavioral theory of twisted thinkers. That particular error in thinking generally originates when overconfidence produces misjudgments that lead to unavoidable accountability—unless they can escape by playing the blame game. It usually results, also, in some degree of revenge to make others pay for getting in the way.

The Revenge Factor

When traveling through Colorado one time, Judy and I stopped for gas in Fort Morgan. As we pulled up behind a van we noticed a well-built young man who was pumping gas opposite our side of the island. Then, we saw a kid riding down a hill on his bicycle to the station. As he came closer I realized that he was older than I thought. He was a small, angry man in a hurry and on a mission.

Suddenly, this guy leaped off his bicycle and threw it in front of the van before us. He then jumped behind the man pumping gas, who was totally unaware of his presence, and threw a punch. Everyone was stunned, including the victim who dropped the nozzle and almost felt down, holding his bloody face. Meanwhile his assailant yelled out, "You know you had it coming!" Meanwhile, the wounded man's wife ran to call the police while the verbal assault continued. Then the guy jumped back on his bicycle and raced away.

I remember thinking how stupid this offender was. In his own mind he justified what he'd done without thinking about being charged with assault. But there were several witnesses to his crime, so focusing only on revenge, while playing the martyr as an excuse, could have backfired.

Potiphar's wife used the revenge factor in Genesis 39. She was confident that she could seduce Joseph and get him into bed with her. But when she made her move, Joseph ran from her grasp and she pulled off his cloak in the process. Then she concocted a lie to make him pay for rejecting her. Again, that's where combining closed and martyred thinking eventually takes a twisted thinker. They'll use revenge to disconnect from responsible people, even if it's a family member.

Do you remember what Potiphar's wife said? "That Hebrew slave you brought us came to me to make sport of me." Do you see her self-victimization coming? "But as soon as I screamed for help, he left his cloak beside me and ran out of the house." Predictably enough, Potiphar believed her and threw Joseph in prison.

I can't help but think you might know people who've been framed like Joseph. They are real victims of someone else's lie. However, Joseph eventually experienced justice. Genesis 39:20 states, "But while Joseph was in prison, the Lord was with him." By faith, Joseph believed that God was in control.

He had nothing else to go on except that faith. As a result, God worked it out so that Joseph was reunited with his father and the brothers who'd sold him into slavery so many years before. He then spent the last forty years of his life together with his family.

Not all victims of someone else's unfounded revenge see justice this side of heaven, but the Bible does teach that a member of the family of God will see justice in eternity. I think this is why responsible people who understand and accept God's authority don't seek revenge. They know God has said in Romans 12:19, "It is mine to avenge: I will repay, says the Lord."

Hebrews 11 talks about members of God's family who were commended for their faith, yet none had received what was promised. They had to wait, but only because God is planning something far better for all of us when we're together in eternity. That will also leave plenty of time for justice.

However, until that moment comes we will continue to struggle with twisted thinkers who will see themselves only as martyrs when they're held accountable for irresponsible behaviors. Unless, of course, they transform their thinking.

Transforming Martyred Thinking

When a twisted thinker begins to correct martyred thinking, what can we look for as indicators of change? If you happen to be a STAR and want to help in the process, you can start by turning on the lights as they go below the street into the darkness within.

The first thing to remember is how martyred thinking combines with closed thinking. No matter what twisted thinking pattern the person is pursuing, none of them operate without closed thinking. With this in mind, asking them "Are you open to discussing what happened when you thought you were wronged?" is a good way to find out they're ready to go further. If they aren't open, don't argue; come back another time. If they say yes, you've respected the twisted thinker as a person and are now ready to address the thinking itself.

You can often turn on one light by helping them own their part in creating their current situation. Do this by discussing choices they made when responding to someone who blocked their intentions. Search them out for the moment when they made a decision to violate a relationship, and look to see if there were other options. Even in domestic abuse situations, at one time each victimizer usually had an option to walk away, as simple as that might sound. If they can see that there were other options besides acting like a victim, martyred thinking can begin becoming apparent.

You can turn on another light by showing them how playing the blame game, overtly or covertly, violates the personal boundaries of other people. The twisted thinker usually believes that no one else has a right to contradict what he wants, so he precludes their choices by emoting on them instead.

In the very act of refusing to accept a "no" from Joseph, Potiphar's wife violated him further. An overconfident woman played the victim and framed him. If she couldn't have him, then she'd show him who was boss by using the leverage of martyred thinking. Welcome to revenge.

Another way to help the twisted thinker overcome martyred thinking is to help make him aware of how others, in similar situations, chose to act responsibly. This can demonstrate how they *chose* to become a victim when they actually weren't.

Another Road to Change

The above examples indicate how to transform martyred thinking, but there's one other way to get there. It has to do with what happens when a person truly is a genuine victim. Even twisted thinkers can be that.

Remember, I mentioned before that even if relational power can be given back to victims by perpetrators asking forgiveness, there will also be times when justice cannot be experienced this side of heaven. The danger in that scenario arises when a victim uses their "unfixable" victimization as an excuse to live irresponsibly, or to violate others. All the above indicators of change apply to them as well, but one more can be added.

Most dramatically of all, martyred thinking can be transformed by a choice to believe God even in the darkness of our own confusion, when contrary feelings are so strong. In the Bible, Job provides a brilliant example of this.

Job's choice to believe God shows how the martyred thinker can overcome the feeling of being a victim when they aren't—or even when they are. Believing God is good for everyone. Note how Job's decision to believe God stirs up the desire for life and brings about a leap into the light.

> "As surely as God lives, who has denied me justice, the Almighty, who has made me taste bitterness of soul, as long as I have life within me, the breath of God in my nostrils, my lips will not speak wickedness, and my tongue will utter no deceit. I will never admit you are in the right; till I die, I will not deny my integrity. I will maintain my righteousness and never let go of it; my conscience will not reproach me as long as I live." Job 27:2-6

When Job said, "My conscience will not reproach me as long as I live," he spoke as a responsible man and a normal sinner. After all his debates, with friends and with God, about his circumstances, he concludes that he's wrong in trying to contend and correct God. Job finally states that God can do all things, and that no plan of His can be thwarted. He admits to obscuring God's counsel without knowledge, and speaking of things he didn't understand.

However, even though Job certainly argued with God, because of his commitment to maintain it as long as he lived I don't believe his conscience was ever seared. The real sadness, of anyone practicing martyred thinking, is how he or she remains closed to making genuine human connections—especially with God.

Job didn't do this and that inspires me. He wasn't into blaming anyone else as an excuse for living irresponsibly. In fact, God said in Job 42:7 that he was angry with Job's friends because they didn't speak what was right, as His servant Job had done.

Job was transformed and lifted out of his darkness by choosing to trust in a living and loving God.

Chapter Six

INFLATED THINKING

Defining Good/Being Realistic

> *I view myself only as a good person to avoid responsibility for offenses. I fail to acknowledge my own destructive behavior. I build myself up at the expense of others.*

I highly recommend a movie from Scholastic Inc. and Karl-Lorimar Home Video, called *Dead Wrong*. This dramatic portrayal of the life of John Louis Evans III starts out by showing the real Evans videotaping a message to young people four days before his execution. He wanted them to learn the importance of making responsible and realistic choices instead of becoming shipwrecked by irresponsible ones, as he was.

The story begins when Evans was thirteen. His development as a twisted thinker began much earlier, however, inside the secret places of his mind. John's parents saw him as a boy with a lot of spunk through terrible twos, terrific threes, and funny fours. But by the time he reached the age of thirteen they were just trying to figure him out.

Evans' parents weren't aware of how he chose to control them. Like a chess player manipulating pawns, John moved them at will. He used deception, anger, guilt, defiance, in-your-face arrogance, and blatant disobedience to keep family dramas flowing.

I've seen this scenario played out over and over. It involves loving parents assuming total responsibility for their children's actions, worrying about where they went wrong while being completely ignorant of their child's twisted thinking patterns. Evans made choices at age thirteen that people trained in forensic counseling say are well-ingrained by age sixteen. Imagine the advantage of knowing about this earlier in the life of a child who's been tearing the family apart via habitual irresponsible behaviors.

When young twisted thinkers accompany their parents to my office they often get very upset when their thinking errors begin to be revealed. On the other hand, parents are typically strengthened via the relational integrity being brought back into the family. Whereas before they had unknowingly cooperated with their child's game, now there's hope for restoring the broken relationship.

Sadly, the parents of John Evans never figured him out until it was too late. John was deeply loved by his parents, but he used that against them. Nothing worked! In his early twenties he called home from another jail, expecting to be bailed out one more time. In the past, John's parents had found ways to do so. Now, literally, they couldn't afford another bailout and a decision had to be made. The father visited the jail, told him it was over, and Evans went back to his cell, furious.

He then shook the bars of his cell, and with hate swelling up in his heart began to complain about his family's abandonment to an inmate named Ridder. Evans fantasized about getting revenge and came up with the idea of a crime spree.

Now—doesn't that sound familiar? Once again it's the combined pattern of closed and martyred thinking we saw in the last chapter. Overconfident and anticipating the bailout, Evans played the victim when his dad refused to pay the bill. Then, something unusual happened in the story when Evans apparently decided to turn his life around. Except that he'd actually made no such decision at all.

A Turn That Was Only a Spin

Three years later Evans was living the "straight life" and was about to be married. One can only imagine the family's joy at the turn they thought he'd taken. But Evans was still disconnected from reality, as all twisted thinkers are. Only this time, no one knew it.

At home with his fiancée, John then got a surprise call from Ridder, who had just been released from jail. Ridder started talking about the crime spree they'd discussed three years earlier. John tried to resist but Ridder shamed him verbally and hung up. After the phone call, you could literally see the wheels turning in Evans' head while he ran an errand. The tension built. Then clearly, consciously, deliberately, and with plenty of forethought he made the decision to call Ridder back.

What followed was the tragedy of a man descending farther into crime than he ever thought he would. The two men's fantasy of a crime spree mainly involved armed robbery, but John Louis Evans III wound up murdering a gun shop owner in front of the man's two little girls.

In the last gut-wrenching scene before his execution, Evans talked with his mother. By now, though the movie doesn't reveal how the transformation occurred, it's obvious that he has finally made a human connection. Sadly, it was too late. He was a "dead man walking" at the age of thirty-three. All he could leave behind was a video of his testimony.

What Happened?

How could John Evans have thrown away what looked like three good rebuilding years, and abandoned a beautiful young bride, for a crime spree? This is the same question many people ask when they look for reasons behind the horrific behaviors of outwardly good, solid, law-abiding, even churchgoing individuals without criminal records. There was no warning that anything was wrong. So what happened?

The answer provides a major key for understanding how twisted thinkers consistently break faith in their relationships. However, that understanding also requires us to go through another manhole into the soul, to the place of *inflated thinking*.

Twisted thinkers believe that good behavior—all by itself—will establish their legitimate goodness. They then mix that belief with secret, irresponsible fantasies, and combine all that with closed and martyred thinking. At that point, whether their excitement comes from criminal or other types of habitual, irresponsible behavior, the impact on everyone else will be the same: Shock!

And yet, at the same time the pride that twisted thinkers have regarding what they believe is their private stock of goodness, allows them to completely dismiss the shock. To them it's no worse than what everyone else does: maybe not great but certainly not evil. Clearly, everything depends on their own definition of goodness.

However, the following biblical principle completely contradicts their own flattering view of themselves.

Any good behavior used to establish goodness is twisted thinking inflated.

THE TWISTED STOCK OF GOODNESS

All twisted thinkers believe the following: "If you get to know the real me you'll see that I'm a good person like anyone else." What no one catches is how they must be the person who defines both (1) what is good and (2) the essence of goodness itself. This creates a barrier, founded on denial that prevents them from acknowledging personally destructive behaviors even as they continue to build themselves up at others' expense. When they define goodness they retain control; thus they become chess masters who like it that way.

On May 11, 1996, a newspaper story in the *Green Bay Press Gazette* about Saddam Hussein reflected on his twisted stock of goodness. He praised the slaying of a defector who had returned to Iraq, yet said he would have stopped the killing if he'd known about the plan in advance. Clearly, Saddam was referring to his son-in-law, Hussein Kamel al-Majid, although he did not name him.

Clan members killed al-Majid and other former defectors when they returned to Baghdad from exile, after Saddam pardoned them. Listen to what the article quotes Saddam as saying and see if you can spot his twist of inflated Thinking: "If they had asked me about it (the killings), I would have prevented them, and the good thing in this matter is that they didn't, because when I pardon, I mean it."

Is there any question about Saddam being a chess master who likes it that way? Did you catch the inflated thinking keeping him in control of whether someone lives or dies?

Shocked By Twisted Goodness

I have a memory of sitting in a car parked in front of my cousin's house in Indianapolis. I was nine and my cousin, about the same age, was standing near the car window, cracking jokes. I noticed a young black boy who looked about six or seven, walking by. Out of nowhere, my cousin began to physically assault him.

I was shocked! When the boy ran away I asked my cousin why he hit him. I said, "He wasn't doing nothing!" He responded with a racially explosive statement, implying that he was a better piece of work than black kids.

One might blame the racial unrest of the 50s and 60s as the cause behind my cousin's attitude. But why didn't I make that choice? If I lived in the same time period, how come I was shocked by his decision? Why didn't I have the same thoughts? No, the fault lay deeper, within secret places in my cousin's heart.

The phrase "racial prejudice" wasn't in my vocabulary but I saw it happening in raw form. Knowing what I now know, I realize that my cousin was living out his own inflated view of superiority. He defined his own goodness and mixed it with an irresponsible fantasy of power and control. What hostility!

In the Bible, inflated thinking sets up a huge wall between responsible and irresponsible people, between Jews and Gentiles, but most of all between God and humanity. The apostle Paul wrote about Jesus Christ's coming to destroy that view of self. His coming was an expression of God's longing to be connected with humanity, and for us to be connected to each other.

> "For he himself is our peace, who has made the two one [*speaking of Jew and Gentile*] and has destroyed the barrier, the dividing wall of hostility, by abolishing in his flesh the law with its commandments and regulations. His purpose was to create in himself one new man out of the two, thus making peace, and in this one body to reconcile both of them to God through the cross, by which *he put to death their hostility.*" (Ephesians 2:14-16, emphasis added)

Inflated Thinking

In order for the above to be true, "good" or "goodness" has to be defined by an external authority. The definition must uphold the highest standard, which must then reject any twist upon it.

Defining Good

I believe the ultimate reference source for defining "good" is the Bible. It's able to penetrate interior recesses of twisted thinking by reflecting God's character—who and what He really is in all His goodness. Without that source the definition of "goodness" is up for grabs, and we're in Dodge City where twisted gunslingers with the fastest draw become tin gods. I believe the Bible as the best possible foundation for determining all this, and Psalms is a great place to start.

> "Many are asking, 'Who can show us any good?' Let the light of your face shine upon us, O LORD." (Psalm 4:6)

> "Remember not the sins of my youth and my rebellious ways; according to your love remember me, for you are good, O Lord. Good and upright is the Lord; therefore he instructs sinners in his ways." (Psalm 25:7, 8)

> "Taste and see that the LORD is good; blessed is the man who takes refuge in him." (Psalm 34:8)

> "You are forgiving and good, O LORD, abounding in love to all who call to you." (Psalm 86:5)

> "For the LORD is good and his love endures forever; his faithfulness continues through all generations." (Psalm 100:5)

We also see "good" defined in chapter 10 of Mark's gospel when Jesus talked to a rich young ruler. The man ran up to him, fell on his knees, and said, "Good teacher, what must I do to inherit eternal life?" "Why do you call me good?" Jesus answered. "No one is good except God alone."

This is the only account in Scripture that records a person going away from Jesus "sad." The pitiful thing about the rich young ruler is that he doesn't get beyond his own bias. Quite possibly he went out into eternity, not only sad but also lost. He wasn't necessarily a twisted thinker, but inflated thinking caused his demise. According to the Bible, that error in thinking has eternal consequences for everyone.

CHOICES

Frankly, inflated thinkers have only three choices if they insist on defining their own goodness. They can (1) continue irresponsible behaviors or (2) change into responsible citizens. Or, (3) they can commit suicide, which sometimes amounts to a demand to control others after they die.

However, I want to be careful here. Not everyone committing suicide does so for the above reason. For some, the pain related to severe depression or a deep sense of loss is more than they could bear. It is not about ego building—It's about being unable to find a way out of despair except by ending their lives. They simply have no hope.

This is not the case for twisted thinkers. They truly believe that they're superior to others. But, when they're no longer able to manufacture their own brand of excitement, and also unable to control other people, their last *Big E* can be suicide. Talk about being totally disconnected from humanity and God . . . they're like the wicked man described in the passage below:

> "An oracle is within my heart concerning the sinfulness of the wicked: There is no fear of God before his eyes. *For in his own eyes he flatters himself too much to detect or hate his sin.*
>
> The words of his mouth are wicked and deceitful; he has ceased to be wise and to do good. Even on his bed he plots evil; he commits himself to a sinful course and does not reject what is wrong." (Psalms 36:1-4, emphasis added)

Twisted thinkers love to shock others with their evil. Eternity is not the focus. Living for *Big Es* is.

"Shocks" From Evil Choices

Our country was shocked when a day-trader in Atlanta killed his wife, children, co-workers, and then himself. The man's suicide letter was rank with the smell of his own self-inflated goodness, even as he committed to a sinful course. Clearly, he flattered himself too much to detect or hate his own sin.

Our country was also shocked by someone's inflated thinking when we heard about a tragedy in Texas, at the Wedgewood Baptist Church. During a Christian music concert for young people, a man deliberately rolled a pipe bomb down the aisle. Then he opened fire on the crowd, killing several and wounding others. In one final act of defiance he shot himself. By choice, this man committed himself to a sinful course by not rejecting what is evil. Clearly, he flattered himself too much to detect or hate his own sin.

The Bible speaks of Judah's breaking faith with God while holding that same view. Malachi rebukes Judah's definition of goodness. He notes how it harmed them by desensitizing the Judeans to any concern for responsible and right living as God defined it. They flattered themselves too much to detect or hate their sin. Listen to Malachi hold Judah accountable.

> You have wearied the Lord with your words. "How have we wearied him?" you ask. By saying, "All who do evil are good in the eyes of the Lord, and he is pleased with them" or "Where is the God of justice?" (Malachi 2:17)

Proverbs 16:2 says, "All a man's ways seem innocent to him (an inflated view) but motives are weighed by the LORD." This reveals that we have enough problems being normal sinners without having more sins come from inflated thinking. Thus the sludge of inflated thinking creeps along, exposing the motives of everyone who believes all their ways are innocent.

I want to encourage you to be like Malachi. He was in a position to make a difference by pointing others to the goodness of God. He knew inflated thinking was a repugnant sludge, keeping Judah from detecting or hating sin. Now let's go further and consider what this sludge is made of.

The Sludge Behind Inflated Thinking

Previously I said that there's an answer to how Johnny Evans could throw away three good rebuilding years and a beautiful young bride. The answer will be the same for any habitually irresponsible person whose shocking behaviors range from producing dark tragedies to small, instant, "passive/aggressive" triumphs. Look at some past public and private moments representing that range of forbidden excitements.

Public Tragedies: from Jonesboro, Tennessee (massacre by two middle school boys) to Jones Borough; from Charlie Manson to Richard Speck; from Adolf Hitler to Saddam Hussein; from Waco, Texas to the bombing Oklahoma City bombing; from the Columbine High School Tragedy to New York City on 9/11/01. All of these are huge scars.

Private shocks brought about by twisted thinkers: What about kids who come home from school and are afraid of walking on a certain path for fear of some bully? What about the children who are defiant in the home but not in public, creating nightmares for the family? What about sexual abuse coming from a family member? What about extra-marital affairs? What about the person with a habitual eating disorder? What about the person who logs onto the Internet and sees his computer ruined by some hacker who sent a virus? What about going to a movie and not expecting Hollywood to insert some flesh scene totally unrelated to the story? What about going to the grocery store and having someone take your grocery cart after you spent an hour selecting food?

Twisted thinkers aren't unique. They're all skilled at making choices that violate relationships, like the man who divorced his spouse of thirty years. "I had it planned before I married her," he said. "I always planned to divorce her after all the kids were gone."

What treachery! No one ever saw it coming. But more important, does it always have to be that way? Not if we're realistic and can identify the elements of sludge within inflated thinking.

If we're going "below the street" into the intents of the heart, we need a roto-rootering process to shake the sewage loose, and it starts with the principle we've already established: "Any good behavior used to establish goodness is twisted thinking inflated."

That principle explains how and when the human connection can be lost in broken relationships within society. But a formula that explains the corrosion of the character of people caught up in inflated thinking will be critical in the transformation of this error.

The Formula of Corrosion

This formula can routinely trace failures to acknowledge destructive behavior on the part of any twisted thinker. Whether in counseling or ministry, I have seen this equation be absolutely foundational to understanding their negative effects on communities.

When twisted thinkers mix irresponsible fantasies with their own definition of "personal goodness," it initiates the process by which all spiritual and moral deterrents can decay. All the twisted thinking patterns mentioned in this book reinforce those fantasies. So, with the above in place, the twisted thinker eventually shocks those around him by pursuing *Big Es*. What was once below the street, in secret, is now above the street in public. Here's another view as an equation.

> Dwelling upon irresponsible fantasies + A personal definition of "goodness" decaying spiritual and moral deterrents + Development of twisted thinking patterns + Determined choices to pursue the *Big E* = Their above-the-street shock

It's one thing to know how the corrosion of character happens, but that knowledge alone is not sufficient to deal with being stunned by inflated thinkers. That's because we need to understand a second bit of sludge behind inflated thinking.

THE IRRELEVANCE OF TIME AND SPACE

Time and space is irrelevant to the twisted thinker. If we don't understand this reality the shock of their *Big E* will leave us even more staggered. On the other hand, understanding it allows us to walk with wisdom as we handle being shocked by them.

We're still appalled, disgusted, angry, sickened, and hurt, but we are not slaughtered by their "behavioral stun guns," which they continue to fire even after we thought they were changing for the better. We can still move because we'll not be controlled by their behaviors. Why, then, is time and space irrelevant to the twisted thinker? The answer is simple but profound.

A corrosion of conscience starts the very moment they choose to entertain irresponsible fantasies. Since that moment originates in a private and secret place, maintaining the fantasies is easy because they can cover them up with responsible behaviors. Why not? The twisted thinker is in total control of those fantasies. No one else knows they're entertaining them.

Ironically, the inevitable decay that results also remains unseen by twisted thinkers (via self-deception), just as it is by any straight thinker. If the twisted thinking fantasy was never rejected it lies lurking, waiting to be re-embraced. For the twisted thinker it's like calling up a favorite game on the hard drive of your computer when you're ready to play. We don't think about the game every waking moment, but when we want to play we can, because it hasn't been deleted.

Thus inflated thinkers are able to mingle an undeleted irresponsible fantasy with a twisted thinker's definition of goodness—all below the surface—while they simultaneously demonstrate good behavior above the surface. However, this doesn't make them well even though they can behave like they are.

Ever see signs saying, "Stuff Happens?" Well, it's not true with respect to *Big E* moments. Those moments come from the sludge we're talking about. There's fantasizing and thinking that no one observing above-the-street behavior will ever see, until the filth of its sewage surfaces. That's the major reason behind the "shock" we feel when people who—without warning—do something totally irresponsible.

Most people live like they believe that they can "Give it a little time, a little space and everything will be OK." Even Johnny Evans could honestly say he hadn't preplanned the murder of a gun shop owner. But, being out of jail and away from Ridder for three years didn't help him. And neither Evans, his family, nor his fiancée knew it.

Once a hurricane hits the shore the filth from sewers, dead animals, and destroyed houses appears. The filth of John Evans' past, involving undeleted fantasies, twisted thinking, and irresponsible behaviors, unexpectedly surfaced in his life during one destructive moment in time. The resulting hurricane shocked even him.

According to the movie, not until six years after he committed murder would viewers ever know that John Louis Evans III had accepted full responsibility for being "dead wrong." He had been transformed into a STAR, able to make human connections. What helped in making that happen, even though he couldn't change the past?

Returning to Time and Space

This next statement is extremely important because it's the key to understanding what happens when twisted thinkers begin disconnecting from others. During the moment certain fantasies enter their consciousness, a twisted thinker must be disgusted by the harm they would do if indulged. That's called "empathy." Then, they need to respect themselves and others by making choices to be responsible in thought and behavior, often with open, public commitments. Again, this must be done at the time of awareness. If it isn't, they have begun to disconnect from time and space—the real world.

John Evans did not do this while in his jail cell, during the moment when he and Ridder first fantasized about a crime spree. No matter how good his behavior toward family members around him became afterwards, that was irrelevant because, during the moment he made the commitment to go on a crime spree, he never stopped to reconsider and change the direction in which his thinking was taking him. It became an emotional, seemingly rational personal reservoir waiting to be accessed. If he had repented in the moment he fantasized this foolishness, an innocent man (and perhaps Evans, his killer as well) would not now be dead. But three years later, when Ridder called, the filth in the reservoir of Evens' soul came forth.

In Proverbs 6:18, God says He hates "a heart that devises wicked schemes and feet that are quick to rush into evil (the shock above the street)." Jesus put a high premium on understanding where wicked behavior comes from in the 15th chapter of Matthew. He said it comes from within or out of the heart (the deep parts of man—our polluted humanity). Change must happen in that place if it's going to last.

Meanwhile, one last bit of sludge that twisted thinkers use to shock unsuspecting victims still needs to be discovered.

THE COVER UP

Remember, twisted thinkers are defining goodness (and using "acts of goodness") to maintain the belief that they are "good." The Bible directly opposes that view of self in the following passages.

> "For it is by grace you have been saved, through faith—*and this not from yourselves, it is the gift of God*—not by works, so that no one can boast. For we are God's workmanship, created in Christ Jesus to do good works, which God prepared in advance for us to do." (Ephesians 2:8, 9, emphasis added)

> As it is written: "There is no one righteous, not even one; there is no one who understands, no one who seeks God. All have turned away, they have together become worthless; *there is no one who does good, not even one.*" (Romans 3:10-12, emphasis added)

> "The fool says in his heart, 'There is no God.' They are corrupt, their deeds are vile; there is no one who does good. The LORD looks down from heaven on the sons of men to see if there are any who understand, any who seek God. All have turned aside, they have together become corrupt; *there is no one who does good, not even one.*" (Psalm 14:1-3, emphasis added)

These passages are all talking about "good" as defined by God and exemplified in Jesus Christ. But, the twisted thinker says, "If you got to know the real me, you would know I'm a good person." To prove it they'll get involved with charities and religious observances, they'll be artistic or mechanical, they'll hold down jobs, they'll abhor particular sorts of crimes and addictions, and they will demonstrate sentimentality toward animals or people, all of which are above-the-street behaviors. It's amazing how many of us get caught in this inflated view of self.

Losing My Own Stock Of Goodness!

A number of years ago, Judy and I were going to dinner with some friends in Sheboygan, Wisconsin. While driving to a restaurant near Lake Michigan, I saw a squirrel starting to run across the road. My thought was to have some fun with our friends by playing a game of "chicken" with the squirrel. I was certain that squirrel would quickly run away from the van I was driving. It didn't. In fact, this poor little animal stopped right in front of the van and the next thing you know we hear a small "clump" under one of the wheels.

My friend's wife gasped. "Jerry! Jerry! Jerry! I can't believe you did that!" Judy seemed just as alarmed. Immediately I tried to explain that I hadn't planned on killing the squirrel, but to no avail. Finally I began feeling shame but tried to hide it.

Once we arrived at the restaurant I started to talk about buying a bamboo birdcage for my parakeet. I embellished my goodness by taking credit for giving "Peety" more freedom to fly. Again, my friend and his wife looked at me with shock. Then he said, "Jerry, I'll bet you think you are a good person because you take care of your bird. But, I want you to know you are nothing more than a squirrel killer!"

Ouch.

I think my friend was kidding (?). Still, he had me dead-to-rights. I could no longer define my goodness as a man who cared for his bird. Even as a licensed professional counselor, I wasn't aware of being in the sewer of inflated thinking. But to avoid more embarrassment, I tried to come off as superior by playing my own game of lickety-split. The fact is, I killed that squirrel! Not intending to was immaterial. What I intended to do was go for a *Big E*, but I got caught instead.

They wouldn't let me escape. Several weeks later, I received a card in the mail. When I opened the envelope, one of those plastic toys you get in a box of Cracker Jacks fell out. It was a squirrel folding his hands in prayer. I was held accountable, again!

Although I'm having some fun telling the story, I did feel the discomfort of two things: killing the squirrel and being exposed for an irresponsible decision. I had to deal with the discomfort just like any twisted thinker must when overcoming the sludge behind inflated thinking.

Overcoming Inflated Thinking

It takes time to work through layers of this thinking pattern, but it begins with the following corrective. The very moment we see inflated thinking being practiced, the twisted thinker needs to have it exposed.

When done out of respect for the person it's the right and courageous thing to do. In fact, as an expression of love, God does the same thing in His Word. The Bible exposes our sins, from Genesis to Revelation, for the purpose of connecting with Him. The exposure is redemptive.

Transforming twisted thinking calls for the same kind of exposure to see what's broken on the inside first, where human connections with each other and God happen. Fortunately, a couple of practical tools can help expose inflated thinking.

When twisted thinkers have been caught in a *Big E* (whatever the irresponsible behavior is), making or discussing a ripple effect chart will show whom they hurt with the hope of developing empathy. Being realistic by recognizing the pain they've caused others will strike a blow to inflated thinking.

Another tool to use is the "rap sheet." On a piece of paper, make two columns. In one column, have them list all the good things they can remember doing. In the other column, have them list all the bad things they've done. You might be surprised to find some twisted thinkers won't come up with a whole lot of good things, versus the bad. At other times, however, they write nothing but good things compared to, perhaps, only one bad incident. Whatever happens the point will be made, and it is this: Can all the good things make up for the bad? If they're open and realistic, the answer will be no. That will strike another blow against inflated thinking.

Weighing the bad against the good allows the twisted thinker to view the whole picture and get beyond tunnel vision. That tunnel vision can be seen when they consider themselves to be above what they believe are low-lifes, as in the story of my cousin. They're actually indulging in inflated thinking and defining their own false goodness.

Weighing the bad against the good in the twisted thinker's life helps them understand that we truly are all made of the same mud. No one is superior in worth. John 3:16 says that "God so loved the world." Everyone is on the same level in God's eyes, all sinners needing redemption. Who can be inflated with that? I believe that no can be, and it's foolish to think otherwise.

Jesus was never impressed by shows of superiority, whether put on by Pharisees or anyone else. In Matthew 23 He said that everything they did was for men to see, but they didn't practice what they preached. They needed to come off their high horses and do things from the heart. God simply isn't impressed with the efforts of "mud" trying to impress Him. Mud doesn't define God or goodness. God defines both Himself and goodness.

Being Realistic

Overcoming inflated thinking is critical, because this is the pattern justifying closed and martyred thinking. It blinds a person to their impact on others. It also hinders the development of empathy, so crucial in making the human connection.

We need to consider the highest possible definition of goodness to understand that all man's ways are not right, even in his own eyes. And I believe this definition is found in the person of Jesus Christ. He's not against good behavior but he's against using good behavior as the only criteria for defining goodness. When that biblical principle is understood and acknowledged on a regular basis, inflated thinking will be deflated and there will be hope for twisted thinkers to become STARs.

"Taste and see that the LORD is good; blessed is the man who takes refuge in him." (Psalm 34:8)

Chapter Seven

STUBBORN THINKING

"I won't"

*I won't make any effort to do things I find boring or disagreeable.
When I say "I can't" I'm really saying "I won't."*

In a favorite *Calvin and Hobbes* by Bill Watterson, Calvin approaches Miss Wormwoods' desk with a compensation contract. Demanding income for wage losses that he might suffer as an adult, Calvin blames it on a poor first-grade education. Miss Wormwood points a finger at him and says, "If you get a poor first-grade education, it will be from your lack of effort, not mine. Get back to your desk." Then, we see Calvin sitting at his desk, mumbling, "By golly, somebody ought to pay me if I don't learn anything."

Calvin's plan is cute, but if an adult tried to live out that fantasy we'd think, "How immature!" To hear older people say, "Somebody owes me even if I don't work or can't learn," means, "I won't work or learn but pay me anyway." As an adult, Miss Wormwood is willing to do responsible things in life. To me, Calvin represents anyone locked into a never-ending relational immaturity.

His childishness can also apply to individuals who are very responsible people in society. Some might be high-profile leaders in our churches, communities, or country, making decisions that affect all of us. Yet they keep repeating selected moments of irresponsibility.

However, I'm not talking about developmental issues surrounding learning disabilities or emotional traumas. Instead, I'm referring to states of immaturity brought on entirely by choices to practice twisted thinking, which no one knows about until they opt for some *Big E* and are discovered.

Those decisions point to failures to grow up and lead to behavior needing correction.

Fortunately, it is possible to get beyond this kind of small mindedness. This chapter will provide keys for releasing immature thinkers from self-inflicted captivity, via which they can then have a chance to be a STAR and restore broken relationships.

Shackles of Immaturity

Using the bookend principles of chapter two, if an individual is convinced he's good via personal definitions of goodness, and then chooses to act like a martyr, transforming him will be very difficult. Moreover, it can be downright debilitating. Whether adults are newcomers to responsible thinking or are harebrained like Calvin, it's imperative to understand the dynamics behind stubborn thinking because they are chained in shackles of narcissism.

Other important questions should also be considered, such as the following:

- "Why does the stubborn thinker's unwillingness to change hurt God?"
- "How does God's pain reflect the suffering responsible people experience at the hands of stubborn thinkers?"
- "What shackles of relational immaturity need to be unlocked, offering freedom of soul to connect with others—and most of all—with God?"

Let's begin with the first shackle, the use of shortcuts.

Shortcuts

Did you ever look for the easy way out of a problem? At some point in our lives, I think we all do. But, twisted thinkers live to find shortcuts so they can avoid being inconvenienced or held responsible. It's their way of controlling anything that's boring or disagreeable. In reality it's a form of laziness.

Twisted thinkers can begin to unshackle themselves from stubborn thinking shortcuts by learning to distinguish between the concepts of effort and energy. This was obvious with Calvin but it's a more sophisticated scenario for twisted thinkers. Let's start with clear definitions for each concept.

- **Effort** requires us to use energy for doing something goal-oriented but distasteful, as in taking out the garbage. This chore doesn't make anybody's motor run!
- **Energy** can also be used for doing something goal-oriented that is exciting, fun, and non-boring. In that context, expending it can seem to require *no effort at all*.

Anything twisted thinkers find boring or disagreeable requires an effort that doesn't seem worthwhile, and therefore it won't be done. Or if attempted, it won't be done well. Yet the same people expend endless amounts of energy for irresponsible and illegal behaviors—*Big Es*. Overall, their constant goal is to find shortcuts for making life work their way. That's why it's narcissism because it's not about you but about them—always.

I've already admitted to being a redeemed twisted thinker who's still transforming his thinking. I don't do stubborn thinking as much as I used to, but sometimes I still find myself taking counterproductive shortcuts. I was guilty of it when helping my grownup son.

Nathan called one day and asked if I'd come over and help him hang an entry door in his house. I said, "Sure, but I don't have much time." I'd watched other men at our church hang doors, and that was enough to make me feel confident that I could do it myself. So I went over to help.

We ripped out the old doorframe; we shimmied in the new door-frame; we caulked the threshold down; we screwed the unit to the house; and it was all done in about an hour. Did you notice how I said "We?" Nathan had been going along with me, possibly because he felt some pressure coming from me as his father. Maybe he thought I knew what I was doing. I certainly thought so. Hey, maybe he was a chip off the old block. Then, the moment came to shut the door and see it all marvelously come together, securely latched. It didn't happen. Something was wrong.

So, I decided to realign the shimmies. This meant unscrewing the door and getting the latch to fall smoothly into place. We were now about two hours into the project. Fussing with this became a bit painful because it was becoming clear that Nathan's father was incompetent. Did you notice I didn't say that *I* was incompetent? It's easier to talk in the third person. But the real stickler to this revolting development came when Nathan finally realized what was going on.

To make matters worse, Heather, our lovely daughter-in-law, was sitting in the next room hearing the grunts and groans of one stubborn, know-it-all guy working with her husband. Alas, after three hours of frustration, Nathan said, "Dad, maybe we ought to read the instructions!"

I was busted, and so I read the instructions. They weren't very exciting, but a strange phenomenon called "enlightenment" then occurred. Instead of lining up the door by putting shims all around it, the instructions called for only one shim at the bottom right. I thought, "Hmm, that's interesting!"

Then, we noticed one screw purposely missing at the top right of the doorframe. The instructions explained that this screw should be used to secure the door, but only *after* the bottom right shim was put in and the spacing was equaled. Again I thought, "Hmm, that's interesting!"

I still had doubts about the instructions, but by then Nathan was convinced that we had no other options. So, we did everything according to those boring instructions. To my surprise the door actually looked lined up, and then came the big test. You wouldn't believe what happened . . . or would you? It worked! I mean that door was tight and gave no resistance. We're talking *smoooth*!

We secured the rest of the frame to the house, caulked it, and gawked at our masterpiece. Did you notice I said, "Our?" Then, Nathan turned and offered the final blow to my ego. "Dad, from now on, we read the instructions first." A one-hour job had taken almost four hours, thanks to my shortcuts.

My precious wife thought this story was funny. On the phone, she told it to our daughter Jana, living in Australia at the time. I couldn't believe it but this whole dynamic was further confirmed when Judy repeated what Jana said. I heard it all the way from down under. "Mom, I've seen Dad do that a lot of times. It's like he does stuff backwards, wasting energy."

And she was absolutely right. Too often I've looked for shortcuts. But now, I have Jana's comment to help me stop wasting endless energy in irresponsible ways, which is the precise definition of stubborn thinking. The truth is that I was expending *no real effort at all*, because reading the instructions would have been boring or disagreeable. Working on Nathan's entry door without instruction, like some Mr. Handyman, was more fun.

Sadly, shortcuts for twisted thinkers always seem more exciting until they fail to work. That's when they usually bail out or play lickety-split.

The impact of what happened at Nathan's house might be less severe than what has happened to other twisted thinkers, but in principle it's all the same stinking thinking. On the other hand, the more twisted thinkers understand this pattern the less surprised they'll be when they discover that what looks like *needless* effort actually isn't. Instead, it's a *productive* burst of energy, used as a *legitimate* shortcut to achieve a worthwhile goal.

Conversely, whenever a twisted thinker says "I can't!" he's really expressing his unwillingness to endure adversity, which can often be as innocuous as reading the directions first.

Lack of Endurance

Years ago, I worked as a chaplain in the Caddo Parish Correctional Facility of Shreveport, Louisiana. During a Sunday chapel service, an inmate still in his cell decided he wanted Tylenol to relieve some discomfort. We could hear him yelling from the cellblock upstairs. Guards usually refused to distribute meds on weekends because the staff doctors were not there. The man kept yelling anyway, for some time. After the chapel service, I went home.

On Monday, when I checked back in, a guard said to me, "Did you hear what happened to the man yelling for his meds?" After I left, the inmate was still upset at not getting the Tylenol he demanded. Then, this prisoner made a self-destructive decision. He doused the lower half of his body with alcohol (who knows where he got it) and set himself on fire! Believe me, that guy then got his meds. Thinking stubbornly, he one-upped a guard who said he couldn't have them.

Let me ask you a question. Did that take effort on the inmates' part, or was it just a waste of a huge amount of energy to avoid an effort to endure adversity? In other words, was this the easy way out? Because he was committed to stubborn thinking, paradoxical as it might seem, the answer is yes.

The prisoner was unwilling to do anything he thought was disagreeable, but he was perfectly willing to deliberately self-destruct to get his way.

Responsible people will wonder how this guy could do what he did, but stories like his are common in many penal institutions.

Now . . . what belief provided the energy for this drastic behavior? That's a good question, because we get an enormous amount of energy out of what we believe. This twisted thinker's lack of endurance, combined with his hunt for shortcuts, resulted from the following belief.

> *Real living is occurring when I control whatever I want, even if it might hurt.*

Because he demands to be in control of his own pain, without any effort he will endure the very pain he inflicts upon himself rather than tolerate anything he thinks will be disagreeable, such as not getting the Tylenol. Now, that's stubborn thinking! Yet I've seen thinking like this by many inmates, such as those who cut on their own bodies because of the same belief. People wonder how a person can do that. Well, look at the belief, combined with the stubborn thinking that goes with it, and that will help you see why it can be done.

Obviously, this was a maturity issue in the inmate's life, which is also true of anyone unwilling to endure the adversity of boredom, or of living with what is disagreeable. Responsible people get bored too, yet they still go to work, pay their bills, and obey the law instead of pursuing what's forbidden. Twisted thinkers don't.

This book is about transforming twisted thinking and becoming a STAR, but the need for every twisted thinker to be connected with God and others is also on my heart. Stubborn thinkers do make connections, but those connections are only to themselves even if they perpetrate self-destructive stunts endangering their life. It's another shackle, which must come off.

Connected Only to Self

Sometimes a twisted thinker actually feels disconnected from a special someone. Yet even when they long to be humanly linked to that person they'll purposely create distance and stay disconnected. Because, it's easier to connect emotionally and sometimes physically with oneself, rather than give someone else a choice to reject them.

For example, I've counseled men who said they secretly used pornography because of feeling hurt or rejected by their wives. Usually, men who have that issue bring the pornography into the marriage and conveniently choose not to disclose the sin pattern to their brides.

Stubborn thinking in those moments is all about certainty. It centers on the thought that "At least I can fill me up and not cheat myself when I feel hurt by someone else, even if it's my own wife." Rather than risking (and thereby having to endure) any dissatisfactions that might arise from being rejected by someone else, they'll stay connected to themselves and reject others instead.

Does that sound like what happened in Genesis chapter 3, with Adam? Adam kept his genuine thoughts hidden from Eve and therefore lied by omission. Clearly, he didn't love her in the way God did, by being open and honest in the relationship.

The Bible also speaks about Moses displaying the same stubborn attitude on four different occasions. In each incident (Exodus 2:10-12; 32:19, 20; 32:21-35; Numbers 20:7-13) he indulged in an illegitimate expression of anger. During those moments, it's my feeling that Moses was defining his own goodness. When he felt hurt by the people he'd led out of Egypt he became becomes dangerous both to himself and his nation.

It didn't take *effort* to do what he did on those occasions, but only *energy* to maintain his stubborn thinking. The Bible makes it clear that Moses never seemed to completely resolve his anger. Because of it, God refused to let him enter the Promised Land (Deuteronomy 26:21-28). I don't necessarily believe that Moses was a twisted thinker at the time those consequences were applied, but they demonstrate the potential cost for any stubborn thinking as a means of connecting only to self. This is so important to see because I don't believe we can think about who God is, and what man was created for, unless we think about the dynamics involved in relationship.

In chapter 14 of John's gospel, Jesus said, "I and my Father are one. He that has seen the Father has seen me." He talks about the Father sending a "Counselor, the Holy Spirit in His name." He then said, "The world must learn that I love the Father and that I do exactly what my Father has commanded me." It doesn't sound like Jesus was connected only to self. His highest priority was being connected in the context of a relationship with us, and most of all with his Father.

I once heard a man say, "Jesus is God all dressed up in flesh." That statement struck me as a wonderful expression of how God wants to be connected with humanity. But not so for the twisted thinker. Instead, without any accountability for how they attempt to control their relationships, they are left open to their own grandiose standards—the last shackle on maturity.

GRANDIOSE STANDARDS

When they automatically say "I can't" they are usually afraid of not reaching their own self-imposed, grandiose standards. Therefore they take the easier way out rather than making responsible efforts. I saw this option demonstrated in a favorite commercial for Monday Night Football.

A junior high school boy is standing in front of some hallway lockers, being pushed by three others into asking a girl for a dance. Looking at the three so-called friends makes me wonder if any girl would have danced with them, but there they are, pep-talking this kid. One of the peers starts singing "Da, Da, Da, Da" to the tune of Monday Night Football, with the other guys joining in. Then the terrified boy gets a wild-eyed look, as if to say, "Yeh, right, go in like a man and ask for a dance. Show some confidence and she'll dance with me!"

In the next scene we see him barging through the door. He points his finger at some girl we can't see, and shouts, "You! Dance with me!" I had the impression that he was a linebacker barking at a quarterback. But here's my question. Did it take *effort* for this boy to shout at the girl, or *energy*?

While admittedly funny, this commercial was not about how to win the girl. And as far as the audience can see, she doesn't come over to dance. Good for her! Maybe that's why the commercial ends at this point.

Seriously, the point of this boy's grandiose standard is that it can become a shackle upon his maturation as a young man. Certainly it promoted a disconnect with the girl. This sort of thing represents what twisted thinkers do in broken relationships. They bark out orders. They act stubborn. They do everything possible to avoid accountability by adhering to pretentious standards binding themselves via the other shackles of immaturity. Thus they stay humanly disconnected from everyone. They lack true perseverance, and that's a maturity issue.

Persevering

The apostle James talks about the need for perseverance, especially for persecuted Christians in his day. It's clear from Scripture that the lack of perseverance is a maturity issue. If only those believers would persevere, they would see that the Lord is full of compassion and mercy.

> "Consider it pure joy, my brothers, whenever you face trials of many kinds, because you know that the testing of your faith develops perseverance. *Perseverance must finish its work so that you may be mature and complete, not lacking anything.* Brothers, as an example of patience in the face of suffering, take the prophets who spoke in the name of the Lord. As you know, we consider blessed those who have persevered. You have heard of Job's perseverance and have seen what the Lord finally brought about. The Lord is full of compassion and mercy." (James 1:2-4; 5:10, 11, emphasis added)

Luke also writes in chapter 8 of his gospel on the need to persevere. In verse 15 he says, "The seed on good soil stands for those with a noble and good heart, who hear the word, retain it, and by persevering produce a crop." It takes effort to persevere in difficult situations when your paradigm changes from "I Can't" to "I Must."

I've been a pastor in rural communities and know about the good, noble hearts you'll find there. Judy and I could go to the grocery store to pick up some bread and a gallon of milk any time we want. People with good hearts in our society provide that for you and me, despite having trials and tribulations of their own. Luke talks about the people of God who believe the crop will come in, if they persevere. It takes maturity to carry on in a responsible way until it does.

In chapter five, I mentioned that the options for twisted thinkers are limited to three choices. I don't need to repeat them, but when I'm talking to any twisted thinker stuck in the sewer of stubborn thinking I'm not shy about presenting those options in an accountability moment. Why? Because they are the only options available and they need to be identified if the maturity issues in twisted thinkers' lives are going to be addressed. They need an image of perseverance, and it goes without saying that the cross of Christ provides it.

As I look at the cross of Jesus I see everything He went through as an act of complete maturity. His suffering personifies perseverance. It is also clear to me that Jesus relied on the Father to do for Him what He could not do for Himself. That meant the Father's power would raise Jesus from the dead.

He had to make a mature faith decision to trust the Father, and because He did, Jesus was able to persevere. He lived, died, and rose again as the only human connection for you and me with the Father. And what a connection it is! It lasts forever, because the Eternal One made it.

I think that's one reason why stubborn thinking hurts God as well as people. Individuals thinking this way are disconnecting from Him and from others, even though God—and many others also—go to the max to connect with the twisted thinker. But there are more reasons for the pain God and responsible people experience from a twisted thinker.

God's Pain and Ours

The pain of being ignored, forgotten, and disregarded by people we long to have a sense of community with is sharp. God knows how that feels because He has so much to offer us if we're willing to connect with Him. But there's more. As with a child in His hand, He wants everyone to need the connection for relationship.

That's why it's sad when someone won't choose to have one with Him. I also note a similar sadness in wounded people in broken relationships with twisted thinkers. Whether they're married partners, children, parents, extended family members, or just friends in general, they often have much to offer. But just as God is, they're rejected via the stubborn thinking of individuals who won't see what they're pushing away.

Stubborn thinkers maintain their distance because they don't want the inconvenience of a responsible relationship. That causes God's pain and ours too, as you well know if you've ever longed to see a twisted thinker become a STAR . . . but they won't.

In Judges 2:6-23, we see God's heart disturbed because His people refused to give up their evil practices and stubborn ways. He provided leaders to care for Israel throughout their history. Yet when leaders like Joshua died, whole generations, either indifferent or outright stubborn, grew up without hearing or knowing about Him. This pattern alarmed and disturbed God. Why?

We find the answer in I Samuel 15:23. "For rebellion is like the sin of divination and arrogance like the evil of idolatry." The word for "arrogance" is the same word for "stubbornness" in another biblical translation. Samuel called it "idolatry" as he spoke to a stubborn, arrogant king of Israel. Saul's stubbornness came from a perverted twist on being "God-like." Only it was not about being "like God" in character but about *being* God instead.

The very thing Lucifer was guilty of—marching through the sewer of stubborn thinking—was also King Saul's undoing. I can't help but think of God's pain and yours, if you've ever longed for a twisted thinker to reconcile with you and they would not, simply because they liked playing at being God.

How sad. God has made it abundantly clear that He longs to be our refuge. In Psalm 91:4 the writer said:

> He will cover you with his feathers, and under his wings you will find refuge; His faithfulness will be your shield and rampart.

In verses 14 and 15 he added:

> "Because he loves me," says the LORD, "I will rescue him; I will protect him, for he acknowledges my name. He will call upon me, and I will answer him; I will be with him in trouble, I will deliver him and honor him."

What a refuge! I also love what Zephaniah said about God in 3:17.

> The LORD your God is with you, he is mighty to save. He will take great delight in you, he will quiet you with his love, he will rejoice over you with singing.

Stubborn Thinking

To me, it's like Zephaniah is saying, "When I walk into the room, God sings." When has that ever happened to you? If you've ever had people sing Happy Birthday when you walked into the room, then you get a little of what Zephaniah was saying.

In chapter 15 of Luke's gospel the father of a stubborn thinker ran to meet his prodigal son, after the son came to his senses and returned home. What's interesting about the father's sprint is how he had to run in his robe. The robe would fly up, exposing him, and would be seen as a shame.

Yet, he ran anyway! The Heavenly Father is ready to run toward any stubborn thinker who has come to his or her senses. Can we see why it hurts our Lord when anyone chooses to be a stubborn thinker? That's also your pain when the person you love rejects you via stubborn thinking.

How, then, can these shackles on maturity be removed? Here are several keys.

Unlocking the Shackles

The first key is simple and I won't have to say much about it. It's to identify and challenge the excuses a twisted thinker uses to avoid giving an effort. In Romans 12:18 the Apostle Paul said, "If it is possible, as far as it depends on you, live at peace with everyone."

However, "live at peace with everyone" doesn't mean you should ignore stubborn thinking. On the contrary, identify phony excuses and challenge those who make them. Bring them back to the real world, with real people who care for them.

The next key in challenging stubborn thinkers is to help them realize that when they say "I can't" it's the result of angry, power-oriented thinking. It comes from self-pity, which usually induces a false sense of fatigue. This is especially true when we see *stubborn* thinking following in sequence right behind *closed* and *inflated* thinking (Bookend Principle Two).

It's a common ploy to act tired when they're not, because it builds them up at your expense. Don't accept the fatigue game. The "I can't" really means "I won't." I'll say, "You mean, you won't?" Even if they mean, "I won't" I still want them to own it. If they say, "I can't" again then I'll deal with closed thinking and ask, "Are you open to discussing some possibilities?"

However, the primary key for unlocking the shackles of immaturity will need to be used, if there's any hope of transforming this thinking pattern. That key is emphasizing and applying consequences for any lack of effort to embrace responsible living. That's how twisted thinkers can be guided into coming to terms with the pain they've caused others.

The writer in Psalm 99:8 said, "O Lord our God, You answered them. You were to Israel a forgiving God, though You punished their misdeeds." God applies consequences. It's the loving thing to do and is an essential part of the transformation process.

Pleasantly Surprised in Houston

In 1998, according to an article by Stefanie Asin of the *Houston Chronicle*, Judge Ted Poe handled a drunken driving accident in a classic way for unlocking the shackles of stubborn thinking. He ordered strict probation conditions for a 19-year-old who had killed a 45-year-old father of two and their 28-year-old nanny. This teen-ager was a senior in high school when his speeding car slammed into a van driven by the man. Only the man's wife survived the crash.

The teen pleaded no contest to intoxicated manslaughter charges and, after serving six months in jail, was released on ten years' probation. However, before the teen's release the judge imposed the following conditions:

- Attend boot camp.
- Erect a cross and a Star of David at the accident site.
- Maintain the symbols and the area around them.
- Carry a sign for five days outside a bar that reads, "I killed two people while driving drunk."
- Carry pictures of the victims in his wallet for ten years.
- Refrain from driving for ten years.
- Speak to students at his high school about his experience.
- Observe an autopsy of a person killed in a drunken driving accident.
- Send $10 every week for ten years to a memorial fund in the names of the victims.
- Place flowers at their graves on their birthdays for ten years.

The wife of the man who died agreed to all of these conditions. She said, "It's appropriate for him to be exposed. People locked away in prison can forget about it."

I believe Judge Poe was wise to apply these consequences, because they would help develop the empathy this young man needed for the victims of his irresponsibility. The same consequences would also help develop the self-disgust this young man needed. It's a mark of character to say, "I'm sick about anything that would hurt another person in any way, and I want to think about that in advance of my actions."

Using consequences can be redemptive when applied out of respect for the twisted thinker's dignity and humanity. I say this because I've heard many a parent say, "What's the use? Consequences don't work. I get tired of trying to apply them." My response: Consequences are more about teaching and having respect for the humanity of twisted thinkers. Sure it's disappointing when they don't seem to work, but persevere! God uses consequences and so should we when we respect people as He does.

The apostle Paul wrote about this principle in Galatians 6:7-10.

> "Do not be deceived: God cannot be mocked. A man reaps what he sows. The one who sows to please his sinful nature, from that nature will reap destruction; the one who sows to please the Spirit, from the Spirit will reap eternal life. Let us not become weary in doing good, for at the proper time we will reap a harvest if we do not give up. Therefore, as we have opportunity, let us do good to all people, especially to those who belong to the family of believers."

Last but not least, if any twisted thinker is to overcome stubborn thinking by enduring adversity, stopping the excuses, stopping the use of shortcuts, and by forgetting their grandiose standards, they have to make solid commitments to be held clearly accountable for their own successes or failures.

Contracts—A Follow-Through of Commitments

For those of us who have gone down into the manhole of stubborn thinking to connect with twisted thinkers, it's absolutely necessary to insist that they follow through on any commitments they agree to make. "Contracting" is the last key to use when insisting on the follow-through of any stubborn twisted thinker.

Contracts are necessary because stubborn thinkers need something concrete to remind them of their commitment. Without a contract the commitment will be out of sight, and you can count on it being out of mind. Here's a perfect example from the book of Joshua.

Joshua was old and well advanced in years, but before he died he summoned all Israel, including the elders, leaders, judges, and officials, to present themselves before God. In Joshua 24:14, 15, he identified the stubborn thinking of the past and called for a commitment to serve the LORD. The contract was recorded in the Book of the Law of God. Then, he took a large stone and set it up under the oak near the holy place of the LORD. Finally, he insisted on their follow-through in Joshua 24:27.

> "See!" he said to all the people. "This stone will be a witness against us. It has heard all the words the LORD has said to us. It will be a witness against you if you are untrue to your God."

That large stone Joshua used to mark the spot of their commitment was concrete, and everyone could see it. There couldn't be any misunderstanding; none of Israel's twisted thinkers could claim later on that "You didn't tell me," or "That's not the way you said it!" Contracts are good to have. God gave us one in the person and work of Christ on Calvary's cross. I'm counting on it and my hope is that you are too.

However, beyond all the above, actually contracting a twisted thinker *on paper* can go a long way toward transforming them. Indeed—stubborn thinking is impossible to address without a contract. Otherwise, rather than something concrete, *felt emotions* will be used as the criteria in decision-making. Plus, when contracts are used the person's actual willingness to overcome stubborn thinking can be objectively measured. In short, it can't be faked.

As an aside, I think that's why many churches fail to understand the repentance process. They're not willing to *contract for change* in the lives of people caught in sin. But based on what God has shown us in His word, it's one of the most spiritually mature things to do for people who say they are repenting.

Contract for Marge

Look at the contract below, made up by a set of parents for their teenage daughter who was arrested for credit card fraud. Before the public became aware of her illegal behavior, her parents had been suffering for some time because of her stubbornness and rebellion. Now, with the support of the legal system, they were able to measure their daughter's commitment for change. Here's how the contract read.

> I know I face a court date to address the charges of fraud. I may be given a Probation Agent, as part of my sentence. What I want to do is work on a program for change, and in order to hold me accountable I want a "Net Work" to be established for evaluations to see if I'm consistent. This contract is made in regards to living with my parents."

1. Pursue counseling. That means I call and set up the appointment within a week of signing the contract; and then, with the counselor develop a treatment plan. It will run as long as the insurance will hold out or if I can make personal payments. If the courts assign me to counseling, that will be in addition to this responsibility.
2. Meet with_____ the Pastor once a week for spiritual awareness issues.
3. Fulfill requirements of Probation and Parole if I'm assigned to them.
4. Abide by the curfew set for me by my parents.
5. Do daily chores assigned to me by my parents. A list will be prepared.
6. Disassociate from any felons. Other individuals are to be negotiated by my parents and/or Probation and Parole, if assigned an officer.
7. Attend classes on my thinking errors.
8. Get a job.

Accountability Network: I give permission for the following people to talk freely about me while in my program for change. My parents;

my pastor; a professional counselor; Probation and Parole, if assigned; any program the courts may assign me for additional counseling.

If at any time I fail to work my program, the immediate consequences will be removal from my parents' home and other "Net Work" members will be notified. If I decide not to sign this contract, the immediate consequence will be enforced today.

Signed_____ Witnessed_____

The whole process was very difficult for these parents, but they did it out of love and respect for their daughter. If Marge was going to live at home she had to contract her commitment.

I want to finish by saying that unless the twisted thinker is vulnerable, to the extent that they'll lose something dear to them, like freedom, contracts won't hold much water. If the stubborn thinker won't sign a contract and become vulnerable, at the very least, offering them a contract will reveal to the people around them that a concrete choice has been made. No more can they said "I can't" when it will be clearly understood as "I won't."

And, because this is "on the table" for everyone to see, the twisted thinker can't hide behind feelings. Just one word of word of caution. Even if a commitment to walk down a responsible path is signed, sealed, and delivered by the twisted thinker, we still need to remember that they are sprinters.

In Marge's case, she signed and completed her commitment. Marge was 17 at the time and eventually made the human connection with her family and society. Today, she and her parents enjoy the freedom of soul God longs for everyone to have when they're willing to become a STAR

I have seen many parents in counseling who've had the courage to make a contract like this, and then persevere. I can't tell you that every time a contract was made the twisted thinker in those families saw the need to transform his twisted thinking, but I've also never seen it happen without one.

A Personal Note

For me, I'm grateful for the freedom of soul I have. I believe this liberty comes from being connected to others longing for relationship with me, who had the respect, the love, and the courage to go below the street of my own stubborn thinking. What's beyond me is how they committed to stay involved with me over the long haul. I think that's grace. Frankly, there are many I can thank, but most of all, thank you, God, and thank you, Judy, my dear wife.

Chapter Eight

RECKLESS THINKING

"What's in it For Me?"

I think living in a responsible way is unexciting and unsatisfying. I have no sense of obligation but I'll get you to obligate yourself to me. I'm not interested in being responsible unless I get an immediate payoff.

In 1996, our small Bible study in Sturgeon Bay, Wisconsin, grew into a new church, and eventually we had to look for property in Door County. Later, we discovered that the Racquetball Club was up for sale in Sturgeon Bay. How God provided necessary funds to purchase the property debt-free is an awesome example of His grace. What a way to begin, with three-and-one-half acres of land, a 10,000 square-foot building, two racquetball courts, two saunas, and a bar. Being the pastor was going to be a lot of fun with that arrangement, in addition to enjoying the company of open, loving people.

We remodeled the club, making it into a warm, inviting, comfortable environment for worship, where relationships were strengthened. Support came from Green Bay Community Church. They provided oversight plus additional funds for remodeling. Although there was some angst about meeting deadlines, spirits were high as people worked hard to make our church feel like home.

During the summer, after we moved into the building, one of the men noticed the church's riding lawnmower had been vandalized. It came as a bit of a shock, because Door County is one of the safest places on the planet. Some of our men investigated and concluded that rookies—possibly budding young criminals—had done the damage.

Apparently, they attempted to start the mower without success. Next, they tried to push the thing uphill, toward a nearby home. That didn't work. They then poked the tires with a knife and left the mower sitting there. Evidently, one goal was making sure no one else could move it. Reckless stuff!

This event affords an opportunity to go below the street of twisted thinking as we analyze the reckless thinking these perpetrators engaged in while messing with the mower. Maybe these weren't their actual thoughts, but if they weren't, their irresponsible behavior reveals the general direction of their thinking.

Such thinking goes like this. "Hey, getting to that mower is simple. These people must want us to have it. If that's the way we think it is, then it is! Man, this is going to be easy." Do you see the *Big E* here? Now, picture in your mind the change in their thinking as the difficulty of succeeding slowly became apparent.

"Nuts, this is tougher than we anticipated. I can't believe these church people made it so hard to get our mower out of here!" (Do you see the Martyred Thinking?) "But they're not going to put one over on us! If we can't have it we'll make them pay. Besides, sticking a knife in the wheels will show them who's boss."

As you can surmise, that reasoning reveals the kind of bitterness residing in every reckless thinker. Even if they're strangers to the people they hurt, their hostility always defiles them in some manner.

BITTERNESS AND RECKLESS THINKING

Reckless thinking is clearly visible in the above story, and is defined by the following: "I think responsible living is unexciting and unsatisfying. I'll obligate others to me, but they can forget about me being obligated to them. If I do respond, it'll be only to net an immediate payoff."

Isn't that a perfect setup for developing the egotistical bitterness that resides in the reckless thinker's mind? But they're held captive by that thinking—ignorant of its power over them. Proverbs 2:12-15 speaks about this kind of bitterness.

> Wicked men . . . leave the straight paths to walk in dark ways, who delight in doing wrong and rejoice in the perverseness of evil, whose paths are crooked and who are devious in their ways.

Doesn't that sound like responsible living, to a reckless thinker, is unexciting and unsatisfying? Doesn't that sound like they're absorbed with self? Proverbs 4:16, 17 also talks about reckless thinkers having no sense of obligation.

> For they cannot sleep till they do evil; they are robbed of slumber till they make someone fall. They eat the bread of wickedness and drink the wine of violence.

Then, in Proverbs 10:4, 5 we see the reckless thinker failing to respond to anything unless they're the only beneficiary.

> Lazy hands make a man poor, but diligent hands bring wealth. He who gathers crops in summer is a wise son, but he who sleeps during harvest is a disgraceful son.

Like a disgraceful son, the reckless thinker has difficulty sustaining a positive approach toward any responsible goal. When work needs to be done he's the only one sleeping, and he believes it *should* be that way. As far as he's concerned, someone else can harvest the crop. "It's no skin off my nose!" might be another way of expressing his indifference. Sleep is also more exciting because there's a forbidden element to it. What a disgrace to the Father!

When a twisted thinker gets to decide between being responsible and doing what's forbidden, the *Big E* will always win out. That's because, if they did what was responsible, their immediate gratification would be delayed. And, even though they typically adopt this thinking pattern long before they become aware of it, whenever they encounter a conflict of interest their decision becomes a conscious choice.

What troubles me more than the wrecking of a riding mower by adolescents is the direction they're heading toward as adults. How would you like to be married to one? Clearly, they chose to substitute violence for their failure to steal a lawnmower. In the future, where will that go when they decide they don't like the way their wife looks? What happens when they decide she's unexciting and unsatisfying? How would you like to be their son or daughter, when it becomes easier to hit you than to talk to you in a respectful manner?

Those young criminals sent a message all right—all about how they'll conduct future relationships. Without a doubt they were disconnected from humanity. That troubles me more. Think of the pain those closest to them are going to suffer if these wannabe thieves don't correct their reckless thinking.

Their bitterness runs deeper than a poked tire on a riding lawnmower. You connect reckless thinking to stubborn thinking, as already mentioned in the last chapter, and you could have the basic ingredients for a class A extortionist. They become bloodsuckers absorbing the essence of your life. No wonder it's such a delight to see them brought to justice when they've broken the law.

Gary's Chronicle

A married couple, struggling with a builder who was reckless in his thinking, charged him with "theft by contractor." To recoup money stolen by overbilling and undercutting the quality of their new home, Gary and Danielle took the contractor to court. Gary sent me emails detailing the trial as it progressed. Welcome to "Gary's Chronicle."

> **The second day:** Greetings from Day Two of our trial: Today went pretty quickly, despite a long day in court, from 8:30 a.m. until 5:45 p.m. Today, there were eighteen witnesses, six times yesterday's three.
>
> The first three were two auto dealers and a marina dealer where the builder bought his vehicles and has his boat repaired. Four and five were representatives from a log home business; six was a representative from the state Department of Revenue (which we're sure is interested in investigating the builder further); seven through twelve were the builder's work crew; thirteen was a representative from a lumber

yard; fourteen through sixteen were subcontractors; seventeen was myself and eighteen was the police investigator. Danielle was also recalled for a few questions.

My testimony was about an hour total, and wasn't as strenuous as Danielle's yesterday, due to the fact that Danielle's was already in-depth, and there was no need to go into the same stuff again. No major gaffes. Tomorrow, the D.A. will be presenting his last three witnesses, and then the defense starts their side. Although, from what I understand, there are only two witnesses, a guy from another lumber yard and the builder's accountant, and then, the builder himself, which should take a long time. Thursday afternoon/Friday morning will be the closing arguments, jury instructions, and then deliberations, which shouldn't take long before the guilty verdict is in.

Today, I kept track of the builder's courtroom antics, starting at mid-morning. There were 5 instances of crumbling paper; 11 excessive pen clickings; 11 loud throat clearings; 6 leaning back with arms behind his head; 16 examinations of fingernails; 3 instances of knuckle cracking, and 18 yawns.

The next day: Deliberations began and ended, little more than an hour later. Danielle and I are guessing that they probably took about fifteen minutes getting coffee and soda; fifteen minutes to look through our photo album and other evidence; fifteen minutes to decide he was guilty of "theft by contractor," and then, fifteen minutes to make it look good.

The Verdict: When the verdict was read, the builder threw his pen on the table, and turned his chair to face away from everybody, so we couldn't see his face. He was very angry! The jury was then dismissed and the bond was set. The builder was ordered to have no contact with us between now and his sentencing. Travel restrictions were imposed on him (no leaving the state). Sentencing is set for 4-6 weeks; we don't know exactly when yet. Restitution for us will be decided at the time of sentencing.

I believe this story demonstrates how the contractor's reckless thinking ruined him. You can see the effects of reckless thinking portrayed in his attitude and his behavior during the trial. His antics demonstrated how he really viewed people, and how being held accountable inconvenienced him.

Gary and Danielle's story brings up a question I have when addressing reckless thinkers who've wreaked havoc on victims. The question has to do with moving too quickly to a state of forgiveness.

As Christians, how do we handle this question when the impact of a person's behavior truly harms others, as in the case of this builder? In chapter four I discussed being willing to forgive. However, the timing of when to forgive is also important; it must not preclude justice.

Moving too Quickly to Forgive

Sharon H. Ringe addressed the matter of forgiveness between people and society in a book entitled *Jesus, Liberation, and the Biblical Jubilee*. "To move too quickly to forgiveness . . . without addressing the way the patterns of oppression have become institutionalized, risks simply perpetuating the status quo. Before forgiveness can find its way back into the lexicon of liberation, it must be linked to justice."

If the building contractor had said "I'm sorry" I don't think it would have been good enough for Gary and Danielle. And not because Gary and Danielle were hard, unforgiving people. But, unless justice was applied in some concrete form the man's "I'm sorry" would have been untrustworthy.

Because, it's one thing to say "I'm sorry" when you've been caught, but it's another thing entirely when you've come to the end of yourself and are broken and disgusted by what you've done, which was clearly not the case with the contractor. Only when the whole picture of a reckless thinker's past, present and future is open for inspection will they do whatever it takes to make amends, restitution included.

Isaiah confirmed this when he was exposed by the presence of God. Everything unclean in him was uncovered, and he cried out, "Woe to me!

I am ruined! For I am a man of unclean lips" (Isaiah 6:5). Only then was God ready to use him, as a man at the end of himself and his sin pattern. Liberation linked to God's justice (represented by a seraph touching Isaiah's lips with a live coal, to remove guilt and atone for sin) now meant that God could trust Isaiah to be His prophet.

I've also seen the principle of justice applied in marriage counseling when one partner says, "I'm Sorry" or "Will you forgive me?" Many spouses respond by saying, "For what?" In other words, unless the sin pattern of how that mate hurt them is addressed, it will be repeated again. Also, even when a person is able to describe the sin pattern and understand the damage they've fostered, that doesn't necessarily mean they'll stop.

But the status quo is less likely to continue when the offender is broken in their understanding of the sin pattern. That means they are disgusted by how they got there and what they did to others. Then, in their brokenness, they surrender and accept accountability. Forgiveness applied when the offender is not broken and accountable results in liberation without justice. In such cases, twisted thinkers think they have a license to offend again. I believe God is quick to forgive but he doesn't forgive too quickly. Sharon Ringe had it right, and Scripture supports the thought: Liberation is linked to His justice.

Society says it doesn't want sin patterns repeated, but liberation has been granted to twisted thinkers many times, at the expense of the victims, before any justice has been applied. But God goes further by thinking in terms of eternity. The Scriptures teach that we are justified by faith alone via the finished work of Christ on the cross. Otherwise there would be no way out of sin's eternal grip.

Instead, God holds humanity accountable by moving deliberately, righteously, and lovingly to the only absolute justice available. In Christ, our debt is paid in full—through Him we are forever liberated from the penalty and power of sin. God's love is unconditional, but forgiveness isn't. That's the deal! Therefore, what is true about man's relationship to God is true about every human-to-human relationship that's been broken and twisted by a sin pattern. And that pattern begins with thinking and fantasizing in the mind. Be careful of moving too quickly to forgive unless liberation is linked to justice.

Becoming a STAR is about understanding the twisted thinking behind sin. It's about going beyond the surface and measuring repentance through clearly visible changes in thinking. Such transformation can then open up real possibilities for genuine reconciliation of broken relationships within society. As God Himself says in Ezekiel 33:11, "As surely as I live . . . I take no pleasure in the death of the wicked, but rather that they turn from their ways and live."

God searches the heart of man, which is another way of saying that He's analyzing the twisted thinker's depravity. But God does so to *promote* life by being connected with you and me. I believe that understanding patterns of oppression coming out of twisted thinking is absolutely fundamental in order to have and enjoy that connection. But it's also no different in any other relationship. We must be willing to forgive by applying justice, which is another term for accountability. Only then can a legitimate hope for change be anticipated. That's the heart of what I'm trying to say in this book.

I'm enjoying freedom of soul because I became conscious of my darkened mind without Christ. By being connected to Him I then recovered my conscience. I want that for you, and for any other twisted thinker. But, the deep below-the-street levels of twisted thinking must be examined and transformed until there's a solid relational connection. That's where God was going when He asked Adam "Who told you that you were naked?"

God's question implied that the place for deep change was on the inside. I believe this is also what the apostle Paul meant when he encouraged the Philippian believers to let the mind of Christ be in them. When twisted thinkers become straight thinkers, allowing His way of thinking/loving/conducting relationships to become *theirs*, then responsible living can begin. The "What's in it for me?" mode of reckless thinking begins to fade away and the result is incredibly liberating!

What's in it for Me?

What do patterns of this syndrome look like? It's important to recognize them because they promote a general lack of commitment for building responsible relationships, whether they're intimate or casual. I'm going to begin with the central factor in resisting responsible living for reckless thinkers. It's all about belief that they are "nobody's sucker."

I remember experiencing good times while growing up in Saginaw, Michigan. Sometimes my father would spend weeks away, traveling as an evangelist. So, when he was home those moments were significant for me, especially when we played ping-pong. Although I've acquired some of my father's competitive spirit, in hindsight I can also see that some of his reckless thinking patterns from his pre-Christian days were a part of me, too. They would show up when we played ping-pong, which reveals that even in fun, reckless thinking is still *Reckless Thinking*.

I learned to play ping-pong while practically living at the Saginaw YMCA. My twin brother and I were competitive and we enjoyed some success in YMCA tournaments. We also had a ping-pong table in our basement. I remember the first game I ever played against my father there. I was excited, feeling somewhat like a puppy dog waiting for his master to pet him.

I usually volleyed for serve, but this time my father said something that confused and rankled me. He looked at me from across the table with a matter-of-fact, in your face style and said, "Suckers serve first." No longer was I a pup looking for his master to give him a pat on the head. In my mind I determined to be the pit bull of all ping-pong pit bulls, because he was going down! I couldn't wait to win and return his comment with a little twist of my own.

The game was close. I could tell he was sweating and I loved it! Then, after my eventual victory, I looked at him with the same matter of-fact, in-your-face style and said, "Suckers serve second; you want to play another one?"

People might have thought we were Sonny Liston and Mohammed Ali, staring each other down. Then, he smiled with a good-natured smile. I'll never forget the moment. Maybe it was a "right of passage" in my manhood. Whatever it was, not until years later would I understand that in a small though humorous moment, my father, a redeemed man, lapsed into reckless thinking while playing the "pit bull of all ping-pong pit bulls."

As I said, it was all good-natured but it brought out the unique psyche involved in the Price way of competing. I can only imagine what my father was like as a criminal during his pre-Christian days, but being nobody's sucker had to be at the top of his list. I've talked to many inmates who also thought they were nobody's sucker. That's how they survived in crime.

However, this is not just about crime. I've talked to many men who've argued with their wives trying to prove they were no *woman's* sucker. That's why some wives have such a difficult time dealing with the reckless behavior of their twisted thinking husbands. If you're in a relationship with someone like this, I might be attaching words to something you already know. Typically, this form of twisted thinking combines one, two, or even three components that I want to mention next.

The first component is *being the main man*.

THE MAIN MAN

Don't be surprised when twisted thinkers seem very responsible in their behavior, because they can be. But they view doing what's responsible as drudgery compared to pursuing their *Big Es*. Thus they may be willing to participate in responsible activities but often want to assume the top position when they do.

In the movie *The Longest Yard*, a prison football team was scheduled to play a prison guard team on the penitentiary gridiron. Until Burt Reynolds became the quarterback on the football team, you saw eleven quarterbacks, each telling the other guys what to do. Each inmate thought they should be the main man. Welcome to the world of the twisted thinker.

Simon used the same modus operandi in Acts 8:9-24. For some time, Samaritan people amazed with his sorcery had supported Simon's main man identity. But when his groupies stopped following him because of Philip's preaching about Jesus, Simon tried the old "If you can't beat them join them" routine. At that point, the great signs and miracles he saw while following Philip astonished him.

Luke says that Simon saw the Holy Spirit being given to people by the laying on of the apostles' hands. Simon was impressed by this but failed to understand its divine origin. When he tried to use money to buy the same ability, Simon exposed his own reckless thinking.

Peter answered him by saying, "May your money perish with you, because you thought you could buy the gift of God with money! You have no part or share in this ministry, because your heart is not right before God." Peter then, said, "I see that you are full of bitterness and captive to sin."

This all came about because Simon demanded to be the main man. It was about his gain at anyone else's pain.

My Gain, Your Pain

Another component of reckless thinking appears when twisted thinkers have no sense of obligation toward anything they deem unworthy. They just won't tolerate the mundane and ordinary aspects of life. That means appointments will be broken. They'll fail to support their spouse and children. They'll be inconsiderate of parents and anyone else blocking them from immediate gratification. And, if they do seem to have a sense of obligation it'll be motivated by a fragmented sentimentality or a need to build their own self up.

Instead of being obligated to others, the twisted thinker more often will try to obligate others to them. For example, while talking to a group of adolescents in trouble with the law, I once noticed how one young man was giving chewing gum to certain members in the group and withholding it from others. Since we were addressing reckless thinking in the meeting, I challenged him.

"Tim, why haven't you shared your gum with the rest of the group?" The young man didn't like that and went immediately to martyred thinking, trying to act like I'd victimized him. But it soon became apparent that the group members taking the gum were in Tim's pocket. In other words, they owed him. Tim became angry with me for exposing him, and quit coming. What was "His gain our pain" was now "My Pain so I play lickety-split."

Welcome to reckless thinking. If they can't be in control they're out of there!

Only What's Guaranteed

The last feature of reckless thinking is how twisted thinkers will avoid responsible initiatives when there's no guaranteed success. That's why opportunities alone do not provide positive motives for them, as they do for responsible people. Only guaranteed successes will interest them. I think the older brother of the prodigal son fit this scenario. I believe that was the thinking behind his anger when he rebuked his father.

> "Look! All these years I've been slaving for you and never disobeyed your orders. Yet you never gave me even a young goat so I could celebrate with my friends. But when this son of yours who has squandered your property with prostitutes comes home, you kill the fattened calf for him!" "My son," the father said, "you are always with me, and everything I have is yours. But we had to celebrate and be glad, because this brother of yours was dead and is alive again; he was lost and is found." (Luke 15:29-32)

Oh, the expectations arising from what twisted thinkers believe should be guaranteed for them. When they think it's all slipping away, look out! Clearly, we can see the older brother playing "What's in it for me?" It didn't seem to matter that he had everything the father could give him, materially. It looked like he was a responsible man for the right reasons, until his younger brother came home. Then we saw a combination of The Main Man—My Gain Your Pain. How reckless! No human connections can be made when those games are played.

So what do you do with people like that? Do you go for reforming or transforming?

Reforming or Transforming

There's no doubt in my mind that our world would settle for the reformation of twisted thinkers. Billions of dollars are spent for more expensive prisons, more expensive mental health treatment centers, and more expensive community programs. I was a part of all that when I worked for the social services department in Wisconsin.

Saving taxpayers' money was one of the big pluses that sold Sheboygan County on the program I developed for inmates. Even if it never had a success rate better than ten percent the county still felt the program would have some value. Our success rate was based on the possibility that an inmate would not re-offend, which would cost the taxpayers even more money. In those days, if we had thirty inmates going through the program and three didn't re-offend, that meant a savings of $60,000. If a hundred inmates went through the program and ten didn't re-offend, that meant a savings of $200,000 a year. It mounts up!

The world is willing to pay for programs like that, just so you might feel comfortable living next door to one of the graduates who remains free and cuts his grass like everyone else. There were good counselors in that program, some who cared deeply about their clients. We worked hard, and statistically the program was successful, but were the clients truly transformed?

On some level we helped the inmates deal with the pain they'd caused others, and I'm not minimizing that. But, in my heart I believed we were *reforming* but not *transforming* them. That conviction resulted from my relationship with Jesus Christ. I can't help remembering what my father used to say after he became a Christian. "Jesus Christ saved the state of Indiana a lot of money." Something happened so deep inside him that he was transformed.

Compared to what happened to my father, what we accomplished with those inmates went deeper than most ever thought it could, but not deep enough. If there is no personal relationship with God, the growth may seem genuine but it becomes just another fig leaf called *reformation*. In contrast, when God's in the picture we get transformation—something that can last forever.

We can be clinical all we want but I've never seen anything, without God, that could truly transform anyone.

That's why I sincerely hope that you will be empowered by inviting God to participate with you in your struggle to identify and correct twisted thinking, either yours or someone else's. Without Him, reforming twisted thinkers will only "manage" them. With God leading the way, transforming twisted thinkers can make each one a masterpiece in His own image.

That said, what are some of the indicators that reckless thinking is really being overcome?

The First Indicator of Change

The first indicator of change involves comparing the quality of *performance* to the reckless thinker's degree of interest for doing what's responsible. Generally, if there is an interest in doing something that isn't forbidden, the twisted thinker's degree of interest will equal the quality of their performance.

However, this is like saying that if McDonald's hires me for $6 an hour they'll get a $6-an-hour effort out of me because that's all I'm interested in giving. On top of that, I determine what the effort is supposed to resemble. Or, if my interest is very high, I'll give it a greater effort. Or, if I'm doing something to score points and get my attaboy, then I'm not interested in doing what's responsible.

It strikes me as a very subtle thing, but questioning where we're going and what's behind the things we're doing can lead to being self-centered. If it does, we're into reckless thinking. For example, one winter night, I stayed with my brother-in-law in Green Bay, Wisconsin. The snow in his driveway was deep and needed shoveling. I thought, "I'll do it for him." But then, while shoveling, I had another thought, that "Joe will be impressed with me!" Fortunately, I immediately asked myself, "Jerry, who are you shoveling the snow for, you or Joe?" That's what it means to examine the direction of our motivation.

I really wanted to do it for Joe, but if it had been about "point scoring," or obligating Joe to give me an attaboy, I would have stopped until I got my motivation/heart right. Reckless thinking can be very subtle, and usually the quality of the performance only equals the degree of interest in the reckless thinker. But, change is beginning to happen when the degree of interest for doing something is less, yet the commitment to quality performances is high and sustained.

This means that when we don't get the attaboys or attagirls, even though it's all right to want them, we don't complain or push for recognition. We'll perform the responsible thing, doing the best we can. I think this is what the Apostle Paul meant when he said, "And whatever you do, whether in word or deed, do it all in the name of the Lord Jesus, giving thanks to God the Father through him" (Colossians 3:17). Being responsible brings glory to the Lord because it promotes the maturity process already mentioned in chapter six.

The Second Indicator of Change

Another major advance in changing reckless thinking takes place when the twisted thinker realizes how obligating himself to others is the opposite of being controlled by others. Again, Jesus Christ is the best example.

He obligated Himself to the will of the Father and, surprisingly, to us. The cross was His choice. He was not a victim. But in Ephesians 1:4, the Bible teaches us that the Godhead got together on this, before the foundation of the world. It was their will to obligate themselves to humanity so we could be redeemed. There was, however, no guarantee that every human would respond to Him. In fact, He already knew that many would reject Him.

Obligating ourselves to others must come out of a choice to love and respect a person, instead of using them, as I saw demonstrated in a *Frank and Ernest* cartoon. We saw a sloppy room with clothes and garbage laying everywhere. Frank said to Ernest, "I'm environmentally friendly. I don't mop it, sweep it, dust it, or wax it."

I thought, "Right, Frank! By not doing what's responsible you're obligating others to do it, if they want to live with you." That's reckless thinking.

The Christian struggling with reckless thinking grows best when he accepts the reality that the Christian life is all risk. So, we can't guarantee success by having "no risk" policies in relationships or at work. To obligate ourselves to any relationship out of love and respect for others means that no one controls or victimizes us, because we were in control of that choice. It's wonderful when that decision is intentional, and it's a pretty good indication that reckless thinking is being overcome.

The Third Indicator of Change

The third indication a twisted thinker is overcoming reckless thinking shows up when one who wants to change avoids associating with other twisted thinkers. The writer in Psalm 1:1, 2 speaks about this.

> "Blessed is the man who does not walk in the counsel of the wicked or stand in the way of sinners or sit in the seat of mockers. But his

delight is in the law of the Lord, and on his law he meditates day and night."

This passage doesn't teach about being isolated from reckless thinkers. Jesus sat and ate with them whether they were Christian or not. The psalmist didn't mean that we shouldn't go to vendors or support public officials unless they're Christians. I believe Psalm 1 is speaking about not taking on the lifestyle or twisted mind-styles of the wicked, because doing so rejects God. On the contrary, delight in His relationship and His law. Visit with Him, day and night. It's wise to emulate sound, responsible people and God is the most sound, responsible being I know.

When reckless thinkers stop associating with other reckless thinkers, work on responsible living with responsible people, and listen to responsible suggestions rather than chasing some *Big E*, they can begin to transform this thinking error. Because, as huge as the required changes are, they are "above the street." When those behaviors are matched with the other indicators of change this book addresses, then we're watching a legitimate metamorphosis. The reckless thinker is becoming a STAR, and because his progress can be measured his chances for major improvements become progressively brighter.

Proverbs 4:18 says, "The path of the righteous is like the first gleam of dawn, shining ever brighter till the full light of day." Here we are at the midpoint of discovering what twisted thinking is, and how a true transformation can be recognized. You've already worked hard to get this far in the book, but my desire is that everyone reading this will know about the healing grace available to anyone struggling with twisted thinking.

There's hope for any twisted thinker who intentionally chooses to walk a righteous path.

Chapter Nine

IMPATIENT THINKING

Assumptions

*I do not use the past as a learning tool when it gets in the way of my plans.
I expect others to act immediately when I demand it. I make decisions
based on assumptions, not the facts.*

Many years passed before I felt I could needle my father about his incarceration, but eventually I was able to use a "gallows sense of humor" on him. However, when I say that, I'm not talking about anything sadistic. Gentle kidding eventually allowed me to connect with my dad, because if anyone had that kind of humor, he did.

A Gallows Sense of Humor

A few years before my dad died I saw something in a store that intrigued me. I didn't want to offend him but I thought he would like it. Maybe I was making a subconscious effort to see if he could laugh at something I really thought was funny—in a twisted sort of way. So, I bought a little padlocked birdcage about six inches high and five inches wide.

Inside the cage was a crow with an extremely large head, sporting two beady eyes and cocked to the side like a wise guy. He was smoking a cigar, and his huge yellow beak filled up most of the cage. He was wearing a blue-striped outfit and a cap. On the front of his shirt were the numbers AB5756. He had his hands behind his back above large, yellow feet. He looked arrogant even with a sign on the front of the cage, reading "Jailbird."

I remember showing it to my mother to see what she thought. Mom was a bit startled but didn't discourage me from giving it to dad. When the big moment came I said, "Dad, I saw something I thought you might like as a reminder of your early days." When he opened the package he gave a small quizzical laugh, but he must have liked it because he kept it until the day he went home to be with the Lord.

I prefer to think this jailbird reminded him of "BTOs," or Big Time Operators in prison. In a story he often told, dad mentioned how they'd take it among themselves to school new criminals, called "fish." Their job was to show the fish where they went wrong in getting caught. The BTOs would then re-educate them (as they would say it) so those "dumb cops" on the outside wouldn't catch them the next time.

My father always said that he was amazed at how all those wise guys were on the inside and all the dumb cops were on the outside. The crow reminded him that he was no longer locked up with those wise guys. They were on the inside and he, a redeemed, transformed man, was on the outside.

After he died, the birdcage and his Bible were the two things I treasured most. Years later, when treating the criminal population in Sheboygan, Wisconsin, I decided to use my gallows sense of humor again. I brought the birdcage into one of their therapy sessions. Every prisoner walking through those doors saw the jailbird sitting on the table and gave either the same quizzical laugh as my father or called it "My little buddy."

If you just smiled or laughed you also have a gallows sense of humor. However, my purpose for bringing the crow was to challenge them on the issue of impatient thinking. I'd start out by presenting a question coming from Proverbs 1:17, and I'd like to ask you the same question.

THE QUESTION

Why is it foolish to spread a net in full view of a crow? Some inmates thought the crow would see the net and fly away. Others commented on how he would have to be stupid to not see the net. Inmates loved saying the word "stupid." Then I asked, "What if the crow deliberately flew into the net? Why do you think he'd do it?" Their answers revealed whether they were involved with impatient thinking or not.

Typically, responsible people would say, "Maybe the bird wants help." Or, "Maybe he wants out of the present life because he can't cope." Or, "Maybe he's alone and it doesn't matter anymore." In other words, responsible people try to empathize with the crow.

But these inmates came up with answers that showed how twisted thinkers generally pursue *Big Es*. "Maybe the crow thought he wouldn't get caught. Or if he did, he thought he could escape." "Maybe he just saw the food and wanted it, not thinking about the consequences."

But the next batch of responses revealed the hidden agendas that some inmates had. "Maybe he wanted to get caught because he'd get three squares a day, clean laundry, and if his wife was pregnant, the state would pay for it because he couldn't get out on work release." Obviously, they had no empathy for your tax dollars.

Psalm 106:6-15 reveals the same dynamics of impatient thinking, but the writer was talking about God's people, the Israelites.

> "We have sinned, even as our fathers did; we have done wrong and acted wickedly. When our fathers were in Egypt, they gave no thought to your miracles; they did not remember your many kindnesses, and they rebelled by the sea, the Red Sea. Yet he saved them for his name's sake, to make his mighty power known. He rebuked the Red Sea, and it dried up; he led them through the depths as through a desert. He saved them from the hand of the foe; from the hand of the enemy he redeemed them. The waters covered their adversaries; not one of them survived. Then they believed his promises and sang his praise. But they soon forgot what he had done and did not wait for his counsel. In the desert they gave in to their craving; in the wasteland they put God to the test. So he gave them what they asked for, but sent a wasting disease upon them." But they soon forgot what he had done and did not wait for his counsel. In the desert they gave in to their craving; in the wasteland they put God to the test. So he gave them what they asked for, but sent a wasting disease upon them."

Whatever the inmates thought concerning the crow, or whatever God's people thought in Psalm 106, both are classic examples of impatient thinking.

It's the "Whatever I want, give me now—I'm not going to wait!" attitude. A more detailed definition would be like the following:

> I won't use the past as a learning tool because I make decisions based on assumptions and not the facts. If I think something is such-and-such, then that's the way it is. So, I expect others to respond immediately when I demand it.

Unmistakably, the writer in Proverbs 26:11 describes the impatient thinker. "As a dog returns to its vomit, so a fool repeats his folly." In other words, the sense of self-disgust, for pain caused to others, is not operative within impatient thinkers. Not having it allows them to fragment their view of time and space when making decisions. That means what is disgusting in one moment may not be in the next, so folly is repeated. Their wiring for decision-making is faulty.

This chapter will expose that faulty system so twisted thinkers can turn on the lights and change.

The Wiring for Decision Making

At times, twisted thinkers feel compelled to do strange things, like birds deliberately flying into nets. What they seem to operate from, however, is really a thinking pattern bent into their own decision-making system. It's the wiring of "impulsivity" and it's connected to impatient thinking.

As an aside, I'm aware of people suffering with Obsessive Compulsive Disorders who need medication to assist them in controlling the physical feeling required to do something. But, I've also known people medicating OCD who are impatient thinkers. In other words, medication alone didn't settle them down. They continued to make irresponsible decisions and eventually had to take ownership of their thinking errors.

In *A Beautiful Mind*, Russell Crowe played a man who won a Pulitzer Prize for his theory on economics. I believed he was a code buster and felt angry at his arrest and subsequent treatment for schizophrenia. After he came home I still believed he was a code buster, even though his imaginary friends kept showing up now and then.

When the movie made it clear that he suffered from this mental disorder, I was pulling for him to ignore his imaginary friends. He finally learned to do that, and when professors at the college participated in the traditional but informal ceremony of laying their ink pens on the table, as a sign of honoring him and his work, I was deeply moved. Even with a legitimate mental disorder, he rewired the way he made decisions. I was proud of him, knowing there are many who fight the same battle.

If people with legitimate organic mental disorders can discipline themselves to make responsible decisions, what about twisted thinkers? Impatient thinking can be rewired. We can start by looking for bad wires.

Disregard For The Future

I have a bias that there is no future without memory. I also think there's logic for saying that if there's no future, then there's no past, and that would mean the only thing that counts is what's going on here and now. It's good logic if you believe there's no such thing as a future, but alas we all have one.

It follows, then, that memory is important to the understanding of future endeavors. But for the impatient thinker, everything they consider valuable is in the present. Pursuing *Big E*s is foremost on their minds as they disregard memories by ignoring tomorrows. Because time and space are fragmented by those choices, this becomes the first bad wire of impatient thinking to undo.

We'll see the disregard in a statement like, "This time, it's going to be different." I think that's why some parents get their children's anger even though they've treated them with respect. The son or daughter expects the parents to hear this statement as fact but parents will hear it as, "Don't get in the way of my *Big E*s." Responsible parents know the statement disregards the future because nothing is offered to establish the statement. The child doesn't talk about what's wrong or how they got there so the history won't be repeated. They don't talk about what will be different: just that things will be.

Kids, making the statement, would prefer to see irresponsible behavior as an isolated event and not as a pattern. But, loving parents remember the past and are concerned for their children's future. They're willing to challenge any blatant disregard for it. I can only imagine the confusion and pain some parents may have because their kids won't use the past as a learning tool. That's a bad wire of impatient thinking.

If twisted thinkers demonstrate any concern about tomorrow it's to pull off what they want to do today. For instance, when asking a twisted thinker "When do you think you are going to die?" I've had the response: "Tomorrow or next year." When I counter with "What about today?" they'll give this look of "Whoever thinks about that? And besides, who cares anyway?" It's because today is all that counts in their minds.

I've also seen a few beer commercials promoting the previous thought. Remember seeing a bunch of guys looking at each other saying, "Whassup?" Or, remember the commercial in which the guy said, "I really love you man?" All he wanted was his Budweiser, and he was willing to say what he thought was needed just to get it. We've seen "Taste Great, Less Filling," The Bud Bowl, a frog's tongue stuck to a beer truck, and "You've only got one life so live it with all the gusto you can!" Okay, I admit to watching super bowls while waiting for these commercials, but in my opinion, they all promote a subtle disregard for the future.

Meanwhile, the Scriptures describe living on earth as being a "vapor" or "grass that withers." The Bible also speaks about destinations after life on earth. It talks about considering where we'll spend eternity—heaven or hell. I think, it's really important to understand how eternity has met today, in the person of Jesus Christ. Because of Him, God's ultimate concern is for any person's eternal welfare. For you and me, there's more to come than the here and now. Solomon describes how eternity will meet the past in Ecclesiastes 3:14, 15.

> "I know that everything God does will endure forever; nothing can be added to it and nothing taken from it. God does it so that men will revere him. Whatever is has already been, and what will be has been before; and God will call the past to account."

In other words, the past isn't just the past. Whatever is past as far as God is concerned will be called into account. I think that provides hope for the victims of twisted thinkers, who know justice in eternity is still available. Psalm 49:7-15 speaks to this.

"No man can redeem the life of another or give to God a ransom for him—the ransom for a life is costly, no payment is ever enough—that he should live on forever and not see decay. For all can see that wise men die; the foolish and the senseless alike perish and leave their wealth to others. Their tombs will remain their houses forever, their dwellings for endless generations, though they had named lands after themselves. But man, despite his riches, does not endure; he is like the beasts that perish. This is the fate of those who trust in themselves, and of their followers, who approve their sayings. Like sheep they are destined for the grave, and death will feed on them. The upright will rule over them in the morning; their forms will decay in the grave, far from their princely mansions. But God will redeem my life from the grave; He will surely take me to Himself."

It's a foolish thing to disregard the future, especially eternity. Categorically, however, twisted thinkers do. Unfortunately, discounting the future and combining that with the next bad wire of impatient thinking can precipitate even more excursions into irresponsibility.

Going for the Big Score

By now you know I love cartoons—for example, a *Born Loser* showing a heavyset bandit wearing a polka-dotted hat and an eye mask, hoisting his handgun and barking an order. "Dis is a stick-up! Hand over your cash!"

In the next frame he says, "I said fork it over! Don't make me use dis thing! Do youse hear me?" Finally, in the last frame we see him with the handgun lowered, thinking, "Sheesh! I'm afraid I need some occupational retraining to stay competitive in my fast changing field!" The reason? He tried to rob a Kwik-Kash automated banking machine.

Someone would truly have to be a born loser to try to rob a machine! Twisted thinkers, however, aren't born that way—they *become* like that. Each one deeply believes in his own demand for instant gratification. That belief promotes all kinds of big-score fantasies, because for them the alternative is nothingness.

Putting this belief and those fantasies together helps us understand why they feel compelled to do what they do. Watch this operate in King Saul's decision making. In 1 Samuel 13, Samuel writes about the Philistines who were assembling to fight Israel, with three thousand chariots, six thousand charioteers, and soldiers as numerous as the sand on the seashore.

They went up and camped at a place called Micmash, east of Bethaven. In verse 6 Saul writes, "When the men of Israel saw that their situation was critical and that their army was hard pressed, they hid in caves and thickets, among the rocks, and in pits and cisterns."

The men of Israel were prime candidates for *foxhole religion*. They were scared! In fact, verse 7 describes how Saul and his troops remained at Gilgal, quaking with fear. He waited seven days for Samuel to come, which was the time Samuel had set before they could go into battle and win. Samuel's job was to offer up burnt offerings. Unfortunately, Saul became impatient and decided he'd do Samuel's job for him, hoping to achieve God's blessing. Just after Saul finished making the offering, Samuel arrived and Saul went out to meet him. In my mind I can see Saul with an egg-on-the-face look, wondering how he would get out of this.

Samuel was appalled. "What have you done?" Saul then used the bookend principles of twisted thinking by applying martyred, inflated, and impatient thinking to give his answer.

> "When I saw that the men were scattering, and that you did not come at the set time, and that the Philistines were assembling at Micmash, I thought, [here comes the impatient thinking] now the Philistines will come down against me at Gilgal, and I have not sought the LORD'S favor. So, I felt compelled to offer the burnt offering." (1 Samuel 13:11-12, emphasis added)

Did you notice how Saul used the "I couldn't help it" line? Remember with me: For twisted thinkers, impulsivity is directly connected to impatient thinking. But Samuel didn't buy it. Even if Saul had claimed OCD, he couldn't get by the thinking behind his choice. Samuel knew it and responded:

"You acted foolishly. You have not kept the command of the LORD your God gave you; if you had, he would have established your kingdom over Israel for all time. But now your kingdom will not endure; the LORD has sought out a man after his own heart and appointed him leader of his people, because you have not kept the LORD'S command." (1 Samuel 13:13-14)

The demand for instant gratification became Saul's downfall. In reality he had no genuine regard for the future when he disobeyed God, because only priests were to offer up burnt offerings. If he had stopped to think about that, things would have been different. Impulsivity (or feeling compelled) controlled his thinking. In his mind and in his fantasy world, defeating the Philistines would be a big score, so he used his brand of foxhole religion to rationalize his behavior.

Before I go to the next bad wire leading to impatient thinking, I don't want to mislead you with the idea that twisted thinkers *always* push for instant gratification without regard for the future. I can see how this might be assumed.

Therefore, be aware that the only time they have regard for the future is when it's manipulated to serve their own purposes. For example, if they think they'll get caught in crime, drug use, or some other irresponsible act they'll do something *less* wrong but just as irresponsible. They do this to minimize the risk of apprehension. In exchange, they will delay gratification for the big score. Remember Satan, the biggest twisted thinker of them all, waited thirty years to tempt Jesus.

In our humanity, sometimes we want what we want and we want it now! To the twisted thinker, however, it's their way of life to demand triumph now. That's why they don't respect themselves or others. I've seen those attitudes expose the unhealthy high self-esteem they really have.

Satan certainly didn't have low self-esteem when he stirred up a rebellion in heaven. However, he did have low self-respect, with no respect for God or for us when he went for the big score. God then dealt with Lucifer's so-called impulsivity, prompted by impatient thinking. Twisted thinkers will also have to address their own impulsivity issues, sooner or later. My concern is that they don't use the line King Saul tried out on Samuel.

Meanwhile, we need to discuss one more bad wire. This one, connected to a disregard for the future and repeatedly going for big scores, can actually produce a false feeling of immediate gratification. It's the bad wire of making assumptions.

Assumptions

In 1995, a report appeared in the news about how a pedophile had been trapped on the Internet. The report related how a 14-year-old girl logged on and said "older guys treat you grown up." This piqued the interest of a convicted pedophile—a truck driver from Las Vegas.

After nine months of communicating with this girl, inquiring about her sexual experience, and sending sexually explicit pictures of himself, the man traveled to a Wisconsin motel room for a rendezvous. But instead, FBI agents arrested him for traveling across state lines to engage in a sexual act with a minor.

It turned out the girl was an on-line concoction of a female private investigator communicating to federal authorities that she was alarmed at the sexually explicit exchanges on the Internet. This man communicated on the Internet more than 200 times between September, 1994 and May, 1995. He agreed to plead guilty to the charges, which carried a maximum sentence of 10 years in prison and a $250,000 fine.

The example is extreme, but this man's decision is characteristic of twisted thinkers who disregard their future, fantasize about scoring big, and pursue a *Big E*. It really doesn't matter if the example is extreme or minor. Whether the big score is about telling a lie, cheating on income tax, stealing chewing gum, or trying to impress Christians with a hypocritical life, the way those decisions are made will be the same.

The last bad wire empowering irresponsible decisions is the wire of Impatient Thinking, involving decisions made without facts. I'm reminded of a sign I once saw on the back of a car: "God is dead, Nietzsche." I read further because I'd heard of Nietzsche's statement before. The next line revealed Nietzsche as an impatient thinker. It said, "Nietzsche is dead, God."

I've also read that Nietzsche didn't mean that God was literally dead, but that God was dead in Europe, culturally, at the time he made the statement in

1882. Those words were written for a character, a madman no less, as if in a Shakespearian play, to suggest that the *Christian notion* of God is dead. Either way, we can still see this bad wire of making assumptions. Neither God nor the Christian notion of God is dead.

However, when this wire of assumptions is connected to the other two we have an impatient thinker as described in Proverbs.

"He who answers before listening, that is his folly and his shame." (Proverbs 18:13)

"The way of a fool seems right to him, but a wise man listens to advice." (Proverbs 12:15)

"The plans of the diligent lead to profit as surely as haste leads to poverty." (Proverbs 21:5)

In the beginning of the book I said that closed thinking was the foundation of all other twisted thinking patterns. Now, we'll see it as it networks to impatient thinking (The Bookend Principles), and how it is cultivated.

The so-called impulsivity issue for all twisted thinkers is cultivated in secrecy. That secrecy is the incubation chamber for irresponsible fantasies. In that context, when twisted thinkers think something *is*, then that's the way it is for them whether they have the facts or not.

They don't need or want facts anyway, especially if they get in the way of their fantasies. So, they're *closed in thinking first,* before networking other twisted thinking patterns such as *impatient thinking* and the *irresponsible behavior* it promotes.

The failure to get facts before making decisions also keeps the impatient thinker from setting realistic goals. For responsible people, a goal involves pursuing a responsible objective while weathering setbacks. Thus they attain a degree of self-respect and satisfaction even if they don't reach the absolute pinnacle of success. But, as already mentioned, goals for twisted thinkers are based upon immediate gratification, like what the adolescent perpetrators tried to get when they shot an eleven-year-old girl in the head with a pellet gun.

Riding in a van three blocks away from the girl's home, they opened up the rear doors and started firing. Asked why they did it, the boys said they just wanted to see if they could do it. For them, the girl was nothing more than an object in a Play Station or Nintendo game. Their goal of providing instant gratification came with a twist of power and control over an unsuspecting girl.

Were they fragmenting time and space in their thinking? Yes. Were their goals unrealistic and not responsible behavior? Yes. Were these young men with low self-esteem? No. Did they have low self-respect and low respect for the girl? Absolutely. They were impatient thinkers interested in one thing only: their big score.

The assumption that they would not be caught, and whatever else was on their minds, was cultivated in the secret chamber of an irresponsible fantasy. The girl was fine physically, but think of the trauma she had to work through to feel safe again.

How can we determine if twisted thinkers have rewired/corrected this irresponsible pattern of decision-making? What can we look for to see if "the light is on" and twisted thinkers are respecting themselves and others? We'll look for solid connections. The process of rewiring the apparatus of impatient thinking begins with realistic goals.

Realistic Goals

Twisted thinkers must develop the ability to review choices, related to goals, that consider the future. We see this happening in the apostle Paul's life. Before he became a Christian his zeal for God wasn't according to knowledge. In other words, he didn't have all the facts. Therefore, his goal of shutting down "The Way" by persecuting Christians was unrealistic, especially in view of eternity. But, when Paul met Jesus on the road to Damascus he got the data necessary for realistic goal setting. Then, years later, Paul wrote to the church at Philippi about his understanding when he set new goals.

> "I press on to take hold of that for which Christ Jesus took hold of me. Brothers, I do not consider myself yet to have taken hold of it. But one thing I do: Forgetting what is behind and straining

toward what is ahead, I press on toward the goal to win the prize for which God has called me heavenward in Christ Jesus." (Philippians 3:12-14)

It's extremely important to reveal the future impact on decisions impatient thinkers will make. That was the whole point behind Ebenezer Scrooge's change in *A Christmas Carol*. Solomon's words in Ecclesiastes 10:1-3 are also especially poignant with respect to thinking about the future before decisions are made.

"As dead flies give perfume a bad smell, so a little folly outweighs wisdom and honor. The heart of the wise inclines to the right, but the heart of the fool to the left. Even as he walks along the road, the fool lacks sense and shows everyone how stupid he is."

If a twisted thinker wants to change, they can. Someone showing the way will help, though—and I'm not talking about education alone. That "someone" must be willing to make a human connection by providing an authentic relationship with them. That "someone" cannot be afraid to talk about realistic goals with them.

In my mind, deep personal changes always come within the context of authentic relationships in which those changes can be substantiated. Jesus Christ set the pattern with the disciples, with my father, with me, and with anyone else who wants a relationship with Him. To progress toward becoming a STAR, that pattern of integrity is what twisted thinkers need. Knowledge alone doesn't do it, but knowledge coupled with relational accountability can get it done, particularly the one with Christ.

Examining the Facts

In order to make responsible decisions you must examine the facts. Doing so is evidence of maturity, which means that potential consequences for irresponsible behaviors can be identified and realistic goals can be set.

So, if inmates in the therapy session I mentioned earlier really saw what was going on with the crow in his birdcage they might have been able to say the same thing my father said about wise guys. But they weren't so wise after all, because they were on the inside of a jail. Not caring about the facts and making irresponsible decisions exposed those inmates' immaturity.

Becoming a STAR is impossible without getting the facts. Making assumptions is the lazy way out and is connected to stubborn and reckless thinking. If you're in a relationship with an impatient thinker, go for the facts. Keep digging as if facts were golden nuggets—doing so will help rewire his thinking patterns.

By the way, when you're doing this, I hope you don't mind if I encourage you to be patient. It's wonderful when impatient thinkers start to identify a genuine sense of harmony within their relationships. How will we know when it's developing?

Experiencing Harmony with Impatient Thinkers

When realistic goals are being set, supported by examinations of the facts, as helpful as that is it doesn't provide a sense of deeper change or give as much hope for experiencing relational harmony with changing twisted thinkers as the next breakthrough.

When they consistently consider potential injuries to others instead of making irresponsible decisions, the apparatus of impatient thinking has been rewired. It's the first "above the street" behavior indicating an end to going for big scores. Meanwhile, they have become more patient with themselves, and with others and their situations. They're now willing to change a decision if they think it would hurt another person.

The transformation is happening because they're beginning to care about other people. We'll begin to see the caring when they become more obligated to others. That means they'll be consistently willing to give others their word and do whatever it takes to keep it. For instance, if they say, "I'll see you tomorrow at three o'clock," they won't mean they'll keep the appointment only if nothing comes up.

It's Worth Waiting For

You wouldn't be this far into this book if you didn't care about the person who broke your heart. I think it's also possible that you wouldn't be this far if you were the person who broke someone else's heart.

If you're the one whose heart was crushed, are you thinking about the journey and the difficult work involved in going "below the street" to connect with a twisted thinker? If you are the impatient thinker who broke someone else's heart, are you getting ready to take the "leap into the light" I talked about in chapter one? Either way, it's worth the wait to be humanly connected and enjoying the harmony available within a healthy relationship.

If you happen to be the impatient thinker this chapter describes, there's also another reason for staying the course and becoming a STAR. In Isaiah 55:6-9 the prophet offers that reason:

Seek the LORD while he may be found; call on him while he is near. Let the wicked forsake his way and the evil man his thoughts. Let him turn to the LORD, and he will have mercy on him, and to our God, for he will freely pardon. For my thoughts are not your thoughts, neither are your ways my ways," declares the LORD. "As the heavens are higher than the earth, so are my ways higher than your ways and my thoughts than your thoughts."

We are all made of the same mud. I don't know of anyone who doesn't need the mercy of God, and to be freely pardoned. I don't believe we can experience the level of harmony God meant for us to have in our relationships until a connection has been developed with Him. He's ready to have a relationship with us and He's ready to boost our self-respect, all the way to heaven. What a joy to be connected to Him and others!

If you happen to be the person who has been hurt, I don't want you to forget what I've already mentioned in other chapters. Transforming twisted thinking is tough, but it's worth it. When the apostle Paul wrote to a group of previously twisted thinkers in the Corinthian church, some of them were still struggling with the mire from that sewer. Here's how he encouraged them:

It is written: "No eye has seen, no ear has heard, no mind has conceived what God has prepared for those who love him" but God has revealed it to us by His Spirit. (1 Corinthians 2:9, 10)

Paul talks about the fact that none of us has the capability to go to heaven on our own. He enhanced our longing to be there when he said that whatever we know, hear, think or experience about heaven is because of God's willingness to have it revealed to us by His Spirit. Thus Paul encourages those believers to be patient. He says that heaven is worth waiting for.

God is in the place where change can happen for you and me. Paul was in the place with Corinthian believers where change could happen for them. It's wonderful to watch God transform twisted thinkers, just as He did for Paul, for the Corinthians, for my father, and for me.

But that transformation doesn't happen unless someone is willing to go "below the street" into the darkness of a twisted soul. Choosing to be patient with twisted thinkers, while God also does His work, is worth it. What a breakthrough when they are transformed! Heaven sings!

Chapter Ten

FEARFUL THINKING

Being Balanced

I have irrational fears but refuse to admit them. I have a fundamental fear of injury or death when I'm not in control. I have a profound fear of being put down. When I'm held accountable I feel lousy and experience a "Zero State."

On her first birthday, Elizabeth was deciding if walking would be more productive than crawling. Her curiosity for going into brave new worlds, previously uncharted, was peaking. But, whenever "Papa" would ask her to come she'd shake her head sideways and look elsewhere. It was clear to me that she was going to decide on the time and place to walk, and if anyone happened to be around they'd just be lucky.

On another occasion, while I was strumming my guitar she was sitting on the floor with her back to me, rocking to the music. To Elizabeth, my talent was wonderful because she didn't know any better. You know it's bad when a favorite nephew says that if he were sitting in a bar, inebriated, my guitar playing might sound great. The opinion of my granddaughter though, was quite different. The sounds coming from Papa's guitar mesmerized her.

ELIZABETH STANDS

Suddenly, she stopped rocking. I could almost see the wheels turning in her head, but for what I didn't know. Then, with her legs spread out in front and falling forward, Elizabeth began to do something like a push-up. Slowly she then stood upright, balancing herself via her bow-legged stance. She reminded me of one of those little plastic cowboys you take off toy horses.

Checking my watch, I timed this historic moment for one full minute and then began cheering. Startled, she fell back on her bottom. Not to worry, though, because she then sat there, smiling. Whatever fears she'd had seemed to be conquered. Perhaps Elizabeth was thinking about the multitude of options before her now that she'd realized she could balance herself on two feet. I had just witnessed an application of responsible decision-making, counterbalancing the way twisted thinkers manage fear.

Responsibility and Fear

At the ripe old age of one, like a mountain climber inching across her first wall of rock, Elizabeth negotiated her fear and achieved a tenuous balance. First she visualized the cost and the consequences. Afterward she evaluated the results. In the process she demonstrated how responsibility and fear fit hand in glove for anyone who achieves a relational balance in life. In fact, there is no responsibility without fear. The Apostle Peter supported the same concept, in his first letter to Christians living in Asia Minor.

> "*Prepare your minds for action; be self-controlled;* set your hope fully on the grace to be given you when Jesus Christ is revealed. Since you call on a Father who judges each man's work impartially, live your lives as strangers here in reverent fear." (I Peter 1:13, 17 emphasis added)

Perhaps you've seen *The Dead Poet's Society*, the movie in which a professor played by Robin Williams translates the Latin phrase "Seize the day" to encourage a group of students to live life fully. They called him "Captain O' My Captain" for teaching them to use their poetic ability to express themselves as free individuals, even while facing rejection.

"Seizing the day" can be compared to the biblical phrase in Ephesians 5:16, 17 (making the most of every opportunity). But there are times when Paul and the professor may mean different things. The difference has to do with what we base our hopes on while seizing our own day.

I believe that whatever one does or doesn't hope in will determines how our lives will be lived out. Peter's comment encourages right living through our hope of seeing the resurrected Christ. I know people can find other kinds of hope to go on in life, but in chapter eight I talked about the ultimate question of where we spend eternity, because wherever we ultimately finds ourselves I believe we will stay. Hebrews 11 speaks about people who've suffered for their faith and were willing to do so. It was because they were sure of what they hoped for regarding eternity and, certain of what they did not see.

What's interesting about hope is how the Bible reconciles it with a reverent fear. In other words, "No fear—No hope!" Having hope with reverent fear is a part of what it means to walk by faith, in a responsible manner. In fact, where there's no hope I've observed people choosing irresponsible paths in life because they eliminate reverent fear along with other legitimate fears. But Christians are encouraged to run their race with perseverance, trusting the Father to do for them what He did for Jesus at His resurrection. Seizing the day or making the most of every opportunity takes on new light when we are in possession of that eternal hope.

Yet there are times when seizing the moment may characterize the spirit of the age we live in, indicating that hope is absent. In that state, people do incredibly wicked things when seizing their moments.

FEARFUL THINKING

Working as a minister and counselor, I have discovered that individuals who have false hopes—or no hope—usually lean toward fearful thinking. This mentality advocates seizing the moment with an all-or-nothing attitude to avoid lousy feelings, or any other instances of personal pain.

The concept of no responsibility without fear seems to be affirmed in Simon and Garfunkel's song, "I Am a Rock." The character in the song isolated himself from others because of fears of relational pain. He expressed how touching no one—and having no one touching him—happens because he's a rock and an island. A rock feels no pain and an island never cries. Relational fortresses and walls were built deep and mighty, so that none can penetrate.

Welcome to fearful thinking, where fear must be cut off at any cost.

I've been given the opportunity to work with many professional athletes. Ken Ruettgers, CEO of GamesOver.org, a ministry to athletes in transition, states that seventy-eight percent of those who retire from professional football will be divorced or bankrupt—or both—within two years after leaving the sport.

I often get calls from athletes in different sports, too, when their marriages are at risk. This also happens with many professionals outside of sport, whether they are ministry people, doctors, lawyers, law enforcement people, and business CEOs.

When we finally meet for their marital intensives they frequently tell me unimaginable stories of infidelity and/or domestic abuse. And sometimes spiritual abuse as well. I might be tempted to wonder how these things could happen, except that virtually every account has one important element in common. Invariably, the adulterer or abuser isolated himself (or herself) from their spouse and created a fantasy world in which they were in complete control.

At that point, the twisted thinking patterns mentioned throughout this book become the foundation for their decision making. Then they get caught! The fantasy of living a forbidden life suddenly comes crashing down, colliding with the real world of their marriage. Now they are no longer in control and about to lose their marriage and family. Living in duplicity isn't an option anymore.

My job is to uncover it all, to go to the secret places of the heart and mind where it started. However, even though I get the call and the offender seems ready and willing to do what it takes, that doesn't mean they've stopped cutting off their fear at any cost, unlike Elizabeth who embraced her fears and made a sound, responsible judgment in her decision to stand for the first time in her life.

Many professionals I work with are sincerely open to facing the music and hoping to restore their marriages. Maybe this is why over seventy percent are reconciled and restored. But those who are still playing the "game" of deflection, or lickety-split, will look me in the eye and lie. They will do everything they can to make sure I know they are a good person, and if I don't buy that they'll try to intimidate or manipulate me in ways I will mention in the next chapter.

If they try to keep that up within the process I give them for reconciliation and accountability, they'll pull out all the stops to control their spouse and me.

And yes, I've had moments in which the danger of being physically assaulted was a real possibility. Those marriages don't make it.

It's incredible to think that, at such a moment, an athlete could be more concerned about maintaining their forbidden fantasies than saving the marriage. Responsible living is not present, and when they fear their gig of duplicity is lost they won't tolerate that fear.

Combining Hope and Fear

The challenge facing practicing twisted thinkers is how to reconcile fear and hope. And if hope, the most vial element for responsible living, is absent then it will lead to avoiding any fear at any cost. The end result will be a person committed to fearful thinking.

However, if hope and fear are combined and balanced against each, then we can understand how believers in Christ should be encouraged to live responsibly while operating in a reckless world. Instead of existing on a rock or an island, oblivious to human connections, people walking with God embrace their personal and relational fears because they have hope in Him. "Lord, to whom shall we go? You have the words of eternal life" said Simon Peter in John 6:68.

With Him we can embrace our fears and live free of their control. Twisted thinkers believe they're free when fear is cut off rather than embraced, but in fact they aren't.

Embracing Fear

In II Timothy 1:7, Paul's comment to a nervous young preacher named Timothy is encouraging. "For God did not give us a spirit of timidity, but a spirit of power, of love, and of self-discipline." In the King James version the words "timidity" and "self-discipline" are rendered "fear" and "sound mind." I believe Paul is describing the "spirit of fear" to mean allowing the thought of being afraid to intimidate us into doing something irresponsible, or to hide from others (closed thinking). God doesn't give such a spirit of fear to anyone.

In addition, Paul wasn't saying Timothy shouldn't experience the emotion of fear, as if something were wrong when he did. To say that God has not given us the capacity to feel fear doesn't make sense. On the contrary, God built this potential into everyone, as a *correct* and *prudent* response to something frightening, disturbing, or painful. I don't go to the dentist and say, "Go ahead, drill," unless that dentist gives me something to deaden the pain. I don't get into a car without putting the seat belt on. I don't monkey with electrical outlets in my home unless I turn the power off first. Embracing the reality of fear helps us make good, sound, responsible decisions.

In healthy minds, separating out the "spirit of fear" means not allowing the thought of being afraid to keep us from the power and love that God gives to those who trust Him. On the other hand, He wants us to experience the emotion of fear both as a protective mechanism and as an indication that we are physically and emotionally healthy. Fearful thinkers, however, allow the *thought* of being afraid to predetermine (and often to limit) their choices. That's when they reject the emotion of fear. Given such thinking patterns, one can only imagine how twisted such person will get in his relationships.

Again, *there is no responsibility without fear.* Whether it's a level of doubt, concern, anxiety, dread, or respect for authority, those feelings need to be embraced by anyone who's alive. Moreover, a healthy state of fear is necessary for fearful thinkers, if they're going to become STARs and enjoy relational harmony. Yet, this fear provides the most terror they will ever experience. It's a transient state of self-disgust.

Embracing Self-Disgust

Proverbs 28:14 reveals why twisted thinkers will not for one second be disgusted with or at themselves. "Blessed is the man who always fears the LORD, but he who hardens his heart falls into trouble."

Responsible people are individuals who respect people's boundaries. They are disgusted at the thought of hurting someone, or when they've actually done so. They respect authority.

In contrast, fearful thinkers do not respect or value the preservation of relationships. The writer in Proverbs describes those who harden their hearts as embittered people, choosing to be unaware of another's pain. Mark this down, will you? *Without feeling disgust for hurting others, including God, twisted thinkers are going to fall into trouble.*

Let me repeat: Responsible people are personally and deeply disgusted by the pain they've caused anyone. Their hearts are ripped out, and they'll do whatever it takes to reconcile or restore any relationship they've harmed. That's what I mean about embracing this misery called self-disgust.

Proverbs 1:7 indicates where responsible living begins: "The fear of the LORD is the beginning of knowledge, but fools despise wisdom and discipline." This thought is confirmed in Proverbs 14:16-18:

A wise man fears the LORD and shuns evil, but a fool is hotheaded and reckless. A quick-tempered man does foolish things, and a crafty man is hated. The simple inherit folly, but the prudent are crowned with knowledge.

I believe these verses imply that transforming twisted thinking and untangling twisted relationships won't start until twisted thinkers embrace the misery of self-disgust. In fact, God said the same thing regarding His judgment of Israel in Hosea chapter 5. Clearly, those people were practicing fearful thinking. Whenever they were held accountable they refused to tolerate being disgusted at hurting God and others. But the Lord revealed what Israel was doing by deliberately putting them in that emotional zero state. He gave them an opportunity to be miserable. That's right, miserable! There is something about misery that can help anyone when it comes to addressing fearful thinking and irresponsible behavior.

In verse 3, God said, "Ephraim, you have now turned to prostitution; Israel is corrupt." In verse 4-5, He said, "A spirit of prostitution is in their heart; they do not acknowledge the LORD. Israel's arrogance testifies against them; the Israelites, even Ephraim, stumble in their sin."

Then, in verses 13 and 14, God talked about the time when they knew they were sick in sin and yet chose to turn away from Him. But we don't see God becoming "co-dependent" by taking responsibility for their actions when they justly belonged to them. On the contrary, He pronounced something dramatic in verse 15. They aren't miserable enough! Instead of eliminating the feeling of self-disgust, God wants them to experience it fully.

"Then I will go back to my place until they admit their guilt. And they will seek my face; in their misery they will earnestly seek me."

Eliminating Self-Disgust

My question is, why would twisted thinkers cut off the fear of self-disgust and fall into trouble? Certainly, God's people did so in Hosea. A possible explanation comes from their refusal to admit that they have irrational fears, because talking to others about them spawns the belief that those people will control them. They might also have had fundamental fears of injury or death when they were not in control. And, they could fear being put down. Those are some reasons why self-disgust is cut off, but inflated thinking must be included as a part of the answer to my question.

By this time, you are probably figuring out how each twisted thinking pattern networks to the one before and after it. Using the bookend principles of chapter two, I call that a cluster. You might have figured out how one pattern can skip over several patterns and network with others, such as inflated thinking connecting with fearful thinking. You may also have figured out that, the farther we go into the sewer of these patterns, every preceding pattern may be part of the one being explored. It's a dark place, isn't it?

That's why, whenever we're in a relationship with twisted thinkers, we need to allow the misery of their irresponsible choices to have its full impact on them. It can be profoundly redemptive when it happens. Each twisted thinking pattern has been interpreted to be the way life is for them, but those patterns must be corrected or there's no leap into the light, which is what real living is all about.

Again, what evil added to fearful thinking keeps them from taking this leap? The answer is noteworthy. They continue to consider themselves essentially good in the very moment when they feel lousy while caught in some unloving, irresponsible act. It's a personal conflict they cannot tolerate, because they believe everyone will see the conflict and share their sense of worthlessness and ignore their view of self as good.

They also believe their emotional zero state will never change. So, if they try to reconcile with their momentary depression it means there's no hope for achieving what they want to be satisfied in life. Consequently, they just cut off the lousy feeling and go for broke, not caring about anyone who's hurt by them.

Without a genuine sense of hope during their moment of self-disgust, they set out to manufacture a false one with all-or-nothing behaviors. It's not difficult to understand why twisted thinkers believe being hotheaded, reckless, quick-tempered, crafty, simple, and foolish can all be good things. When they mix inflated with fearful thinking, those behaviors then come out of a person who in essence believes that they are good, and that such behaviors are justified. That's why waiting for misery to take hold of the twisted thinker is very important, as God said in Hosea 5:13, 14.

Waiting for the Misery to Take Hold

I've talked frequently with inmates in my role of a correctional chaplain and a therapist. One inmate lived behind a shield of Plexiglas securely fastened to the cell bars. It was there as protection for anyone walking by, to keep him from defiling them. This man was moved to a different prison every four months, to prevent him from starting riots. Yet, when we conversed he came across as a highly educated, religious, clean man as evidenced by his immaculate cell. His outward appearance, though, hid every heinous crime he'd perpetrated.

Eventually we came to a point in our talks where I could speak about God. On one occasion, after I'd challenged his thinking, he entered an emotional zero state. We were sitting on the floor, next to a small opening in the Plexiglas, when I asked, "On a scale of 0-10, where do you think you'd have to be for God to allow you into heaven?" He went deep into thought and then said, "Hmmm! I'm not there yet, but I believe it's a 10."

I said, "Well, it might seem so, but actually, it's zero."

He looked at me, somewhat astonished, and asked, "How do you figure?"

"Not until you're at zero on this question will God be able to respond to you. No matter what you try to do or not do, you can't earn your way to heaven. Zero means there's nothing you can offer Him. In fact, anything above zero is disgusting to Him because what God offered through His son was enough. All God requires from you is to receive His gift by faith alone."

"I'll have to think about it," he said, for this was (and is) very difficult to grasp for anyone who believes he's good, in spite of what his rap sheet discloses. Sadly, when I returned the following week I discovered that he'd been moved to another prison.

Waiting for twisted thinkers to become more miserable may not seem like you're doing anything, but you are. Without misery there's no reason to believe they will ever come out of fearful thinking in a consistently responsible manner. Remember, God said, "in their misery they will earnestly seek me." Waiting for this to happen is good and productive. The father of the prodigal waited for his son to come to the end of himself, and God waited for His own habitually irresponsible people to do the same. Without misery they ignored the personal and spiritual realities for each to overcome.

A Spiritual Reality

Experiencing the misery of self-disgust, especially when we've hurt others, can teach us to be keenly aware of our own soul's darkness. Hope for living in an eternal heaven depends on being conscious of that spiritual reality and not cutting it off, like the inmate seemed to be doing when I talked to him.

In I John 1:8, 10, John explained what it's like to struggle with the darkness in our souls. He calls for a clear acknowledgement of sin or depravity, even if we claim to walk with God.

> "If we claim to be without sin, we deceive ourselves and the truth is not in us. If we claim we have not sinned, we make him out to be a liar and his word has no place in our lives."

If cutting off the awareness of our own depravity, by believers, is a crucial concern for God, how much more important might it be for twisted thinkers? John's letter was written with that principle in mind. No genuine, lasting, deep, personal or relational changes happen for anyone until they have a healthy respect for that reality. Cutting it out of our awareness is irresponsible and dangerous. That's why the Bible declares that God is willing to wait for us to acknowledge being lost in this condition.

It's also true socially. By refusing to cut off consciousness of our own soul darkness we own who we are and what we do. God teaches this truth out of love, while allowing the misery of irresponsible thinking and behaviors to affect everyone's life—even His own people, as in Hosea 5.

God did this for a friend of mine who once told Him that he was going to do whatever he wanted until it hurt somebody. On Sundays he'd lead a church youth group, but during the week he'd get drunk. His drinking was done secretly and went on for two years. But one night he staggered home, roaring drunk, and there in front of him stood his brother and his parents. Abruptly, he became aware of hurting them.

God allowed two years for this man's behavior to achieve its full impact. But on the positive side, if twisted thinkers choose to be broken and disgusted with their own soul's darkness, as my friend did, they're then ready to be transformed and to make legitimate connections with God, family, and friends. Again, waiting for this to happen is good and valid work, even when it feels like nothing is being accomplished.

Being at zero is good news for those who trust God, but twisted thinkers consider it bad news. In that state, responsible people consistently deal with their emotional zeros by working through them in appropriate ways. They're not like the inmate who believes being a rock or an island is good because it lets him avoid his emotional zeros. Until twisted thinkers remain at zero and can work out of it in a responsible manner, they continue the poisoned living. We need to be aware of this or we'll fail to see how they cut off zero states prematurely, thus forestalling any potential improvement.

Cutting off Emotional Zero States

Understanding the dynamics of fearful thinking removes the mystery of how fearful thinkers cut off lousy feelings. People who've been hurt by twisted thinkers need this perception to gain back some sense of balance, as they look for indicators of genuine change in the twisted thinkers thinking patterns.

When unexplainable or bizarre behavior is viewed in the light of fearful thinking, it provides wisdom to deal with the calm before a storm—and for the storm itself. You may have to batten down the hatches, as if you're Tom

Hanks in *Castaway*, but you'll survive for another day of opportunity while they work out of their own emotional zero state, with maturity.

The calm before the storm arrives when twisted thinkers are confronted and act like everything is fine, especially when you know they should be experiencing self-disgust for hurting someone. Be watchful because the storm is coming. They will act out in some irresponsible manner, sometimes even weeks later. When the storm does rage you need to be aware that they are combining fearful with inflated thinking, to excuse the irresponsible behavior.

When held accountable, it's like they're saying, "I'm good, so don't imply I'm bad or make me feel bad. Because, if you do I'll make you pay!"

Of course they often keep that thought private. In their minds, it's all or nothing because they're either "good" or "bad." They'll admit to doing bad things while never believing they're a bad or wicked person. They won't even admit to being a jerk. They'll tell you, "I'm just like your next door neighbor."

This is why people with addictive behaviors continue to do what they do. Whether it's an eating disorder, gambling problem, self-mutilation, sexual addiction, drug addiction, or any other cruel addiction, mixing inflated with fearful thinking perpetuates the raging storms within.

By using that mix, Ted Bundy and other serial killers continued to do what they did. Israel continued to do what they did in the book of Hosea, via the same mixture of twisted thinking modes.

Twisted thinkers love to keep their stuff going. "You can't really help me because you don't understand." Have you ever heard that line? They'll do anything to remove contradictions to their definitions and perceptions of goodness, even when they're the ones causing the dilemma. I don't want you to be surprised when you feel pressured by them. They use anger, victim-seeking behavior, and lack of true helplessness to erase their emotional zeros, just as often as they act like everything is fine.

To what end? By cutting off their fear of emotional zero states, it keeps inflated thinking going and reinforces secret, irresponsible fantasies. When they purposely cut off the self-disgust they should be feeling, others will then feel the effects of their raging internal storms.

Examples

In a northeastern state, a former church organist confessed to more than 500 church and synagogue burglaries that netted $2.5 million in gold and silver religious objects. When the man was arrested the officer said, "Nothing was ever ransacked or disturbed. The thief carried out the burglary as if he were showing great respect." The man had confessed to lootings spanning more than a ten-year period. Now, my question is, how could this church organist be involved with worship one moment and then rob the church the next?

In a Midwestern state, another man was convicted of causing his eleven-month-old son's death by leaving him in a hot car while he went to smoke marijuana with friends. He said he was hurting inside because he loved his son with all his heart. But the judge said it was difficult to comprehend how someone could have left the boy in a car in such sweltering weather. Then the father told the Judge, "I forgot." How could a father say, "I loved my son with all my heart," be involved with smoking marijuana, and forget his boy who was dying in a death trap? It's inexcusable!

Fearful Thinking

How could another man be a loving husband one moment, then turn into an abuser of his wife and children the next moment? How can a minister stand in a pulpit to preach the Bible one moment, then live immorally or unethically when he gets home? How could any husband or wife act as if their partner were the only one for them, then be unfaithful? How can an adolescent athlete, noteworthy for good character and one of the most popular kids in school, then get caught cheating? It goes on and on.

How fearful thinkers choose to cut off the fear of being found out is connected to every thinking pattern previously mentioned. In other words, they may go directly to fearful thinking from any one of those patterns.

This is not good news but it's honest reporting on how the network of thinking patterns can be accessed, like programs on a computer with any pattern ready to be called up at any time. The deeper we go below the street the darker it gets, but remember that the transformation doesn't happen unless we get all the way "into the sewer."

Society uses the threat of prison or jail, and education on occupational hazards (such as being maimed or killed). But beyond all that, what happens when alcohol or drugs are added to the blend of fearful thinking? Those chemicals supply immediate cutoffs from every external deterrent society offers. External deterrents become impotent even without chemicals, but using chemicals speeds up the process. However, although alcohol and drugs are used to facilitate behavior they are not responsible for it. The twisted thinker himself is responsible, as the following thought declares: *It's always the thinking before the using.*

The fact is that twisted thinkers aren't asking, "What will happen when I get caught?" because they don't think they will. Even so, it's still right and responsible for others to use external deterrents to try to connect fearful thinkers with self-disgust. Doing so could also help introduce God's influence into the equation as we wait for the self-disgust moment to develop.

What does society do to address and/or encourage internal deterrents? There's plenty of education on the dangers of whatever is harmful. The marketing world advertises certain irresponsible behaviors as personal putdowns. Peer pressure is used. Humanitarian features are promoted in the news. Religious communities use standards of conduct that promote right behavior. Other organizations appeal to the sentimental sides of people. Everything is done with the hope that twisted thinkers might care enough to let some of these messages sink in. However, they have an internal means of eliminating any internal deterrents from awareness, by using the cutoff process.

I gave a formula in chapter five to show how internal deterrents—such as stopping to think about who gets hurt, making plans to be responsible on a daily basis, and not dwelling on some *Big E*—can corrode or decay. That corrosion sets up the basic cutoff principles I've detailed below, all of which is very important to understand.

Recognizing "Cutoff" Principles

I want to focus on the phrase, "Determined Choices to Pursue Big *Es*." Those split-second choices are usually made when someone is either in, or is coming out of, a zero state—self disgust. In a flash they make the decision to cut off those emotional zero states. Or, conflicts become the foundation for their lives. That foundation allows them to do whatever they want, supported by the equation mentioned in chapter five. It all starts in their secret fantasy world—a world exerting a huge influence on the way they make decisions. So, the first principle of the cutoff is this: *There must be a Big E to pursue before they do it.*

It is also possible that their decision to pursue Big *Es* might not come from being in an emotional zero state. It could result from taking an irresponsible fantasy and simply transferring it to a real-world experience, like transferring funds in a bank account. The intent, as mentioned in chapter six, is immediate gratification from an instant triumph. In other words, the *Big E* is pursued for the sake of the *Big E*, rather than to escape the lousy feelings produced by moments of accountability. Nevertheless, fearful thinking is operating because it disregards and cuts that person off from responsible living. Whatever the reason, cutoffs of fear will not happen unless there's a *Big E* to pursue.

The second principle advances the last rule. Before the decision is made to eliminate their fear of self-disgust, twisted thinkers must be extremely certain they can achieve their *Big E* and won't get caught, unless getting caught is a part of a self-serving agenda. It's a fundamental part of how decisions are made, even if the person isn't totally aware of the dynamic.

For instance, I didn't presuppose that a man who told me he didn't want to be considered a wife beater was actually thinking of making sure he didn't get put into that list, just so he could continue abusing loved ones. In his mind he was extremely certain that he was not a wife beater, which both *reflects* and *reinforces* the third principle of the cutoff. Fearful thinkers must view themselves as good people or they wouldn't be able to do what's irresponsible. I know it's twisted, but that's the way they think.

Sadly, the man eventually lost his marriage and his family. What foolishness and what irresponsibility! He would rather live in his fantasy world than make a genuine, human connection with those he said he loved.

Many, twisted thinkers are also very aware of making sure they're not going to be caught before committing themselves to a *Big E*. They do think about getting caught, even if only for a microsecond.

Add the corrosion of internal moral deterrents to these three principles of the cutoff and we have the basic mental process for eliminating emotional zero states, or self-disgust. That mental process will always surface from "below the street" as an irresponsible behavior. Then, once they've cut off their fear, one more thing keeps the cycle going. They choose to fragment their behavior from who they are.

KING SAUL'S CYCLE OF FRAGMENTATION

In 1 Samuel 15, Samuel gave King Saul instructions from the Lord to exact justice on the Amalekites. They were guilty of waylaying Israel when they came out of Egypt. God didn't forget that, any more than a government forgets the murderers on death row, waiting for execution. God gave orders to destroy the Amalekites and everything they possessed. Nothing was to remain alive lest any of them might think they could fool with Israel and kill innocent people again.

King Saul disobeyed God and allowed the Amalekite king to live, although Saul and his army kept the best sheep, cattle, fat calves, lambs, and everything else they thought was good. God then expressed His grief to Samuel because Saul's decision revealed how he minimized the murder of Israelites. It also revealed his real thinking about God and indicated that Israel was not safe under Saul's leadership.

But, when Samuel went to confront the king, Saul acted as if everything was fine by using God-talk, saying, "The LORD bless you! I have carried out the LORD'S instruction."

Samuel immediately pointed out a contradiction, at which point Saul introduced the zero state we've been discussing. Saul's behavior illustrated every principle defining the mental cutoff process when he responded by blaming his soldiers for the discrepancy. I can imagine Samuel thinking, "Yeah, right, like you really want to hear what God says."

Samuel then reviewed how Saul had got to where he was, as a head of the tribes of Israel. He asked Saul why he had disobeyed God. At that moment, Saul used fearful thinking mixed with inflated thinking to avoid self-disgust and said, "But I did obey the Lord." Furthermore, he also told Samuel that he did what he did for religious reasons, which again fragmented his behavior from who he really was.

Samuel then told Saul that he was not impressed, and lowered the boom. "Because you have rejected the word of the LORD, he has rejected you as king."

Immediately, Saul came up with what looked like repentance and said, "I have sinned. I violated the LORD'S command and your instructions."

If they'd had television back then Saul would have gone on it to confess, with tears rolling down his cheeks. I mean, everything he said was the right thing to say; it sounded like, "Hey, he really means it!" But true to form with people committed to fearful thinking, Saul followed this comment with an excuse and said, "I was afraid of the people and so I gave in to them." Again, he chose to fragment his behavior from who he was on the inside.

Samuel said that the LORD had torn the kingdom of Israel from Saul. You'd think that Saul would finally get it, but no! Saul was still using the cutoff process when he replied, "I have sinned but please honor me" in public. Well, Samuel did one last public thing in front of Saul and his constituents.

Agag, the Amalekite king, was summoned, and by now he was thinking everything was cool. But in front of Saul and the Israelites, Samuel did Saul's job and executed Agag. Saul was not allowed by God or Samuel to escape feeling lousy because of his disobedience. In fact, because Saul chose to fragment his behavior from who he really was he never recovered. How pitiful, because it didn't have to happen.

THE ART OF FRAGMENTATION

Throughout this book I call certain individuals twisted thinkers because they've learned the art of fragmenting. This is not some mystical "shrink" term implying that twisted thinkers can claim, "I don't know where it's coming from when I'm doing what I do." On the contrary, fragmenting is a functional decision allowing a person to continue investing energies into irresponsible fantasies, as we witnessed with King Saul.

A person going through a cutoff of fear can decide to step back into responsible behavior, but it's not necessarily evidence for the change they want you to think is occurring. Usually, when they start acting or living responsibly, the loved ones who've been hurt are still hurting and reserve doubt about whether they can trust those "above the street" changes. Every irresponsible behavior in the mind's eye of the twisted thinker, however, is viewed as a separate event. Instead, they should be looking at who they are as a person by connecting every event from the past to their current irresponsible behavior, and integrating them all together.

If challenged on the reliability of their behavior, their choice to fragment rises to the surface again in statements like the following: "It's someone else's fault," or "You don't trust me," or "That was then and this is now," or "I'm doing fine, but if you keep pushing my buttons you're going to make me mad, and if I do something it'll be your fault."

Responsible individuals, though, determine who a person is by viewing that person—and their behaviors—as one and the same. That's why the cliché, "Don't do as I do but do as I say" doesn't cut it. Responsible people don't fragment the two as separate entities. Obviously, that approach would be hypocritical. Twisted thinkers, however, separate these two entities via fearful thinking, because the fragmentation sets them up to continue their fantasies. The cycle for practicing twisted thinking will continue until they deal with those fantasies and the thinking that supports them, and then make a commitment to face the self-disgust they should feel for hurting others.

Responsible Christians take to heart the apostle Paul's comments in his second letter to the Corinthians, about irresponsible fantasies. He identifies the struggle we all have with them while walking in the flesh. But he also talks about the mighty weapons we have through God, to pull down these strongholds in the mind. You can hear this in "We take captive every thought to make it obedient to Christ" (II Corinthians 10:5).

In other words, how we deal with fantasies or imaginations is our responsibility. That's the way it is for everyone. But, when someone is functioning as a fearful thinker, we might experience quite a bit of time passing before the next "below the street" behavior comes up. They do not take captive every thought, much less to make them obedient to Christ. They need to de-fragment by pulling together all the compartments of the cycle you see below, as parts of who they are. It has to be done if they're going to find a balance, which overcomes fearful thinking.

THE DEFRAGMENTATION CYCLE FOR TWISTED THINKING

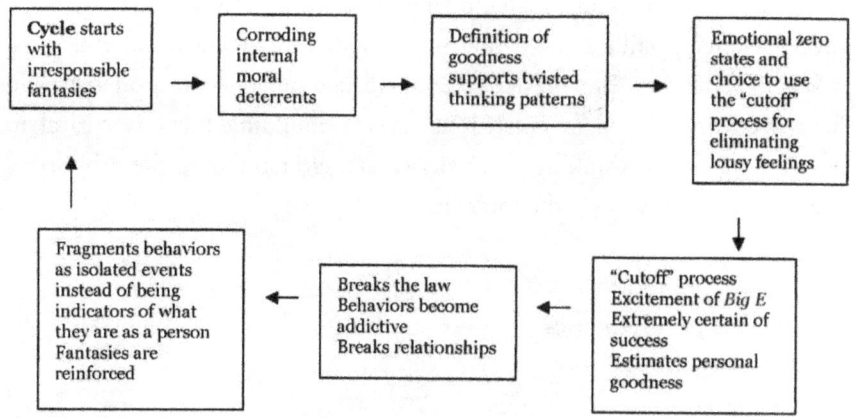

FINDING BALANCE

In I Samuel 16:7, God says, "Man looks at the outward appearance, but the LORD looks at the heart of man." Samuel's decision-making process for selecting the next king was no different from the process for determining whether change is happening for twisted thinkers involved in fearful thinking. Samuel was to look for a "balanced" man by looking inside of him—what the Lord calls the "heart of man." He was to be more impressed by that than by the outward appearance. As you will remember, David, the youngest of Jesse's sons, was the eventual selection—and a very good one, too!

When David went to fight the giant, Goliath looked him over and saw that he was only a boy. In stature he was, but on the inside David had the heart of a man—a *responsible* man, and that's what counted. The balance in his thinking and living allowed him to meet the giant head-on and defeat him.

That balance is what to look for from twisted thinkers who are becoming STARs. You'll see it when they stop fragmenting what they do from who they are. There's also another indicator that this is happening. It shows up when they sharpen their ability to solve problems, as David did when deciding how to fight the giant.

Problem-solving Skills

In the story I told about my granddaughter learning to stand she was using problem-solving skills already built in by God, and what a wonderful thing it was to watch her. But the skills Elizabeth demonstrated as a one-year-old have been diminished in twisted thinkers. Rebuilding them is critical to overcoming fearful thinking. I usually encourage rebuilding them by using the acronym SOLVE, via the following:

- **S**tate your problem
- **O**utline your responses
- **L**ist your alternatives
- **V**isualize your consequences
- **E**valuate your results.

Developing those skills can help identify and challenge fears in fearful thinkers instead of cutting them off. Building those skills also helps in developing sensitivity to others by keeping situations in perspective. I also believe improving on problem-solving skills can assist in opening a door for becoming sensitive toward God. That is especially pertinent when determining how He would like us to handle our emotional zero states.

Promoting Sensitivity to God

The apostle Peter tells us that God isn't dumb. In I Peter 3:12 he says, "For the eyes of the Lord are on the righteous and his ears are attentive to their prayer, but the face of the Lord is against those who do evil." The buck stops at God's desk. Cutting off fears means twisted thinkers haven't understood that God isn't blind. He sees all, hears all, and knows all.

Peter encouraged Christians to hang in there even when experiencing emotional zero-states resulting from a walk with God in a world that didn't like it. They weren't suffering for irresponsible behaviors; they were suffering for behaving right. Peter says, "Do not fear what they fear; do not be frightened. But in your hearts set apart Christ as Lord" (I Peter 3:14, 15).

If a twisted thinker or anyone else is going to be a STAR, I believe it is absolutely primary to develop his or her sensitivity to God. Only a fool says in his own heart, "No, God!" We all need God's participation when making our decisions, not because we can't think for ourselves but rather to understand we're not rocks or islands unto ourselves. Who better to have in our lives than the creator, giving us the balance for living that everyone needs?

Participating with God

Stan Fulweiler, an elderly gentleman and friend of mine, was suffering with cancer in his leg bones. In my view he was a man's man, and I enjoyed his wit, his stamina, his courage, and most of all his fellowship as a brother in the Lord. Stan had great impact on people for good and didn't let his suffering get in the way of it.

Stan invited me over for what was to be our last talk. Even though he was dying I treated him as if the relationship wasn't ending, which I think would be good to do for any dying person. Furthermore, if a dying person is a Christian and has gone from this earth, they're still living in heaven and when we get there we'll have a party because the relationship doesn't end. So we talked about a lot of things, but one topic stood out for me. Typically, Stan was being open and real. I asked if I could share this story with others and he gave me permission to tell it.

He and his lovely wife, Mary, lived on the shoreline of Lake Michigan just south of Sturgeon Bay, Wisconsin. We were sitting outside their house discussing God, heaven, and loved ones, when Stan started opening up about the pain he suffered. He looked at me and said, "Jerry, it took me eight hours yesterday to move my legs so I could get out of bed." "How come?" I responded.

"I was afraid of the pain I thought I'd feel but I decided to risk moving this body out of bed, anyway. Then, I learned something."

It's great when older people tell me they learn something. The notion that you can't teach an old dog new tricks isn't true. Then Stan said, "I learned that the pain was nowhere near what I thought it would be."

After eight hours of his own personal "Mexican standoff" Stan made the choice to embrace the pain. Quite frankly I'm glad he did. I think it was straight, solid thinking on his part to take the risk. I told him I was going to miss him and asked him if he'd say hello to my dad when he got to heaven. We shared some more intimate moments and then I left, but my impression of how he overcame the fearful thinking connected to his pain remains with me. His decision to stay connected with Mary and others, by not avoiding the fear, showed me the balance of mind he had.

Sometimes quite a bit of change can happen for twisted thinkers who develop problem-solving skills, and even more can happen when they acknowledge God. But I don't believe we find the balance needed for really overcoming the zeros of life until actually inviting God to participate in them, as Stan did.

Without that hope, twisted thinkers will jump out of their zero states and into the next thinking pattern.

Chapter Eleven

MANIPULATIVE THINKING

Power Without Being Powerful

I have a compelling need to be in control of others and every situation. I use manipulation and deceit to get into and take control of situations. I refuse to be a dependent person unless I can take advantage of it.

It doesn't matter if the power that man possesses is mental, physical, spiritual, or emotional—the responsible use of any kind of power is legitimate and should be enjoyed. I also don't believe it's wrong to either *have power* or to *be relationally powerful*, but those are two different concepts.

I do believe, though, that God longs for everyone to have and to be both. Now, that might almost seem sacrilegious if we think of His longing to mean that He needs to be filled up because He is personally empty. On the contrary, it's out of His fullness that we are given life, plus the capacity to express the powers we possess. Ever since Adam's fall man has been empty before God, meaning we all fall short of God's glory. The neat thing is that God literally wants to "fill" all of mankind.

The apostle Paul put it another way in a letter to Christians living at Ephesus. In Ephesians 3:19 he wanted them to "Know this love that surpasses knowledge—that you may be filled to the measure of all the fullness of God." In a letter to the Colossian believers, Paul further describes how that fullness was revealed to humanity, and where it could be located.

> For God was pleased to have all his fullness dwell in him [Christ], and through him to reconcile to himself all things, whether things on

earth or things in heaven, by making peace through his blood, shed on the cross. (Colossians 1:19, 20, emphasis added)

Then he said, "For in Christ all the fullness of the Deity lives in bodily form" (Colossians 2:9). It's amazing how God is willing to put Himself in a position where His longing to fill you and me with Himself could be rejected. He's not an empty person but I think it must be heartbreaking, or feel something like a void, when anyone does reject Him.

In reality, if God were a twisted thinker being rejected wouldn't mean much because He wouldn't care. However, Scripture shows that He does care when it says, "He's not wanting anyone to perish, but longs for everyone to come to repentance" (II Peter 3:9). Yet, for a lot of people, His longing to have them safe in heaven remains unsatisfied because He's given them the power to say no. It's sad to think that anyone would, yet many do. On the other hand, when a person says yes to God's way of securing eternity in heaven with Him, the angels sing and He rejoices.

I also believe God is pleased when anyone exercises whatever power they have to affect others for good. He's given us the capacity to do so and loves it when we care about others. It reflects what He's all about and, in fact, moves His heart.

THE POWER OF MOVING GOD'S HEART

The Bible reveals how one man in particular moved the heart of God, in II Chronicles 20:7, Isaiah 41:8, and James 2:23. There it tells us that Abraham was a friend of His. God's desire to have His heart moved by us can also be seen in John 11. That account describes how Jesus returned to Bethany to wake Lazarus from the dead. He mentioned to His disciples about being glad He had not been there when Lazarus died, so they would believe when He performed the miracle. When Jesus arrived, one of Lazarus' sisters met Him. While standing before Jesus, Martha noted that if He'd been there her brother wouldn't have died.

Jesus asked if she believed He was the resurrection and the life. Still in the standing position, Martha answered as if she were in a catechism class. Even though she was right her response sounded more like a theologically antiseptic, religious exercise. Then, she went back to get her sister and Mary raced out to meet Him.

When Mary reached Jesus, instead of standing like Martha she fell at his feet and repeated Martha's "if only you'd been here" statement. But the interesting thing about this moment is what happened when Jesus saw her—and those who had come with her—all weeping. John said "Jesus was deeply moved in spirit and troubled." The difference between how Martha and Mary approached him was significant. Jesus seemed barely affected by Martha but deeply moved by Mary.

On another occasion when Jesus was at their house, Martha was distracted by all the preparations to be made. She even questioned His sensitivity by complaining that Mary was sitting at His feet, listening to what He said instead of helping in the kitchen. In Luke 10:41, 42, the Lord answered Martha with "you are worried and upset about many things, but only one thing is needed. Mary has chosen what is better, and it will not be taken away from her."

I believe Martha represents the individual with power who is not relationally powerful. She was using her abilities to make the meal, wash dishes, do the laundry, and clean house. But when comparing her use of power with Mary's non-use of the same power, we find Martha's agenda to be self-serving. Jesus was not moved by that relational style. Instead, Mary moved the heart of Jesus on both occasions. That's why I see Mary as a powerful person.

However, I don't want to get caught up in arguments about whether Mary was more spiritual because she didn't do the things Martha did. That's because I believe the issue for Martha had more to do with motive than behavior. Some people, when acting spiritual or sounding religious, are just as distracted by self-serving agendas. God's heart is not moved by such schemes either. At the same time, if Mary's motive had been to impress Jesus with her spirituality because she sat at his feet and listened to Him, then she would not have been a powerful person. But her motive wasn't manipulative, whereas Martha's did seem to be. That's why I believe Martha didn't move the heart of Jesus, or anyone else for that matter, in those texts.

Yet God still wants people to appreciate the power He gives to them. In that vein, the Apostle Paul prayed in Romans 15:13, "May the God of hope fill you with all joy and peace as you trust in him, so that you may overflow with hope by the power of the Holy Spirit." God's power allows Christians to be at home with Him in spite of all the struggles they still have. When we're at home with God we can be like Mary, who moved the heart of Jesus, or like Abraham who was called God's friend.

RELATIONALLY AND SPIRITUALLY POWERFUL

Paul prayed for the Christians at Ephesus to be relationally powerful while grasping the wonder of God's love.

> "I pray also that the eyes of your heart may be enlightened in order that you may know the hope to which he has called you, the riches of his glorious inheritance in the saints, and his incomparably great power for us who believe. *That power* is like the working of his mighty strength, which he exerted in Christ when he raised him from the dead and seated him at his right hand in the heavenly realms." (Ephesians 1:18-20, emphasis added)

> "I pray that out of his glorious riches he may strengthen you with *power* through his Spirit in your inner being, so that Christ may dwell in your hearts through faith. And I pray that you, being rooted and established in love, may have power, together with all the saints, to grasp how wide and long and high and deep is the love of Christ." (Ephesians 3:16-18, emphasis added)

James also wrote about being influential when he said, "The prayer of a righteous man is powerful and effective" (James 5:16). I admitted one Sunday at our church that I didn't believe I had a public ability for praying like some people I know. I've been in all-night prayer meetings and have stories in which God answered prayer in wonderful ways, but when I pray publicly it doesn't come as natural as talking to God in my car.

After I confessed this a lady in my church called me and asked if I'd pray for her and her husband. "I know you mentioned you didn't have the public gift of praying, but I'd like you to pray for us anyway." This wonderful lady had a good sense of humor, so I told her that, in what James said about prayer, he didn't seem to be talking about how much a person prays or how eloquently they pray. Rather, he seemed to be emphasizing whether a person is righteous and walking with God.

So I told her, "If I'm going to pray for you, then maybe you should pray that I'm a righteous man because the prayer of a righteous man is powerful and effective." Then I added, "I hope I'm not trying to twist this and pat myself on the back." She laughed.

We were kidding but I do believe that the Bible emphasizes righteousness above prayer itself. It's a matter of the right motives of the person praying—whether he genuinely pursues a real relationship with God. When he does, God's heart can be moved by that conversation. He loves it!

I think that's why I especially like reading David's Psalms. They are powerful conversations coming out of real life moments, during which his well-being was often endangered but which never limited his pursuit of God. We read about David's desire for God going way back to his teen years. Sure, he eventually had personal and family problems, but on many occasions he was the powerful person God wanted him to be. As a man after the heart of God, David knew where being powerful and having power really lies.

The Source of Power

If we're going to exercise power and make good human connections, it's important to remember the source of that power. Or, we risk being twisted in our thinking and being irresponsible with people.

Years ago, when I was starting out in ministry, God gave me a country pastorate. I think preachers ought to start out in a country church because it has a way of taking them out of the clouds and bringing them down to earth. I know it did for me.

Judy and I had been married for about a year when the opportunity came. Every year the church had an evangelist come for a week of meetings and, on one occasion, my father came to conduct them. Although I'd heard him many times growing up, it was special to have him come and be our evangelist for the week.

People have told me they think I'm bold, but my boldness doesn't even compare to my father's. He took me all over the county and we'd knock on doors, pass out tracts, and do whatever else could be done to get the gospel out. One day we decided to visit a friendly neighbor whose farm was on the other side of the church property. The guy was about the same age as me, so we're talking early twenties.

As dad and I were sitting in the farmer's house they started communicating. Truthfully, I was trying to get some pointers on witnessing but I wasn't ready for what happened. Suddenly, this guy started saying he believed in the power of his own hands and claimed to be the power behind growing a successful crop, not God. I guess you could say the man got right to the point.

My father started a small debate on where the source of power is for anyone, whether they're farmers or city slickers. I'm just sitting there, learning. Then, suddenly, this neighbor starts talking about his grandfather being the one man he respects more than any other man in the world. He said, "My grandfather was the kind of man that if he didn't like what someone was telling him, they'd find themselves out on the street with their rear ends on the side walk."

I'm thinking, "Wow, this guy brought the conversation to a head!" I felt like I was watching the first Super Bowl, just waiting to see what dad would say next.

Dad leaned forward and said, "I'm glad you respect your grandfather and I can hear what you're saying to me, and if someone doesn't like what I'm saying they'll ask me to leave and I will. But nobody is going to put their hands on me."

How's that for a witnessing technique? The guy's eyebrows went up and he became apologetic after a few moments. Then we left on decent terms.

We were good neighbors but I'll tell you—the arrogance of that farmer was incredible. No one was going to tell him anything different from what he'd already decided, about himself versus God. When he said things like "I give life to my corn" I wondered about his views on sunlight and rain and other stuff. But no one could get through to him.

A few months later, that farmer learned a lesson. The man sincerely believed what he said about being the source of power behind his successful farm. Consequently, if he were in a situation on the farm where it might seem otherwise he'd get angry and demonstrate who's the boss—like he tried with my father.

One day I heard that neighbor was in a farming accident. He was discovered in the barnyard, laying in the manure and mud of a cattle pen. A big bull stood over him, snorting, as if saying, "Who's boss now?"

The story goes like this. The man didn't think the bull was moving into a pen fast enough. So, he grabbed the ring in that bull's nose and tried to move him. Need I tell you the bull didn't like it? Bam! Bam! The bull pinned him against the side of the barn and the farmer went down.

It's amazing that my neighbor didn't lose his life. That animal's power had to be respected, but the farmer forgot. From what I can tell, the man never pulled the ring on that bull's nose again. The bull taught him that someone else had a greater source of power.

When we exercise the powers we have in life, I believe we need to respect where they come from. If not, we're liable to make irresponsible decisions out of some twisted idea that all power begins and ends with man. The writer in I Chronicles 29:11 gives us a hint: "Yours, O LORD, is the greatness and the power and the glory and the majesty and the splendor for everything in heaven and earth is yours. Yours, O LORD, is the kingdom; you are exalted as head over all."

Solomon said, "A wise man has great power, and a man of knowledge increases strength" (Proverbs 24:5). Remembering all the above can help immensely when you're exercising any power or authority.

Applying Legitimate Power

I continue to learn how responsible applications of power can come from having knowledge of the Scriptures. Maybe that's one reason why the Bible is the number one best seller of all time. Jesus certainly supported this view when some Sadducees tried to trap Him on the state of marriage, after His resurrection. In Matthew 22:29, His reply pointed out their twisted thinking. "You are in error because you do not know the Scriptures or the power of God." Whatever power or authority they were trying to force on Jesus was illegitimate, because their authority base was not the Scriptures.

I believe there's no other book on the planet, including the one you are reading, that can rival what the Bible has to say about the use of power and being relationally powerful. When that power is expressed in a legitimate and responsible way, it's a joy to experience the wonder of what it does in the lives of others.

But what happens when the use of biblical power, or other kinds of power, is distorted and illegitimately applied? And how different is that between being a powerful person and a twisted thinker? I would describe twisted thinkers as individuals who have power but are relationally impotent, because of a compelling, overriding need to be in control of every situation. They will use manipulation and deceit to maintain that control. They refuse to be dependent upon anyone unless they can take advantage of them. So, let's go further "below the street" and examine manipulative thinking.

The Distortion of Power

Achieving satisfaction by exercising legitimate power doesn't fly with twisted thinkers. They're willing to compromise their principles and integrity to achieve power. Others might benefit from that power, but what they do is mainly for themselves. They make the rules to gain an edge on situations or people, simultaneously doing anything they can to avoid the emotional zero states we discussed in the last chapter. They pursue power for its own sake because they believe they're the source of it. Once their manipulative thinking is discovered they're exposed as being relationally impotent.

We saw this when I talked about Lucifer's invulnerability in chapter three. Remember how Isaiah 14 alludes to Lucifer as an individual with great supernatural powers, yet in the end he's relationally impotent? "Is this the man who shook the earth and made kingdoms tremble?" There you have it, all wrapped up in a package: having power without being powerful!

Lucifer personifies every manipulative thinker. As in his case, rehearsing anger is a basic component to manipulative thinking. Fear, particularly fear of being put down, is the most common source of anger. Twisted thinkers perceive mistakes (their own or those of others) as personal affronts, eroding the expectations that everything should go all right.

It doesn't matter who the manipulative thinker is—male or female, young or old, criminal or law-abider, religious or non-religious. As with Lucifer, their chosen response to any perceived put-down is aggression. They all use hostility to come out of their emotional zeros in one of four ways. Those irresponsible methods, called *power thrusts*, assist them in keeping control over every situation.

What do these power thrusts look like? How can they be confronted and corrected if the twisted thinker is going to take a leap into the light and become a STAR?

Being Tough

On November 28, 1993, The Associated Press came out with an article entitled "Duking it out in the OR." The news clip examined how even well-educated people act tough and use force to manipulate others. Using force is a favorite power thrust for many manipulative thinkers.

The article said that two physicians gave a new meaning to the phrase "fighting a disease." One surgeon was about to begin surgery on an elderly woman when he and the anesthesiologist began to argue. The anesthesiologist swore at the surgeon, who in turn threw a cotton-tipped prep stick at him.

The two then raised their fists and scuffled briefly on the floor. Meanwhile, a nurse monitored the patient who slept through the incident. After the fight the two doctors got up to resume the operation, completing it a half-hour later without complications.

How would you like to wake up from the surgery to find out that happened? I know I'd be checking the stitches or wondering what might have been left inside me.

The state Board of Registration in Medicine fined both doctors $10,000 each and ordered them to undergo (now get this) *joint psychotherapy*. Imagine their emotional zero states, sitting together in a room, talking to a counselor about their irresponsible behavior and having to pay for it to boot! Officials at their medical center state put both doctors on probation for five years.

The reason acting tough appeals so much to twisted thinkers is that it represents immediate outward triumphs in settling their conflicts. In III John 9-11, John writes about the proverbial church boss who tried acting tough with church members when he wasn't getting his way. The man's name was Diotrephes who, the passage says, loved being first and in control. I think he exhibited the bully and loner he really was, even though he fancied himself as a spiritually unique man.

He made consistent choices to disregard the rights of others. He unjustly accused his opponents and misrepresented the truth. When his intimidation did not yield control, I can imagine him resorting to acting tough and using force. One type of force he might use would be the unjust excommunication of others, but more likely it would include a violent expulsion of members from the church. There's no doubt in my mind that he was a twisted thinker.

In a southern state, a high school football player's mother was accused of pulling out a gun and firing into the crowd during a game after another spectator accused her son of unsportsmanlike conduct. The 41 year-old mother was charged with aggravated assault, carrying a concealed weapon, and discharging a firearm in public. Her son was charged with battery.

The boy stormed off the field during a Saturday night game, after his quarterback fumbled in the third quarter. The quarterback's aunt told the youth to calm down. But he leaped at her, punched her in the face and began fighting with some of the lady's relatives. That's when his mom pulled out the pistol.

After the shooting the game (attended by about 200 people) was called off. Being angry because the game didn't go the way the kid thought it should, plus the mother's anger at being put down, resulted in their choice to act tough. Those tough displays are moments in which people with power are actually relationally impotent. Indulging in a big shot power thrust amounts to the same thing.

THE BIG SHOT

Proverbs 21:29, says, "A wicked man puts up a bold front, but an upright man gives thought to his ways." People practicing manipulative thinking don't necessarily look for confrontation, but it's inevitable because people will get in the way of their plans. When that happens they'll tell you it's nothing personal, but business is business. This attitude allows them to be big shots even when they're feeling lousy for one reason or another.

My mother has had to be courageous over the years, especially before my father went to prison. Like my father, her life also changed when she became a Christian. Wherever she went, whenever possible she passed out a gospel tract telling his story. Although we had a good home it wasn't always easy for my parents, who were overcoming the consequences of past sins.

For mom, living with dad had its moments during his transition from crime to Christ. Years later, after being married to Judy, I returned from an Indiana prison ministry with him when we received some news from my mother. A businessman had sent over a couple of heavies to collect on a bill and she was scared. Now, before I tell you this you have to understand that my father was a man who loved the Lord and tried to be as gentle as he could with people. But there were times when he'd rise to the occasion and, like I said in the story about the farmer, I was just along to learn about life.

After being told about the collectors, dad said, "C'mon Jerry, let's take a ride." I'm thinking, "Oh nuts, here we go again" because we were going to the office of the man who sent the thugs over to the house. As we entered I sat down, only two feet away from the guy on his side of the desk. My father sat in front of the desk.

You talk about being a big shot! This man was a classic picture of one in those days. He was heavyset, wore a pinstriped suit, and slicked his hair back over his head with what seemed like Vaseline. He smelled really good, as if his clothes were dipped in "High Karate" or "Brute" cologne. Of course, when we walked into the office he was very jovial and said he was glad to see my father. I just sat there wondering what in the heck was going to happen.

Well, my dad didn't waste time. He leaned forward with his elbow on the man's desk, and said in a calm but low tone, "You impress me." The man smiled at him. Then dad says, "But then again, you don't impress me." The man stopped smiling. Then dad looked him straight in the eye and, still using that calm but low tone said, "If you ever send anyone over to my house again and muscle my wife to pay a bill, you'll have a problem with me."

I'm thinking this guy is pretty big and I'm sitting in the wrong place. Then, he put up a bold front like any wicked person does and responded with, "Okay Don," and invites us out for lunch. Weird!

Any twisted thinker who uses this kind of power thrust loves to flash his stuff, whether they leave the waitress a big tip for everyone to see or invite you out to lunch after being confronted. It's one of those moments in which they get an immediate *Big E*.

They'll do anything to look like a big shot to get rid of their lousy feelings after being confronted. Some flash you by showing their muscle; some by overwhelming you with their intellect; some by waving their wealth around; some by making sure they're wearing the right clothes; some by using sex; and some by cussing you out.

It amazes me how many inmates I've seen with four-letter words inked on their knuckles, and most of the time those letters don't spell "love." It's all about being a big shot and flashing power. The person acting tough demands the immediate gratification of an outward triumph, meaning they like seeing it happen with people knowing about it. But the last two power thrusts of manipulative thinking go inward for satisfaction.

THE SNEAK

Another power thrust they use to avoid or come out of emotional zeros is described in Proverbs 10:18. "He who conceals his hatred has lying lips."

The writer is talking about exercising power through secrets, or misrepresenting the truth. When that goes on for the twisted thinker, they're looking for inward triumphs. In counseling circles it's known as passive-aggressive behavior. They can be like the disturbed cat in the following story.

One of my daughter's friends told her about Henry the cat. Several college students lived in his house, along with two dogs and two cats. Henry was a fluffy orange cat who was used to having his way. One night my daughter's friend let Henry out with one stipulation. "If I let you out, that's it; you're not coming back in tonight."

The friend went upstairs to sleep and, wouldn't you know it, Henry found his way up onto the roof and started meowing. My daughter's friend said, "I ignored him until I fell asleep." Now, here comes Henry's power thrust!

The friend got up in the morning and began to smell something awful. Then, in the bathroom, he found Henry's mark right in the middle of the bathroom rug. A roommate had let the cat into the house when he went to work earlier that same morning.

It's like Henry was saying, "Leave me outside like that again and who knows what happens next. I'll make you pay! I'm the King of Sneak." Henry got his inward triumph in knowing the guy would find the mark. That was his take on what Henry did and I'm inclined to agree. Like the cat, twisted thinkers who use the sneak approach for power thrusting on others look for the same type of perverse satisfaction.

I was in a conversation with a man, talking about his attitude as a short order cook for one of those truck stop restaurants you see off the expressways. We were joking about funny stories involving customers when he told me how upset he got when certain customers or waitresses put pressure on him to get orders out quickly. His way of handling them when they said "Cook the steak a certain way and step on it!" was to obey, literally! He took great pleasure in demonstrating how he'd throw that steak on the floor and stomp it into a Swiss steak before placing it on the grill.

I never forgot what he said . . . and I don't frequent restaurants at truck stops very often anymore.

There's power in exercising irresponsible secrets but that power is illegitimate. Combine being an irresponsible sneak with closed thinking and you get a prime example of manipulative thinking. I've used two stories with twisted humor in them, but this type of power thrust can be very painful for unsuspecting victims. The writer in Proverbs actually called the sneak an individual who conceals hatred. That's why this power thrust can be so destructive.

BEING SLICK

Manipulative thinkers will use another type of power thrust for immediate inward triumphs. It's a little bit different than being the sneak—it's called *being slick*. With being the sneak they say nothing to keep everything a secret. With being slick, they say plenty but make sure they don't say anything of real concern to their listeners. Instead of exercising power through secrets they exercise it through selective silence.

One of the most disgusting passages in the Bible, demonstrating this power thrust, is II Samuel 13:1-22. It's a sordid story of rape and incest in which Samuel exposed Amnon, one of King David's sons, for the sexual assault of his sister, Tamar. Amnon knew that he dared not seize Tamar and fulfill his perverted love fantasies. But another twisted thinker, named Jonadab, came up with a scheme in which he appeared prudent even as he advised Amnon on how to force Tamar "into the moment." At the same time Jonadab found a way of not being directly involved in the plan itself.

Had King David acted on his son's crime, Jonadab probably would have been charged as an accomplice, especially if Amnon needed a plea bargain. Amnon feigned illness and asked Tamar to help care for him, whereupon he seduced (forced?) her into bed. It's a sad story describing the relational ruin of a human being. Obviously, these two guys were both examples of individuals who had power, but they were relationally impotent and humanly disconnected.

The following chart helps put these power thrusts together, so we can gain a better look at manipulative thinking.

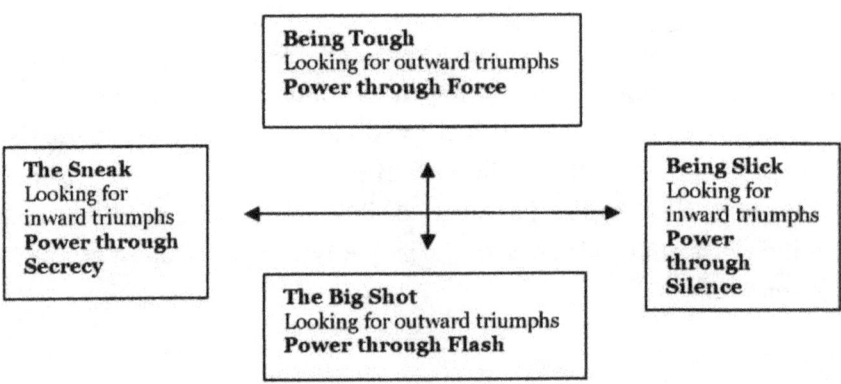

It helps to visualize these methods because we need as much wisdom as we can get to discern how twisted thinkers use manipulative thinking. Notice that we have two continuums. If they're acting like a big shot they're on the same continuum as being tough. The goals are the same. They're demanding an immediate, outward triumph. If they're being slick they're on the same continuum as the sneak and their goals are the same. They're demanding an inward triumph. In each case, there's a compelling need to be in control of every situation, and they use power thrusts to maintain their control.

Every method is in their arsenal, but each twisted thinker has a favorite. Generally, if someone is on the "slick and sneak" continuum, one of those is a favorite thrust but both are used. It's the same for the other continuum.

I've been in groups of twisted thinkers, where we were identifying the favorite power thrusts of various members. "Sneaks" and "slicks" usually see "big shots" and "tough ones" as fools or suckers who give themselves away. "Big shots and "tough ones" will see "sneaks" and "slicks" as smart but weak. All see their own style as being more effective, but in many cases the use of a power thrust on one continuum covers up the favorite method preferred on the other continuum.

One person in one of these groups said, "My favorite power thrust is being tough." I asked if they were open for feedback. They said they were, at which point another person in the group said, "I think you want us to think you are but I think you're really slick." The first individual melted in front of everyone because his con hadn't worked.

It's important to understand the power thrusts manipulative thinkers use, because half the battle is over when they're exposed. The other half is knowing what can be done to transform manipulative thinking.

Transforming Manipulative Thinking

If God wants everyone to enjoy the legitimate use of power and to be powerful people within relationships, what needs to happen for twisted thinkers to achieve that? How can responsible individuals help them to correct manipulative thinking?

Based on what we've already discovered in other twisted thinking patterns, it's apparent that every previous pattern supports and reinforces manipulative thinking. By now you are well "below the street" of twisted thinking and probably have an idea that confronting this pattern is like confronting the others. That is, confronting each thinking pattern places the person at fearful thinking. But it must be done or the hidden dynamic of manipulative thinking remains unexposed.

Discovering it is like using a jackhammer to break up cement. It gives twisted thinkers a chance to go deeper into the transformation process. It starts with honesty, just as much on our part as on theirs.

Honesty

Without responsible people being straightforward and honest about power thrusts that twisted thinkers use, hope for changing it is zilch. Jesus did this for Saul during his conversion in Acts 9 when He said, "Saul, Saul, why do you persecute me? I am Jesus, whom you are persecuting." They then leaped ahead in their relationship because Saul chose to be redeemed and transformed, but when Jesus exposed Saul's power thrust that helped immensely to bring Saul's change about.

Expressing honesty could also be similar to how my father confronted the farmer and the businessman. Simply call attention to the twisted thinker's attempt to use power over you. You can state it differently than my father did by saying something like, "I don't like the manipulation you're using on me when . . ." Then describe the power thrust. Telling them how they're doing it can help turn on lights, like it did at Saul's conversion.

A word of caution is necessary, though. There is the possibility that twisted thinkers will respond in a physically aggressive manner (tough/force) when you try to hold them accountable. If you've pointed out their power thrust and they begin to escalate, it's time to end the conversation and come back to the issues later. You may have to leave or call for help if they won't let you leave. I'm thinking primarily of adults in this case, but some very young twisted thinkers are just as capable of violence. Violence must not be tolerated.

Being honest with them about their power thrust respects the person using manipulative thinking. That respect comes from showing them you aren't going to play their game. Becoming matter-of-fact about the power thrust can be very helpful in defusing the emotions they use to control the moment. You see it happen all the time with referees in professional sports. The athlete or coach does what is called "doing the referee," or emotionally intimidating them to change a call or make things even. The best referee just stands there and shakes his head up and down, communicating that he has a listening ear and then, in a matter-of-fact way, explaining his reason for the call. Things usually calm down.

At other times, manipulative thinkers absolutely and knowingly use power thrusts without displaying all their feelings. If they aren't arguing they'll ignore you, act tired, stay silent, or even stare you down, all to avoid dealing with being caught in a *Big E*. Being honest with them about that power thrust blows their cover.

Once the power thrust is acknowledged it may be possible to assist them in coming out of this thinking sewer and embracing responsible behavior. Again, it's imperative that we be honest in our relationship with those caught practicing power thrusts. Even if they will not be truthful, unless we are candid about their power thrust they will go on believing that no one sees or cares about it.

I've talked to men who've been angry with their wives and can present all the reasons for their right to be angry. But when I ask questions such as "What were you trying to accomplish by tossing the magazine down when you were arguing with her?" they get this confused look on their face, unable to understand why I'd ask that. I follow with "What do you think the message to your wife was when you did that?" Obviously, it's a message about being in control of her. When I ask, "Do you think the message could be that you're next?" they usually say, "I wasn't thinking that."

It doesn't matter if they don't have those actual thoughts because acting tough eventually goes there if not stopped, and it's naive to think otherwise. By the way, most women I've talked to about this sort of incident don't have any problem getting that message. Being honest with how we see twisted thinkers pursuing power can be huge in opening doors for constructive changes. That's especially true when they are honest about their power thrusts and willing to do the hard work to build responsible relationships.

Hard Work

Twisted thinkers need to distinguish between the use of legitimate power by working hard to achieve personal satisfaction versus their struggle to emerge as top dog by doing the easy thing. The apostle Paul used this approach with the Corinthian believers when some were trying to one-up each other's spiritual gifts.

Paul presents an analogy of the human body to remind them that God has arranged all the parts of the body just as He wanted them to be. He explains that no one can say they have no need of others in that community, and that everyone should have equal concern for each other. Among many things Paul is teaching here, one shows how having power and being personally powerful will always be in the context of respecting people, even twisted thinkers. Paul is also teaching Corinthian believers that, when this occurs, it reflects well on their relationship with God.

Power thrusts keep twisted thinkers from being honest and working hard. They customarily send the sometimes subconscious but demanding message that everyone else should appreciate their appetite for being top dog. But the hardest work of all is committing themselves to entering emotional zero states and then, when coming out of them, finding responsible ways to use power for helping and not hurting others. I have no doubt that, when this is done consistently, the twisted thinker will become more of the STAR God intends them to be.

Chapter Twelve

ARROGANT THINKING

Blessed Are the Humble

I think I'm different and better than others. I expect out of others what I fail to deliver. I'm super-optimistic because it cuts my fear of failure. I will quit at the first sign of what I consider failure.

"None of us is as smart as all of us." This statement, seen on the wall of a treatment center for offenders, reveals the humility twisted thinkers must develop in transforming themselves. But the task is gigantic because their arrogant thinking provides a cornerstone for image building—one of being different and better than others. It's the opposite view of Christians who believe they will never "arrive" until they see Jesus, which shows there's always room for growth. Yet, this thought doesn't preoccupy the minds of twisted thinkers. Consequently, for them, unless they overcome arrogant thinking they won't recover their conscience. The following story illustrates this.

In March of 1995, a nineteen year-old man, along with his father, faced nineteen felony counts. One of those crimes included the murder of a police officer in Waukesha, Wisconsin. Under direct examination the young man said he began training in earnest to separate himself from humanity at the age of seven. Imagine: age seven!

He talked about living with his dad on the dark side and starting his criminal career. For them it was the ultimate place to be for achieving status in a "different" realm. He said that once they'd entered this particular "dark side," death was the only escape because morality no longer got in the way. In fact, nothing got in the way. He had no conscience; he simply disconnected from society and his own humanity.

Listening To Conscience

In I Samuel 24, the story of another young man reveals a completely dissimilar picture. David, innocent but under suspicion for wrongdoing, was hiding in a cave from King Saul to escape certain death. When Saul entered the same cave for personal business, David crept up unnoticed and cut off a corner of his robe. The message he sent seemed to be: "Hey Saul! Watch me use my power to mess with your mind and teach you a lesson!"

It might be interesting to theorize about why David did this. Maybe he thought he'd been running long enough from a king he'd once fought for, who in turn had disdained his loyalty. Both martyred and inflated thinking would support such thoughts of a sweet sense of justice. But then, however, David became conscience stricken about his act of rebellion because he knew that Saul was still the anointed of the Lord.

What are the implications of all that? David's rebellion exposed a spiritual and personal issue with God. It would have been good if he'd understood this before cutting Saul's robe, but that wasn't the case. In earlier years David's life reflected complete trust and dependence upon the God of Israel.

Now, his theology was tested in a new way. What do you do when someone in your own ranks becomes an enemy? Can God be trusted then? Jesus proved he could be when betrayed by one of His disciples, but David's act of rebellion was an expression of anger, indicating that wasn't so for him. He assumed the position of "Top God" when he cut the king's robe. It was essentially the same as trimming God's robe for not coming through, as David might have thought he should have.

Ever been there? I know I have.

There's no doubt in my mind that David's act was understandable from an emotional point of view. But he was much more than the sum of his feelings, and so are we. On a deeper level I think he recognized his arrogance by understanding how he communicated to God. It's amazing to see what happens when a person is broken about being arrogant, because there's hope for recovering a conscience when the person is contrite. As an act of repentance, David surrendered himself to Saul by calling himself a dead dog, or nothing more than a flea. Saul realized that David could have killed him and took the high road: "May the Lord reward you well for the way you treated me today."

Unlike the previous young man, David listened to his conscience. Sadly, though, after becoming king he chose to disconnect from responsible living, as an adulterer and murderer. His story shows this can happen even with God's people—not just confirmed criminals. And yet, after coming through a great deal of personal and family pain, King David could still be identified as a man pursuing God. Because of this I think it's possible that his testimony might have been the same as the Apostle Paul's in Romans 12:3.

> For by the grace given me I say to every one of you: Do not think of yourself more highly than you ought, but rather think of yourself with sober judgment, in accordance with the measure of faith God has given you.

Thinking More Highly

Rather than having problems with low self-esteem, arrogant thinkers consistently think more highly than they should. Their mindset values self above anyone. We see it demonstrated by the wicked witch in *Snow White and the Seven Dwarfs*. She wasn't beautiful like Snow White, either externally or internally. So, when she asked the mirror, "Who is the fairest of them all," the mirror kept answering, "Thou art fair as fair can be, but there is one more fair than thee." When the mirror wouldn't agree with her own image the witch smashed it.

Sober judgment wasn't in her repertoire, and choosing a narcissistic path failed ultimately because it resulted in self-destruction. Obviously the witch wanted no one's help—a certain sign of arrogance with anyone, let alone twisted thinkers. Yet listen to Solomon talk about how important a good name and sober thinking is:

> "A good name is better than fine perfume, and the day of death better than the day of birth. It is better to go to a house of mourning than

to go to a house of feasting, for death is the destiny of every man; the living should take this to heart. Sorrow is better than laughter, because a sad face is good for the heart. The heart of the wise is in the house of the mourning, but the heart of fools is in the house of pleasure. It is better to heed a wise man's rebuke than to listen to the song of fools. Like the crackling of thorns under the pot, so is the laughter of fools." (Ecclesiastes 7:1-6)

"Do not be over righteous, neither be over wise—why destroy yourself? Do not be over wicked, and do not be a fool—why die before your time? It is good to grasp the one and not let go of the other. *The man who fears God will avoid all extremes.*" (Ecclesiastes 7:16-18, emphasis added)

If arrogant thinkers would only grasp what Solomon said. Instead, they do not avoid the extremes he mentioned. They're either over-righteous, over-wise, or over-wicked, as the man in the next story demonstrates.

In 1993 a thirty-one-year-old ex-con was in a Columbus, Ohio, university class. He had a degree in criminology but decided to take a refresher course. Two police officers were also in the class. The professor asked the man to talk about his crimes in the past because he believed the man's life had become a success story. The professor said, "All his crimes were not violence-related."

The ex-con looked at the officers and said, "Because the statute of limitations is up, I can talk about one that was." He then proceeded to confess to a murder he'd committed thirteen years earlier. Shortly thereafter Mr. Braggadocio was arrested at his place of employment.

Afterward he was asked, "How could you not know that murder has no statute of limitations? Especially a criminology major! How could you be so dumb?"

The answer I'd give is that arrogance makes anyone dumb. Because the twisted thinker never makes decisions until he's certain of guarantees, arrogance blocks his path to responsible thinking. The murder victim's mother told the media that she now believed in miracles. What affected her most was how the murderer did it to himself. "No one told him to stand up and brag about the murder of my son," she said.

Clearly the ex-con didn't believe what the book of Proverbs makes perfectly clear:

"Do not be wise in your own eyes; fear the LORD and shun evil." (Proverbs 3:7)

"Do you see a man wise in his own eyes? There is more hope for a fool than for him." (Proverbs 26:12)

The same ex-con turned also fits the description in Psalm 10:2-6:

In his arrogance the wicked man hunts down the weak, who are caught in the schemes he devises. He boasts of the cravings of his heart he blesses the greedy and reviles the LORD. In his pride the wicked does not seek him; in all his thoughts there is no room for God. His ways are always prosperous; he is haughty and your laws are far from him; he sneers at all his enemies. He says to himself, "Nothing will shake me; I'll always be happy and never have trouble."

Twisted thinkers are common, ordinary, run-of-the-mill yet arrogant people regardless of their age. On one occasion, an adolescent struggling with arrogant thinking gave me a fantasy formula to crack. As I present the imaginary scheme I'm asking you to be patient in reading and working through the problem with me—tongue in cheek. The teen called it his "Genius Algebra Formula," trying to associate himself with Einstein.

Formula

"NIM=LWS=WXTXALT=ALTT=WXTXALT=FSFF=4step evaluation (28-step problem)." Trying to comprehend!!!

"Solution: NIM = possibly 3 unknown numbers X's. The young person gives the following solution to the equation and I want you to see if you can hear the arrogance. The next/equals/LWS = the same numbers but different variables / = / a number multiplied by

X 3 more numbers = either those 3 numbers or equals 4 numbers X each other = the "reverse equation" = 4 different numbers X each one. This, so far, is a 4-step equation that needs to be saved in order to figure the ALTT."

The teen stated: "Getting confused when only reading this is likely, unless you are me, which you are not—unfortunately. Please ask me all your questions about this and I will unconfuse you because, since I wrote the formula, I should know what I am doing, saying, and mean."

In other words . . . are you solving it incorrectly? To solve it in the correct manner is to come to me only and ask. All you have to do is read and do as I say and you'll have the answers. It's not at all hard! It's very easy. But, if you still do not understand I suggest you get some serious mental help.

Not!

This same student had been involved in a serious felony, but he considered treatment for correcting errors in thinking a waste of time. Everything seemed like a joke to him; he pooh-poohed anything that got in his way.

If this person hadn't been guilty of serious offenses you might think he was just some kid, bored during a study hall, who put whatever came to his mind on paper so he could be noticed. Or, as a friend told me when he heard the story, "It could be a kid whose mind has been fried on acid. I've seen it."

But the truth is that this young man was an arrogant thinker void of empathy for victims of crime. Again, all twisted thinkers think more highly of self than they ought to. What astounds me is how early arrogant thinking can start.

I Thought of It

Years ago, when we were living in Sheboygan, some friends were visiting Judy and me. Frank related that, before they came, he'd had to discipline his son for defiant acts at home. He said he told his son that, if he continued to disobey him, the boy's Nintendo game would be taken away for ten days. Frank knew something was wrong when the boy responded by saying, "Make it one hundred days!" Caught up in the moment, my friend said, "You got it!" Then his son said, "Make it forever!" and Frank repeated, "You got that, too!"

By then he realized he'd lost control with the boy and went back to the one-hundred-day plan. He and his wife were in process with that strategy when arriving at our house.

Whenever friends would come to the house for overnights, Judy and I would take them to the Kohler Design Center. This place was loaded with bathroom and kitchen displays that made it possible to build luxury facilities even in grass huts (I'm think I'm kidding about that, although it wouldn't surprise me). They have a museum, movies, and a hotel housing high-level potentates from all over the world.

While touring the bathroom displays, Frank's boy found a loose towel on one of the racks. He then said something that smacked of impatient thinking mixed with arrogant thinking: "It's not glued down so I can take it!"

Judy asked him if he got the idea from TV or from someplace else, and here came the arrogant thinking. The young fellow looked at her with disdain and said, "No, I thought of it myself." His look said, "Come on lady, you should know better than to ask a question like that. You're looking at a genius!" Yet he was only five-and-one-half years old.

Our two friends are good people involved with ministry. They love their children and do not sit around trying to plant irresponsible ideas in their heads. They are the quintessence of responsibility. Frank is so honest he won't cheat on his golf game or score. They have a very good marriage and are well thought of by the community in which they live.

By no means am I saying that Frank's son is a criminal, but his "It's not glued down so I can take it!" approach is scary because it's unadulterated arrogant thinking. The thought seems to come out of nowhere, but the boy claimed it as his own—and it was! That's what's frightening, because the world we live in wants to blame those thoughts on external influences, like parenting, rather than focusing on the intents of the hearts as Jesus would do.

After the incident I gave Frank a crash course on twisted thinking. His eyes grew larger because everything rang true, but he was grateful for the help. They got to the problem early in their son's life and he is growing into a solid young man. Although I'm not thinking about him when making the next statement, I want to say the following: *Few people know what twisted thinkers are like when they practice arrogant thinking.*

Maintaining Uniqueness

When I say that few people know what they're like, I don't mean to say that being arrogant isn't easily spotted. What I do mean, though, is that when they practice arrogant thinking they are calculatingly vague, deceptive, and flagrantly untruthful.

From that position it's not difficult to see how arrogant thinking partners up with closed thinking. To arrogant thinkers, the idea of letting others in suggests that they will be taken advantage of, which won't be tolerated. It gets in the way of their agendas. Keeping others outside their thought bubbles makes sure they don't get in the way of any grandiose view of self—being unique or above others.

So, twisted thinkers are secretive even when there is no apparent need to be. Being separated and isolated from others allows them to be overconfident or super optimistic when making decisions. That serves as an immediate cutoff of any "normal" deterrents for any irresponsible behavior.

Again, secrecy is a huge issue for arrogant thinkers. I'm not against privacy—I'm more of a private person than most may think. Privacy and secrecy, however, are two different concepts. Privacy allows for personal times and personal healing without public involvement, but never without accountability. Proverbs 15:3 says, "The eyes of the LORD are everywhere, keeping watch on the wicked and the good." To me that sounds like God allows privacy but not without accountability. A secret lifestyle won't endorse this.

At the request of parents, I went to a high school basketball game with my daughter, Jana, to observe an athlete. Since I had been a coach and Jana played college ball, we had something to offer as scouts. Both of us were impressed with the player and couldn't figure out why the coach wasn't getting him more involved in the game.

On the way home, Jana said, "The team was told by the coach that he didn't want them going home and talking to their parents about what was going on in practices, or with the team. If they did so there would be repercussions. It was to be a secret."

Can you see the arrogance in that thought? I loved Jana's powerful response to the mother when she stated, "That's what a perpetrator will say after molesting kids."

I understand that high school coaches can have it rough when parents meddle with coaching decisions. But let me tell you, as a parent, if some high school coach is going to play head games with my kid and think they'll not be held accountable, they've got another think coming. There are a lot of great coaches out there, but some pull baloney like that coach pulled. Relational style in coaching is usually responsible for most of the damage done to high school athletes—not the Xs and Os of the game. Any style that doesn't respect family or school systems by suggesting that everyone else must stay out of the picture comes from arrogant thinking.

I'm putting this story in here because I want to remind you that practicing twisted thinking is not just about criminal or addictive behaviors. It can happen with citizens who coach our kids but don't understand the difference between privacy and secrecy. Arrogant people maintain their skewed sense of uniqueness by keeping secrets. They are burglars of the soul, and isolating themselves keeps their arrogant thinking intact. Let me show you a contrast to arrogance by people who were open to being loved.

A Contrast

> How great is the love the Father has lavished on us, that we should be called children of God! And that is what we are! The reason the world does not know us is that it did not know him. Dear friends, (in another text, it says "Beloved") now, we are children of God, and what we will be has not yet been made known. But we know that when he appears, we shall be like him, for we shall see him as he is. Everyone who has this hope in him purifies himself, just as he is pure. (I John 3:1-3, emphasis added)

This wonderful text in I John reveals the hope Christians have. That phrase "Beloved" or "Dear Friends" qualifies the nature of the friendship. It suggests that these people have allowed God and others to love them. Arrogant twisted thinkers won't permit this. As a result, we don't see them asking anyone for help even if they need it. It's one thing to have the Scriptures say, "God so loved the world that he gave." It's another thing to say, "that whosoever believeth in Him (Jesus Christ) should not perish, but have everlasting life." What's my point? Let me make it by asking one or two more questions.

Why don't we see humanity running toward God's way of loving? In fact, why don't we see humanity in general just sprinting toward the God of love? I believe it's because humanity is spiritually polluted at the roots by arrogant thinking. Inherently, man won't ask for help from God. Instead, we'd rather tell God how He should love.

Humanity, like the wicked witch in *Snow White*, says "The mirror is wrong" and then smashes it. Well, God is the mirror and mankind is bent on rejecting God's love as expressed in and through Jesus Christ. It's a spiritual paradox! We want to be loved by God but won't allow it to happen on His terms. I'm suggesting that this comes out of man's penchant for arrogant thinking—it's just another way to resist God.

What I believe is true, spiritually, is also true relationally with twisted thinkers. The arrogant twisted thinker demands his right to call the shots. But when they're down emotionally they'll believe that no one else experiences or understands what they're going through. As a result they have a certain tenacity in making rules, since they think no one else understands what it's like for them. Of course the rules aren't always out in the open, and if you break one, look out! To them, even if they make you pay in an abusive or irresponsible manner, it's not wrong. Why? Because they make the rules!

What a contrast to the people in I John 3. Instead of using arrogant thinking as the cornerstone for image-building, these people received the love of God through Jesus Christ, heaven's Chief Cornerstone for relationship. He makes the rules and His rules of love *rule*. Everyone who has the hope of seeing Jesus purifies himself, which is another way of saying they have allowed themselves to be loved by God in His way. It's a wonderful leap into the light, but arrogant thinkers don't think so. Committed to building on a cornerstone of their own making, they believe no one can have the thoughts they have. Those thoughts are the only lights they'll accept, which creates a serious problem for others.

The Problem

A very amiable young man behind bars told me that he was not guilty of drunk driving or causing criminal damage to property. He felt angry at being let down by a friend whom he'd asked to be his designated driver. While at a party getting drunk the fellow decided to go home. When he couldn't find his designated driver he got upset and then chose to drive home himself. In his new truck he drove down a road packed with other vehicles. Minutes later, after banging into several cars and totaling his truck, he was arrested. I saw him in jail and began talking about being responsible for his decision. He didn't like my reasoning.

I said, "You chose to drink; to get a designated driver; to drive after not finding him; and now you're here." That led to a cluster of thinking errors: closed, martyred, inflated, and especially arrogant thinking.

He kept saying that, if he had been my designated driver, I never would have been guilty of this. He said he expected his friend to be responsible for him. Clearly the man put himself above his friend. In other words, it's okay for the friend to be responsible but the rule didn't apply to him.

That pretty much nails the problem. *Expecting out of others what he wasn't willing to do for himself gave him permission to be irresponsible and break the law.* He used martyred thinking to justify the behavior: "If they let me down, I can blame them and do whatever I want."

Whenever arrogant thinking is involved the person actually believes things are stacked in their favor. That's why the man chose to do what he did. It's not that arrogant thinkers want to get caught. They don't believe anyone else can be like them in any way. No wonder that view leads them to believe they are above the law—*any* law. As I've said before, this cornerstone must be demolished for the transformation of twisted thinking to take effect.

Demolition of Arrogant Thinking

When huge buildings are demolished the principle of imploding is used. Explosives are set in such a way that the building will burst inward as they go down. Once down, clean up then goes all the way to the foundation before any efforts are made to rebuild. Otherwise, new buildings would sit on top of rubble and unsure footing.

In journeying "below the street" of each thought pattern, it's important to realize how the other thinking errors relate to the dominant one being addressed. For instance, if closed thinking were transformed, all other twisted thinking patterns would be rendered inoperative. Since every other thinking error operates in concert with closed thinking, it's logical to address closed thinking whenever possible. Yet many times the other patterns need attention first because they're the dominant patterns at the moment. In such a case, to implode twisted thinking the explosives to dynamite *arrogant* thinking must be set right, or the structure will still stand. So, how do we set the explosive so the structure will burst inward?

IMPLODING ARROGANT THINKING

One of the reasons I started the first chapter by saying we were all "made of the same mud" was to prepare us for this chapter. To prove the point biblically, we took a look at God's mug shot for humanity. The whole idea behind that approach was to discover commonalities of twisted thinking that we all have, by focusing on the darkened mind that everyone possesses from birth. Spiritually, there is no hope for spending eternity in heaven unless that truth is understood. It's part of the lost-ness of sin from which we're being saved. Because we're all made of the same mud we all need to be cleaned up—God's way. No one escapes this.

Again, what's true spiritually is also true relationally. Twisted thinkers need to discover commonalities with others. They must resist believing that they are different and better. One of the ways to accomplish this in the jail program was to put questions in a box—questions that related to the personal lives of group members. It was fun and it exposed the mystery each member established with his or her self-imposed isolation. Sometimes the questions were as simple as "What is your favorite color?"

Afterwards I'd ask the inmates if they were open to questions about their comments. That exercise set the stage for puncturing their false sense of uniqueness. Something good happens when we can identify with each other as people made of the same mud, and it's no different with twisted thinkers. It needs to happen for arrogant thinking to implode.

The willingness to ask for help also needs to be developed. However, I don't mean using it as a method to manipulate others, because that can happen. Sometimes a person will ask for help to get someone else to do his or her personal work. More often than not, however, arrogant thinkers won't ask for help. Because of their fear of being controlled by others, they think they'll lose their own uniqueness. It's another way of saying that they are guarding the possibility of pursuing more *Big Es*.

Group members in the jail also had to memorize the definitions of each thinking pattern. They would have to recite them, word for word. When they failed to remember a word they would have to ask another group member for help. It could be quite humorous at times to see how the game of lickety-split was played during that moment. They'd stand for several minutes, struggling to remember so they wouldn't have to ask. They'd give painful looks at the wall, the floor, and even at other group members. They'd wave their hands at group members to see if someone would give them the answer before they asked. It was amazing what they'd do just so they wouldn't have to ask for help.

Why? Because all the above meant they were just like anyone else and were not as unique as they thought. It blew their cover, yet this had to be done if arrogant thinking was to implode.

This type of thing also needs to be done just as much for husbands who won't stop and ask for directions when they're lost. There's enough arrogance to go around for everyone. We all need help—not just twisted thinkers. Would you agree? Asking for help is important. In fact, God loves it when we ask Him for help, because it indicates there's a balance in our humanity where integrity is at the center. In other words, we face whatever is true in our lives. That will implode arrogant thinking as well.

Confession Time

Another thing to look for shows up when a twisted thinker is overconfident in their problem areas. You'll hear it when they use absolute words or statements: "I never again will," or "I've learned my lesson and I never will." Or, "that will not happen with me like it did for . . ." Whenever they make those statements they're heading in the wrong direction, because the statements indicate they've arrived while others haven't.

One thing that could bother me about writing this book is the fear of giving the impression that I think I've "arrived" in my own process of transforming twisted thinking. I'm still in process and it won't stop until I see my Savior face-to-face.

Thinking we've arrived can do a lot of damage. It happens in Christianity when people try formulas to achieve spiritual growth and believe they've arrived at what they were shooting for. I've especially seen this happen with spiritual gifts in the church.

One man said, "Spiritual gifts mean absolutely nothing unless they are practiced in and out of love. Spiritual gifts are a means of the Holy Spirit to point towards and glorify Jesus Christ." I believe the man is right, because if they aren't practiced for that reason the result is completely arrogant and self-serving. Paul had to write a group of Christians at Corinth and talk about the greatest gift of all, because arrogant thinking was common in the Corinthian's ranks. Those brethren got caught up trying to impress everyone else with their special spiritual gifts. If you didn't have the gift of so-and-so you weren't much. The damage to people, via that thinking, can be enormous.

Over the years, I've seen how this can lead to sensationalism, misinterpretation of Scripture, and divisions just as it happened in Corinth. Whether we're talking about twisted thinkers in jails, families, government organizations, or churches, the belief that we've arrived in life can and does hurt others. The apostle Paul encouraged believers to keep pressing on and to take hold of that for which Christ Jesus took hold of *him*. He said in Philippians 3:13, "Brothers, I do not consider myself yet to have taken hold of it." Isn't that a beautiful statement, showing that Paul demolished any arrogant thinking he'd had as a Pharisee of the Pharisees?

If I met Paul today I think he would support saying, "None of us is as smart as all of us." After the murder of Stephen, while he was heading toward Damascus to clean religious houses of people known collectively as "The Way," Paul met the resurrected Jesus. From that moment it took about seventeen years before he went up to Jerusalem to meet the other apostles. Much ministry was accomplished before he went to Jerusalem, yet going there indicated that they all needed each other. No one was different and better than any other. Blessed are the humble.

Summary

Discovering commonality, asking for help, checking for overconfidence, and understanding how repenting from twisted thinking is a lifelong process implodes arrogant thinking. Although this is a very difficult thinking error to demolish, twisted thinkers open to this course of action can become STARs. If they're not open, then anyone practicing twisted thinking will plunge to the lowest place in a person's soul—a despicable place. It's where the embodiment of evil will be identified. Any anticipation for joy when going to this level "below the street" should come from the knowledge that our Lord was willing to enter it first, for redemptive purposes.

Let's follow Him for the same reason.

Chapter Thirteen

POSSESSIVE THINKING

"I Own You"

I perceive all things and people as objects that belong to me. I have no concept of the "ownership rights" of others. I will use sex for power and control and not intimacy.

On September 12, 2001, the *Green Bay Press-Gazette* displayed three never-to-be-forgotten pictures. A shell of the World Trade Center towers rose above rubble. In another, two women were holding each other as they watched the WTC burn. The last showed the Pentagon in Washington, D.C., just after being hit by another commercial flight as part of the attack. Finally, in bold black print, the headline read: "Our Nation Saw Evil."

Even though the headline and pictures were worth a thousand words, I want to suggest that more will be needed to describe the twisted thinking behind the use of evil as a major force in our world. Evil may be understood via such pictures no more than all the people we know can be instantly identified by their clothes. From the images of 9/11/01 we can learn a great deal about the subject, but they don't necessarily divulge a greater reality.

That reality must be understood if we're going to fight against the forces of evil on any meaningful level. II Corinthians 11:14 supported this thought when Paul portrayed Satan, the epitome of evil, masquerading as an angel of light. His statement presents quite a different view of darkness and implies that we'll need to catch sight of something more.

What is the greatest evil of all? In what form could it come?

Levels and Shades of Evil

Trying to identify the greatest evil of all brings up another question. Could evil be layered in such a way that it would allow us to tolerate the "upper layers" before we encountered their ultimate source? I believe it's reasonable to think so. It's sort of like the fairy tale involving the princess with insomnia. To help her sleep comfortably, someone came up with the bright idea of layering her bed with more and mattresses until it reached an incredible height.

When a subject in her kingdom finally discovered that a small pea under the first layer was causing all the trouble, her problem was solved. Once the pea was removed, all the other mattresses were also removed and the Princess slept undisturbed.

Like those mattresses, layers of evil can cover the original evil. But the underlying pea can't be ignored and eventually must be dealt with.

I believe we can also see the effect of the multilayering of evil via the analogy of color. Evil typically evolves from lighter shades of gray into complete darkness, but it's in all those gray areas where the presence of evil can sometimes remain hidden or unseen.

Many have experienced this when good was called bad or right was called wrong; when the pure was called impure and the just were called unjust. Or, when something pure and honorable was called wicked. Do you know of anyone, except Jesus, who hasn't mistaken good for evil or evil for good?

I think you've come far enough in this book to understand that we can't transform twisted thinking, make human connections, and experience relational harmony unless we look evil squarely in the face. I have no delusions about this. Facing evil without the light of the world is like trying to escape a raging bull by running down a dead-end street.

However, I'm not suggesting we stand up strong by taking it on alone. In Jude 9, Michael the archangel, when disputing about the body of Moses, didn't dare bring a slanderous accusation against Satan but said, instead, "The Lord rebuke you!" Even an archangel wouldn't challenge evil, alone. That would be arrogant thinking for any created being. But evil has to be looked squarely in the face, because its outward manifestations cannot be ignored. The world found that out on 9/11.

Likewise, our journey "below the street" has been an attempt to look at the evil in man's heart—within every soul's dark side. And, because we all have a dark side, the problem exists virtually everywhere. Although many reading this book might not be twisted thinkers at any given time, the truth is that all of us demonstrate what evil can do to people at other times.

With all that in mind, this chapter discusses the last pattern. In my opinion, more than any other, this one represents the embodiment of evil. If we're going to understand the macro concept of twisted thinking we must face it.

A Short Review

Remember: *Twisted thinking shackles the mind and incarcerates the soul.* Secretive and self-righteous, twisted thinkers will only disclose what serves their immediate purpose. We saw how they lie more often by omission than commission. If there's a choice between doing what's responsible or irresponsible, pursuing *Big E*s will be foremost in their thinking. They love playing games of lickety-split to escape accountability.

I've also mentioned that twisted thinkers have no hope for becoming STARs unless their twisted thinking is diagnosed, acknowledged, and corrected. These issues are also central to each person's relationship with God. Our eternal hope is to be supernaturally connected to Him through faith in Christ. But mankind's twisted thinking, in general, exposes how we often struggle with God's plan for redemption, highlighting the need for such a plan even as it works *against* the same plan at the same time.

Now, as we go "below the street" to the last twisted thinking pattern, I want you to remember the bookend principles with me. It's important to note that this pattern will combine and encompass all other patterns in one moment of time, by a single Godlike act.

Twisted thinkers will quickly cross your personal and emotional boundaries as they trigger this thinking pattern. They'll send messages that people are only furniture to be moved or sat upon. Yet man is built to reflect God's capacity for enjoying life, to think clearly, to make choices and feel the full measure of a person's worth. This twisted thinking pattern will deny a person that opportunity. In both a flagrant and a subtle manner it calls for twisted thinkers to be worshipped rather than God.

It is *possessive thinking* concealed by an *ownership attitude*.

An Ownership Attitude

Looking at all things and all people as objects to possess is the core issue in possessive thinking. A moment from *Peanuts* by Charles Schultz gives a humorous example of that. We see Linus walking behind Lucy on the way home. He says, "We have something new at our house. When I get home from school, my dog meets me in the yard with milk and cookies."

As Linus steps into the yard, Snoopy comes to him with milk on a tray. Linus says, "I see the milk but where are the cookies?" Snoopy says, "They got tired of waiting, so they left."

The cartoon is cute, except that what Snoopy said demonstrated an ownership attitude. Obviously, our beloved dog of comic strip history made an arbitrary decision when he ate the cookies. That choice determined what was right for him and Linus.

I don't believe Mr. Schultz meant to reveal the embodiment of evil, but inadvertently, he did so by showing what motivated Snoopy. *When the direction of our motivation is exposed we can determine if the value of our behavior is truly what it seems to be . . . or not.* What we see here is that Snoopy was above the street behavior of bringing cookies and milk to Linus. But, the direction in which his behavior took the dog (a representation of goodness) differs from the direction of Snoopy's attitude while he was waiting for Linus and "suffering" from hunger.

That's when we see the unseen dynamic of possessive thinking. With Snoopy, the trail is covered (lickety-split) as he points out how tired the cookies were when they left. Whether Linus liked it or not, Snoopy gets the cookies while trying to impress upon Linus that he's still a good dog by bringing the milk.

You might be thinking: "Get off the Snoopy bashing. You're carrying this point to the extreme!" Well, I like Snoopy and I'm not trying to bash him. I'm not even suggesting he's an evil dog or that he knows about his level of evil.

But I am saying that the decision-making process that Snoopy employed was evil, even though his behavior seemed charming.

If there's any possibility of evil being multileveled, going to the extremity of where it ultimately ends seems reasonable. That is to say, we need to see gray as another form of black when discussing twisted thinking. We watch for signs of bad weather and prepare for what's ahead, don't we? Have you ever driven down a road without turning back because you didn't believe a sign that read "Road Closed?" We need to know where decisions will take us. So, why not do the same for twisted thinking, even if doing so involves a cartoon icon? Part of me is having fun with the example, but the other part is very serious because any possessive thinking is destructive.

One way to see this grayness is to understand the direction in which the person's motivation is going. Focusing on that is much more important than focusing on where they think good behavior takes them. That's because right or wrong motives are determined within the inner man, and therefore change must happen there first before we can trust that any "good behavior" isn't about an ownership attitude.

THE ARBITRATOR (WITHOUT PERMISSION)

An arbitrator is a person chosen to settle disputes. But twisted thinkers aren't chosen, nor do they ask for the job. Instead, they make decisions on behalf of themselves or anyone else, without permission to do so, like the man who decided to help his wife wash dishes. When she indicated it wasn't necessary he became violent and had to be arrested for domestic abuse. How dare she reject his offer! In his mind she had no rights. So he handled her like a bag of garbage—a disgusting view of arbitration by an irresponsible man.

Many times you won't even notice the subtlety of a twisted thinker's uninvited arbitration, until they've left the room and you're feeling uneasy, pressed, manipulated, or controlled. Then, how you've been used suddenly begins to dawn on you. It becomes clear that God, you, or anyone else won't be allowed to influence or determine what the twisted thinker did do, should do, shouldn't do, or can't do. But you'll have to live with the result, not the twisted thinker.

We need to become familiar with the concept of acting as an arbitrator without permission before talking about any flagrant demonstrations of possessive thinking. It will serve as a forewarning, like the alert Jesus gave in Matthew 16:6 concerning the faulty teachings of Pharisees and Sadducees. Speaking to His disciples, He said, "Be on your guard against the yeast of the Pharisees and Sadducees."

Yeast is internal to the process of baking bread, causing dough to rise. Jesus used this analogy to help his disciples perceive evil with their mind's eyes—where certain Pharisaic teachings of that era came from and what they did to people.

In many ways the teaching looked and felt good, but ultimately it was about puffing up Pharisaic pride with a mental ferment that precluded God's grace. Their doctrinal yeast was meant to control everything in sight by leaving Him out of the mix. Jesus also knew that their twisted teaching would eventually destroy Him on the cross.

So, if you're feeling controlled by someone, as the religious people of Jesus' day tried to do with Him, chances are you might be experiencing a clever representation of someone's ownership attitude. If you are, be on guard. Meanwhile, let's observe a godly prophet guarding against his servant's ownership attitude.

Gehazi's Possessive Thinking

In II Kings 5 we read about a commander in the army of the king of Aram, who suffers from leprosy. His name was Naaman and, after discovering that a prophet in Samaria could cure him, the king provided the means to pay for his treatment. Eventually, Naaman went to the prophet Elisha's house with great expectation and hope for healing.

But instead of speaking directly to Naaman, Elisha sent a messenger to say "Go, wash yourself seven times in the Jordan, and your flesh will be restored and you will be cleansed." Naaman took offense and stomped off. But fortunately for him, his servants finally convinced him to return for the treatment, and it worked!

After the healing, Naaman and his attendants went back to the man of God to express their appreciation. 2 Kings 5:15, 16 gives his tribute to Elisha. He says:

> Now I know that there is no God in all the world except in Israel. Please accept now a gift from your servant." The prophet answered, "As surely as the LORD lives, whom I serve, I will not accept a thing." And even though Naaman urged him, he refused.

What a deal! There was no charge because it was an act of grace. Yet Gehazi, Elisha's servant, had other thoughts. I want to show how Gehazi used several thinking errors funneling to the embodiment of evil and its consequences. You'll see the macro concept of twisted thinking from chapter two's definition. Twisted thinking is a network of thinking errors used in decision making by people who have been irresponsible. We pick the story up in II Kings 5:20-23.

> After Naaman had traveled some distance, Gehazi, the servant of Elisha the man of God, said to himself, "My master was too easy on Naaman, this Aramean, by not accepting from him what he brought. As surely as the Lord lives, I will run after him and get something from him." So Gehazi hurried after Naaman. When Naaman saw him running toward him, he got down from the chariot to meet him. Is everything all right? he asked. "Everything is all right," Gehazi answered. My master sent me to say, 'Two young men from the company of the prophets have just come to me from the hill country of Ephraim. Please give them a talent of silver and two sets of clothing.' By all means, take two talents, said Naaman. He urged Gehazi to accept them, and then tied up the two talents of silver in two bags, with two sets of clothing. He gave them to two of his servants, and they carried them ahead of Gehazi.

An Irresponsible Fantasy

First of all, we see Gehazi's irresponsible fantasy. He had dollar signs in his eyes and on his brain. But there was a problem. He was not authorized to close the deal with Naaman. While entertaining the fantasy, Gehazi didn't stop to think about consequences or about who would get hurt. We can see his closed and inflated thinking as he reasons, "My master was too easy on Naaman, this Aramean, by not accepting from him what he brought."

Gehazi put himself above Elisha by faulting him, and then used the race card to embrace martyred thinking. He did that by referring to Naaman as the Aramean. That recalled how Syrians had hurt Israel in the past, which then justified Gehazi's jealousy of Naaman's possessions.

So, Gehazi planned to alleviate his misgivings over going without by taking advantage of Naaman. That kind of jealousy causes quarrels and divides and destroys relationships. You can read about in I Corinthians 3:3 and James 4:1-3.

Gehazi's attitude demonstrated how jealousy is always the consequence of possessive thinking. We can also see his arrogant thinking supporting possessive thinking when he acted super-optimistically and said, "Everything is all right." That bit of baloney forestalled any fear of failure in his plan to extort the man's goods.

We can see the arrogance manifested in another way, as well. Who made Gehazi the boss man? Of course he didn't talk to Elisha about this, since that would have got in the way of his *Big E*. Instead we see him inflating his view of self by getting religious: "As surely as the LORD lives, I will run after him and get something from him."

The guy is very good at god-talk, but notice that he omits "whom I serve." This is quite a bit different from Elisha's "As surely as the LORD lives," which included that phrase. Elisha's statement reflects grace but Gehazi's reflects the greed behind his god-talk. The man of God had integrity; Gehazi didn't.

Remember my saying, "When the direction of our motivation is exposed we can determine if the value of behavior is what it seems to be or not?" Unmistakably, in this passage we see the direction of Gehazi's motivation and how it differed from his behavior, which seemed right to Naaman.

Naaman had no idea that Gehazi had acted without permission. Here, the servant of Elisha manipulates a very powerful commander; a servant of God. Did you notice that? Surely he'd been around Elisha long enough to understand that no one messes with God. Even if Gehazi's past could show that he was a faithful servant, on this occasion he was twisted by possessive thinking. Clearly, there's no sense of obligation to God, his master, or anyone but himself.

So, "Mr. Slick" power-thrusted the soldier by faking sincerity. Then, with money in hand, Gehazi headed home feeling proud and secure. That was some chase he put on, wasn't it? Did you get any sense of the forbidden excitement Gehazi had in going for money that wasn't his?

Well, for twisted thinkers who are practicing an ownership attitude, just the idea of wanting something is the same as possessing it. In fact, I've heard some say, "They should have protected their stuff if they didn't want me to have it." If I were Gehazi's therapist, I have no doubt he would have said the same thing. That's because he was not unique but was just a common, ordinary, run-of-the-mill twisted thinker.

Back home, he suddenly experienced a zero state when Elisha asked, "Where have you been Gehazi?" Trying to manipulate his master through lying, he said, "Your servant didn't go anywhere." Somehow, Elisha knew what we know and we saw him lowering the boom, describing everything Gehazi did and took from Naaman. Afterwards, the prophet declared the consequences and said, "Naaman's leprosy will cling to you and your descendants forever." Immediately, Gehazi went from Elisha's presence full of leprosy, a calamity brought on by his ownership attitude—the embodiment of evil.

The lesson is before us. Whenever we see possessive thinking we must not ignore it because ruin is waiting for each twisted thinker, along with an incredible amount of damage to victims of that behavior. In this case, Gehazi's victims not only included the prophet, a soldier, a Syrian ruler, but also his descendents. It happened because he had no concept of the ownership rights of others.

There is also one other lingering area of irresponsibility for twisted thinkers that illustrates how this is true. We'll see it often when they use sex for power and control, and not intimacy.

Using Sex for Power and Control

I was sickened when reading an AP writer's report on the rape of an eight-year-old girl. The report said that a nine-year-old boy instigated and then participated in the gang rape of his younger sister. The police said the boy persuaded his sister to enter an abandoned house and "to some degree directed the activities of the others."

He also admitted to raping his sister. Seven boys, ages 6 to 13, were suspected of the attack. Two weeks passed before the attack was reported, but after questioning the seven boys police determined that the girl's brother had been involved. He was the one who told his sister not to tell their mother what had happened.

The above is another reason why I call possessive thinking the embodiment of evil. It attacks the sexuality of a person when they're being controlled as sexual objects in order to meet the demands of perpetrators. The collateral damage to everyone involved in that tragedy is beyond imagination. How sad!

Disgusting as the last account is, another media report involved a twenty-four year-old father and his five-year-old daughter. The man's ownership attitude flooded his daughter and others by a wave of shame when he posed naked with her. The reason: He wanted to launch a modeling career. The man and a female accomplice were charged with the sexual offense after they dropped the photos off to be developed at a store. The judge in the case sentenced the father to twenty years. The Assistant Prosecutor said she hoped the jury's verdict sent a message "that you don't have an absolute right to do what you want to with your children."

Child sex offenders come from all walks of life. We're learning you can't judge a person's private sexual behavior by their public behavior. Having nice clothes, a good job, and a good education has nothing to do with whether a given person is (or will be) a sex offender. Statistics revealing how much child sex offenders offend is mind-boggling. That's why treatment for offenders must involve having external control over them with limited confidentiality. This is so a spouse, family members, and others will know what to look for if the person is beginning to re-offend. Obviously, the perpetrator isn't allowed unauthorized contact with victims, and no contact with pornography.

I believe another necessary ingredient in the treatment approach should be requiring accountability for every twisted thinking pattern that supports the sexual offense. In my opinion, if that isn't done the treatment won't go deep enough because sexuality is underdeveloped in every sexual offender. They have chosen to lock themselves into an immaturity reinforced by every twisted thinking pattern in this book. They've dehumanized victims by making them objects to possess. Intimacy is a foreign concept to them, and without a responsible understanding of intimacy they'll take the easy way out when they express themselves sexually.

We need to be on guard today in places no one would have thought of years ago. Even, the churches of our land are on high alert due to the tragic molesting of children on many such premises. It has rocked our society. Churches are being advised to check for criminal records on anyone caring for children in their nurseries or Sunday schools.

However, it doesn't matter where this happens. When sex is used for power and control, it always represents someone's ownership attitude—the embodiment of evil. Let me give you another reason why I believe possessive thinking embodies evil.

Connecting with the Devil

Proverbs 28:24 says, "He who robs his father or mother and says, 'It's not wrong'—he is partner to him who destroys." The son or daughter who steals from their parents is described as a partner to him who destroys. Do you see the ownership attitude this verse reveals? To rob means the child has made an arbitrary decision to take something from the parent. Over the years, I've talked to many parents who've told me they put locks on bedroom doors to keep a son or daughter from stealing private things, including money. Can you imagine being a prisoner in your own home because a child is partner to him who destroys? It's sad, but it happens.

That phrase "he is partner to him who destroys" is another expression of the embodiment of evil. In fact, the *New Living Translation* renders it as "Robbing your parents and then saying, 'What's wrong with that?' is as serious as committing murder."

The word for destroyer in Revelation 9:11 refers to an angel coming from the bottomless pit. I find the reference to that passage very interesting when I think of what happened on 9/11 in this country. His name in Hebrew is *Abaddon* and in Greek is *Apollyon*. The implication in Proverbs 28:24, of stealing from a father or mother, is equated with being on the same team as the destroyer—Satan and his crowd. That's grave!

Clearly, possessive thinking keeps people from being humanly connected to others. How can they be when it promotes looking at things and people as objects to possess? An uncorrected ownership attitude can lead to the worst things imaginable. And, the writer of Proverbs 28 says it can happen right in our own homes. To be a victim of someone's ownership attitude is essentially to have been relationally murdered. That's why the writer said stealing from a parent is as serious as murder—murder being the ultimate act of possessive thinking.

Whether we're talking about Snoopy's level of possessive thinking, the yeast of the Pharisees, Gehazi's greed, sexual offenders, thieves in a home, or the evil our nation saw on 9/11, all these will rob humanity of dignity—even life itself. Allow me to reiterate: *The only purpose possessive thinking serves is to acquire an illegitimate, god-like power and control over others.*

Someone with an ownership attitude willfully violates personal, emotional, spiritual, sexual, or volitional boundaries. It's the lowest, darkest place "below the street" a twisted thinker can go. Therefore, we need to be more aware of the presence of this attitude in every shade of evil it assumes, from gray to black and possibly even in representations of light.

It can be very difficult to be with people who are this far below the street. Either they've been caught doing the unimaginable or it's clear that they're still viewing you and others as objects to use. Transforming their possessive thinking calls for a complete understanding of how every twisted pattern is activated and undergirds the embodiment of evil. Otherwise, even the smallest act of ownership is minimized and ignored. If that happens, it will come back to haunt relationships of the non-repenting twisted thinker. They need to understand what moving from an ownership attitude to a genuine relationship is like. How can that happen?

The Rights of Others

The first thing to emphasize is putting the accent on the rights of others. I believe God longs to preserve the dignity of mankind. That longing involves His passion to preserve the inalienable rights of others to think and make choices on their own. If twisted thinkers thought more of that—if we all thought more of that—we might get better at building relationships. When their uninvited arbitrations stop, possessive thinkers will get better at relationship building. Instead of stepping over another person's boundaries, they will be willing to honor that person's dignity.

They will also be willing to accept disappointment in their relationships and still be responsible individuals who aren't demanding satisfaction. For instance, I believe Gehazi's thought of his master going easy on the commander wasn't necessarily a wrong thought. To him, that's the way it looked and it wasn't immoral, unethical, or unspiritual to have the thought, per se. What was wrong is how he kept the thought a secret to support his irresponsible fantasy and unreal worldview. That's when he massaged his thought and developed possessive thinking. Gehazi wasn't willing both to be disappointed and to conduct a responsible relationship with Elisha, at the same time. What might it have looked like if he had been?

He could have gone to Elisha and said, "I think you blew it with the commander. We could have been set! Would you give me permission to extract some wealth from him?" A couple things would be in place if Gehazi had done so. First, he would have been open and honest, which means that, although his comments were still self-serving (as a normal sinner's can be) he would not have been hiding. And second, that means he would have been in a position to be helped.

Asking for permission would have indicated that he acknowledged an authority structure and was willing to obey it, even though he was clearly struggling with it. His relationship with Elisha would still have been respected, even if Elisha had responded by saying, "You want me to give you permission to do what? Are you nuts?"

Wouldn't that have been a revitalizing moment between the two? By being open and honest, along with being willing to be disappointed while still embracing the relationship, Gehazi could have defeated possessive thinking.

I believe that what was so refreshing about Jesus in his relationship with the disciples was how he respected them, even when they wore relational and sin issues on their sleeves. In particular, how can we not love the dynamic between Jesus and Peter? Peter put himself right out there—warts and all.

Even so, we see conflicts going on between them, and on one occasion Jesus rebuked Peter, saying, "Get behind me Satan." Just before Jesus is crucified, he says Peter will deny him three times. Many think it was Peter who, in defense of Jesus, took his sword and cut off the ear of a servant of the high priest. Now, that's a picture of uninvited arbitration! But in Luke 22:51, Jesus says, "No more of this!" And he touched the man's ear and healed him.

After the crucifixion, burial, and resurrection of Jesus, the Lord sought out Peter to reaffirm His love for him. By the seashore, He encouraged Peter to keep on growing and to serve Him as a shepherd of God's flock. Their relationship was open and honest. Peter was made of the same mud as any twisted thinker but he continued to grow and correct himself. STARs will do that.

We can see the growth in his first letter to Christians:

> Humble yourselves under God's mighty hand . . . and the God of all grace, who called you to his eternal glory in Christ, after you have suffered a little while, will himself restore you and make you strong, firm, and steadfast. To him be the power for ever and ever. (I Peter 5:6, 10)

That's a wonderful transformation of a man who had been in conflict with Jesus but still wanted to do the right thing by his Lord. If Gehazi had chosen to be as open and honest with himself and Elisha, as Peter was with Jesus, I believe he would have been restored like Peter. If he had put the emphasis on respecting the rights of others, the same grace extended to the soldier would have been there for him. God's grace is worth so much more than the stuff Gehazi wanted to extract from the Aramean, and Peter could have told him so.

But, alas, the consequences for Gehazi's thinking and behavior had to be applied, as they must be if there's to be any hope for a genuine relationship.

Applying Consequences

If a twisted thinker's possessive thinking is discovered, it helps to point out clear consequences of that thinking. If a behavior revealing any ownership attitude has been demonstrated (e.g., borrowing without permission or being abusive to others), then those consequences need to be assessed and applied. They can be redemptive, as they were for me when I played college basketball.

A tough team on our schedule was soundly trouncing us. I had lost my poise and needed to be taken out of the game. After the coach pulled me, I angrily tossed my warm-up at the bench.

Did I think doing this in front of the crowd would hurt the coach and my team? No. Did I think I owned the team and could do what I wanted if the coach disappointed me? No. The fact is, I was angry with myself for goofing up and letting the team down. So, I tossed the warm-up . . . but it was the wrong thing to do.

Although those other thoughts didn't run through my head, the decision to toss the warm-up sent the message that it did. You see, the warm-up wasn't mine because it belonged to the school. We had rules about taking care of equipment and I broke those rules. The team had a reputation for having disciplined and responsible young men. We were champions who became role models for many. On top of that, I was a senior and captain of the team. I knew I was in for some discipline after what I did, but I didn't anticipate what was coming.

The team was in the locker room, licking our wounds from the loss when my coach entered and said, "Price, you're suspended until further notice."

You know, it's a weird thing to be stunned while knowing, at the same time, that what the coach had done was right. I felt immediate shame, got dressed and went back to the dorm. I couldn't get to sleep and decided to take a chance on calling the coach in the middle of the night. He invited me over and we talked. I asked him to forgive me and he did.

Then he applied the consequence for my behavior and said, "Your suspension is for one week." That translated into a two-game suspension. He could have said four weeks but it wouldn't have mattered because a man I deeply respected forgave me.

I'm forever grateful and indebted to him for being strong enough to care for and respect me in the way he did. I have no doubt it had a big influence on how I handled David in my six-minute sports story from chapter four. I learned that consequences need to be assessed and applied for acts of ownership, or individuals practicing possessive thinking won't begin to think about changing it.

Double Standards

Another way of transforming possessive thinking is to examine and challenge a person's double standards. I don't need to dwell on this point, but suffice it to say that wherever there's a double standard it comes out of someone's ownership attitude. Double standards are used by twisted thinkers to increase the control they think they have over others. Hypocrisy is not a subject that enters their mind unless they can point out somebody else's.

Double standards promote paranoia because, instead of doing unto others as you would have them do unto you, you do unto them before you think they'll do it to you. Twisted thinkers routinely discount others, using that philosophy. If you've ever had anyone cut in front of you in a grocery line you've just been a victim of someone's double standard. It shows that the person didn't have empathy for you. If they had, you wouldn't be treated as a pole on a slalom course for their skiing pleasure. So double standards must be challenged. Doing so teaches twisted thinkers to look at situations through the eyes of their victims, which can help build up the shortfall of empathy in their lives.

Who Owns Whom?

Possessive thinking was a problem within the Corinthian church on many issues, but I want to address one in particular. It's the issue of sexual immorality, which I've already said is an expression of possessive thinking. The interesting thing about what the Apostle Paul says is how sexual immorality is not only a sin against others but also against the person's own body. In other words, their ownership attitude would be expressed somewhat like the following: "It's my body so I can do anything I want with it." Paul reminds the Corinthian believers that this wasn't true.

> Flee from sexual immorality. All other sins a man commits are outside his body, but he who sins sexually sins against his own body. Do you not know that your body is a temple of the Holy Spirit, who is in you, whom you have received from God? You are not your own; you were bought at a price. Therefore honor God with your body. (I Corinthians 6:18-20)

The question of who owns whom in Scripture is about choices. In God's love for humanity, the ability to choose or reject Him is never violated. But once man chooses Him, Paul states that the choice to belong to God results from the understanding that they've been bought with the blood of Christ. They aren't their own anymore; they're His.

I want to challenge Christians to reconsider who owns whom and what, especially when it comes to our body. I believe that fleeing from sexual immorality promotes a healthy respect for everyone. It communicates that God possesses me because I said He could, and that means I'm not to make decisions that indicate something to the contrary. To show that God possesses the Christian, Paul calls the body the *Temple of God*, the most intimate place for relationship we can have with Him. It's His place, not ours.

I believe one reason God set standards for sexual morality in the Bible was to help us determine whether we can be morally responsible or not. He has the authority to do so, because God is the creator of the heavens and the earth.

But my point is this: Even if a person's body isn't God's temple, sexual immorality is a sin that causes havoc within any community. To be sexually immoral indicates the presence of an ownership attitude. It communicates that a person is their own god, deciding for themselves and everyone else what is or isn't sexually immoral.

I can hear someone thinking, "But much of humanity continues to go down the same path. Doesn't God allow this?" Obviously He does, but God isn't for it. Nor will He support the decision should a person choose to be sexually immoral. I think His reasons for not supporting sexual immorality are profound.

First, the rules of sexual morality are God's and not ours. As Creator, He built into creation certain consequences for people who break the rules. Second, I believe God applies consequences so that our individual dignity can be preserved, along with that of the human race itself. The account of Sodom and Gomorrah reveals that truth.

Third, God applies consequences because they can be redemptive for perpetrators of sexual offenses. There's always the possibility that a perpetrator's empathy level, temporarily lost from being sexually immoral, can be built back up via the victims of their behavior. Empathy is absolutely essential if they wish to be connected to God and to others. Without it they can't stop searing their own conscience. I believe no other passage in the Bible shows this more clearly than Romans 1:18-32:

> The wrath of God is being revealed from heaven against all the godlessness and wickedness of men who suppress the truth by their wickedness, since what may be known about God is plain to them, because God has made it plain to them. For since the creation of the world God's invisible qualities—his eternal power and divine nature—have been clearly seen, being understood from what has been made, so that men are without excuse.
>
> For although they knew God, they neither glorified him as God nor gave thanks to him, but their thinking became futile and their foolish hearts were darkened. Although they claimed to be wise, they became fools and exchanged the glory of the immortal God for images made to look like mortal man and birds and animals and reptiles.
>
> Therefore God gave them over in the sinful desires of their hearts to sexual impurity for the degrading of their bodies with one another. They exchanged the truth of God for a lie, and worshiped and served created things rather than the Creator—who is forever praised. Amen.

Because of this, God gave them over to shameful lusts. Even their women exchanged natural relations for unnatural ones. In the same way the men also abandoned natural relations with women and were inflamed with lust for one another. Men committed indecent acts with other men, and received in themselves the due penalty for their perversion.

Furthermore, since they did not think it worthwhile to retain the knowledge of God, he gave them over to a depraved mind, to do what ought not to be done. They have become filled with every kind of wickedness, evil, greed and depravity. They are full of envy, murder, strife, deceit and malice. They are gossips, slanderers, God-haters, insolent, arrogant and boastful; they invent ways of doing evil; they disobey their parents; they are senseless, faithless, heartless, ruthless.

Although they know God's righteous decree that those who do such things deserve death, they not only continue to do these very things but also approve of those who practice them.

A Question . . .

For those who've struggled with sexual immorality and other manifestations of possessive thinking, I hope you will be open to the following question. It has a great deal to do with becoming a STAR and freeing you from the embodiment of evil—an ownership attitude. If you haven't already made the commitment, will you allow Jesus Christ to be Lord of your life and honor Him by offering your body as a servant of righteousness, leading to holiness?

When we are set free from sin through faith in Jesus Christ, and become His servant, the benefits we reap lead to holiness and the result is eternal life. This means that choosing to believe in Jesus guarantees a home in heaven. When that choice has been made, God applies His personal holiness to our lives. That's because He's already determined the death and resurrection of His son to be the only thing that can satisfy the question of how we can have a home in heaven. We can't become any holier than that, and His word is good for it.

However, even though we're secure within that holiness we're still stuck on this side of heaven in bodies that won't make it in eternity. We're also still sinners, for the capacity to sin is still with us. It's the truth and the Bible doesn't skirt the issue. That's why, in Romans 12, the apostle Paul encourages Christians to present their bodies as living sacrifices, holy and pleasing to God, which is our spiritual worship.

God is not asking anyone to do something His own son didn't do. Even though he was sinless, Jesus chose to surrender his life and body to the Heavenly Father, for us. I believe the cross is the only path to redemption for mankind, and I also believe that Jesus demonstrated what awaits those who make such a decision this side of heaven. Although there are many benefits leading to holy living, God provides joy through His resurrection power while we live in this world. I believe that joy helps in overcoming the impact of sin, such as twisted thinking and broken relationships. But there's also something to knowing we're just plain *growing up* and *being what we've been made to be* as image bearers of the Most High God.

So much is involved in working through the network of twisted thinking, as you well know by now. But without the Light of the World, shades of evil continue to darken the mind, eventually leading to the foolishness from which relationships are destroyed. Isn't that sad, especially when God is ready to deliver us from this embodiment of evil called possessive thinking? In the light of Christ's cross, surrendering our lives and bodies is a reasonable thing to do. But God won't violate us by giving us no choice in the matter, even though He owns the believer because of that cross. I think that's amazing and I think it's another way of Him showing us how to love well.

Chapter Fourteen

FROM DARKNESS TO DAWN

Becoming a STAR Is Possible

Remember how Jesus told Peter, in Matthew 18:22, how many times Peter was to forgive his brother? "Seventy times seven," He said.

He was teaching that if a brother/sinner keeps pursuing a genuine relationship with people they've hurt or people they owe, even if it's the four hundred ninetieth occasion, when those people forgive they are to forgive from the heart. We can see that pursuit by Abraham, Jacob, Moses, and King David, to name just a few biblical characters. All were engaged in twisted thinking at one time or another, but still worked at having a relationship with God. They were committed to struggling with themselves, and God was committed to struggling with them too. Thus He forgave them from His heart. I'm counting on that and I hope you are too.

However, I think that another lesson comes out of Peter's conversation with Jesus, and it's the following: *There's nothing wrong with having a healthy skepticism about whether someone is changing.* In Matthew 18 you'll notice that Jesus didn't rebuke Peter for his question. I think it's possible that Peter was actually frustrated with a Christian brother—maybe someone among the twelve. Perhaps he'd reached the end of his rope on whether he should go on forgiving, because a brother kept sinning against him.

I also believe it's possible that Jesus saw Peter on the brink of living by a double standard. Peter's concern was how much was enough when sinned against, but Jesus upped the ante, from seven to four hundred ninety times, to make a point. It's as if Jesus was saying, "Peter, do you think you're going to stop sinning against me, at sin number seven? What will you want from me if you don't?"

After being married forty-three years I know I've gone over the four hundred ninetieth mark with Judy, yet what I longed for from her has been granted. I believe Peter found out what he really wanted while talking with Jesus around a campfire on the beach after the resurrection.

Throughout Scripture, forgiveness wasn't extended unless certain conditions were met. I think it's a reasonable assumption to say that when Jesus talked to Peter about the subject, the basic conditions had been met to warrant forgiveness to a brother in conflict with him. Peter's bewilderment comes from being repeatedly sinned against by the brother.

What we can learn from Peter's question is that forgiving people won't necessarily guarantee that their sinful or irresponsible behaviors will stop for good. Nor do I believe that forgiveness was ever intended to be a tool to stop the behavior, even though I've heard many people imply that it is. That's why those folks don't forgive unless they have some guarantee the behavior will stop. But if they had a healthier sense of skepticism, maybe things would be different.

Healthy Skepticism—Area #1

I believe a healthy skepticism toward whether someone is truly changing has to do with two areas of concern. As with Peter, the first arises from the natural confusion of having a person in relationship with us who repeats irresponsible behaviors or sins against us.

Forgiveness doesn't mean that we ignore their behavior or its impact on us, solely because the conditions of forgiveness are met. On the contrary, it means that we don't hold a grudge against them nor become bitter, although being hurt by them was a bitter experience. In other words, we forgive from the heart as Jesus did.

So, skepticism is healthy if it's not about whether we forgive at the appropriate time, but more about how we relate to an ongoing problem of being sinned against, after forgiveness has occurred. If a twisted thinker hasn't changed behavior yet has met someone's conditions of forgiveness, the problem is elsewhere.

It could be a question of ignorance about the deeper parts of the heart, such as this book discloses. Perhaps something could be wrong medically.

Maybe past damages to themselves, from being sinned against by others, haven't been identified and handled. It's also possible that, even though they've met the conditions of forgiveness for particular behaviors, they are still secretly committed to pursuing *Big Es*.

Whatever the reason, relating to such an individual calls for wisdom in determining how to accept the manner in which they are relating to us, or even if we must. And if we don't, what do we do then?

There's nothing wrong with struggling through those issues, as long as the measure of our decision-making is redemptive in nature. We saw this in chapter nine when we talked about How God withdrew His presence from Israel so they could embrace their self-disgust and seek Him in their misery.

Knowing Jesus and being a Christian doesn't eliminate the struggles that arise when relationships are not working very well. There will be times when boundaries must be set for the sake of the other person's growth, and so that we don't get involved with a masochistic version of Christianity in which Christians beats themselves up for not doing enough for the twisted thinker. They take on personal responsibility for the twisted thinker's failure to change by emotionally and spiritually flagellating themselves. Twisted thinkers love to see to that happen, because then they don't have to be responsible for anything!

Area #2

The second area of healthy skepticism involves being with people who haven't met conditions of forgiveness. That might be due to a shallow understanding of what biblical forgiveness calls for. Or, it might be true because they don't care to have a genuine relationship, or because they are relationally incompetent because they lack the tools to build a healthy one.

Also, as always, twisted thinkers caught in irresponsible behaviors might be trying to manage their collateral damage to preserve potential *Big Es* in the future. So, rather than go through the hard work of building authentic relationships they make only minor changes in their behavior because that's easier. They become functional chameleons.

How then, do we measure whether real change is happening for them? How can the power of God fit into that change?

A friend of mine once said, "Jerry, we all like to hear about miraculous changes in the lives of twisted thinkers, such as what happened with your father. But all too often the desired changes just don't come on a sustained basis."

I responded by saying, "I'm not sure what 'sustained' means. Does it mean we don't mess up like we all have in the past? Or can it mean that no matter how much we have messed up previously—or will mess up in the future (not that we're planning on it)—we're still committed to struggling with our issues; continuing to move toward loving God and others better? If 'sustained change' means that, and we don't see it on a consistent basis, I believe we may very well be looking at the need to transform twisted thinking."

What my friend was saying was legitimate. If we're going to talk about changing twisted thinking, doesn't that mean that if behavioral changes are sustained the transformation is real? Doesn't it also mean that if behavioral changes are not sustained then the transformation isn't really happening?

My answer for the first question is "It could be but not necessarily so." And for the second question, "Not necessarily so but it could be."

This might sound like double talk until we look at the radical but biblical dynamic for change. Real change in a person's life will come not only from understanding what motivates people, but also from understanding where that motivation is going to take them.

Here, we all have a problem. Ever since the events of Genesis 3 occurred, humanity has had a strong inclination to hide from God and from others. That's why we cover up the reality of our feelings, our choices, and what we believe instead of being open, honest, and unashamed in all our relationships.

After Genesis 3, God's mandate for openness and honesty didn't change but mankind clearly did. And what we still do is to distort the mandate either by being closed, dishonest, full of shame, or all three. Whether a person is a Christian or not, I believe we're all stuck with the above inclination this side of heaven. But, a major part of being a mature person or Christian is *facing up to it . . . because none of us completely escape.*

BREAKING THROUGH DENIAL

I've mentioned that the Pharisees were trying to impress everyone with right behavior as their means of defining who they were. But they met up with a person who designed the original plan—who could see beyond the behavior into the "why" behind it. What Jesus saw was dark, for they were trying to hide the reality of self/sin.

However, because He had the capacity to forgive, Jesus directed them to what was most important if they were to return to the original mandate for relationship. He told them to look first on the inside of the cup. Isn't that a strange thing to say? It's another way of saying, "Face up to the darkness inside you."

Jesus pointed to where the miraculous really happens. Indeed—the miraculous thing about my father's change was that it happened to him *on the inside first!* Looking within, he saw the damage he'd done to my mother, my twin brother, and me coming right out of his heart and soul—a dark world.

For anyone else on this side of heaven, Jesus is saying that there's no other way to experience the dawn of a new life, and no way to transform twisted thinking unless the darkness is entered first. That's what he meant by "inside the cup," and that's what I mean about "going below the street" into an unseen world we all know.

WHERE'S THE LIGHT?

In the movie *The Abyss*, a scientist must go into the depths of the sea to disarm a nuclear bomb. The suspense is unnerving after he leaves the underwater station, but he finally locates it. However, in order to reach the bomb and defuse it he makes a decision to go farther than what his air supply will allow. His choice was heroic, but I remember thinking, "Please—not another one of these movies in which the good guy doesn't make it!"

After defusing the bomb and just before he runs out of air, the scientist saw a strange light surrounding a strange creature coming toward him. The creature took him to a place of safety on the bottom of the sea, in which the scientist could breathe and could be revitalized. He was then brought back to the surface by the creatures of light and was reunited with his friends, so everything ended well.

For me, that movie provides another metaphor for how a twisted thinker can go from darkness to dawn, transform their thinking, and become a STAR. Allow me to explain.

In John 3, Jesus says that men love darkness instead of light. This is a metaphor referring to spiritual and relational realities in every person's soul/heart. John 1 describes Jesus as light shining in darkness, but the darkness has not understood Him.

That's like saying we're the man in the abyss who doesn't understand the strange light coming toward him. He brings his own light to search for the bomb but this other light seems to have no business being there, because it's completely foreign to the darkness he's in. When Jesus talked about man loving darkness He was describing man's comfort zone as being spiritually darkened, and it's an abyss.

Whether we know it or not we're used to it. Yet every once in a while we'll develop our own spiritual lights and try to penetrate the darkness, but the Jesus light is foreign to us and seems like it has no business being there. We don't naturally understand it but the light is still there, ready to wipe out all the darkness!

Then, I John 1:5 says the following: "God is light and in him is no darkness [spiritual, relational, moral, or intellectual] at all." Spiritual darkness in the heart of humanity disconnects us from God, who *is* light! The Scripture says that darkness loves darkness. It's a way of saying that darkness won't pursue light due to its very nature.

So where can God, who is light, be found? The answer is, in the abyss of man's spiritual darkness. It's a light that seems to have no business being there, but because it's a light that penetrates spiritual darkness it makes hope available for everyone. That hope resides in seeing who God really is, as well as what matters in building a solid, lasting relationship with Him and those we love.

There was no way to do this other than by going into the darkness. God did that when He entered the human race. As in the movie, God's light can be found at the bottom of our own spiritual darkness. That's how committed He is to giving everyone hope for living, when it looks like there is none.

It's revolutionary to understand that I can be personally/spiritually alive and spend eternity in a place where there is no darkness because the light from eternity chose to enter my darkness first, to *connect with me*. Yet even then, we have the choice to reject His light/Jesus. I find that amazing!

I believe that what the Bible says about man's spiritual darkness and where we can spend eternity is also to be a model for what is true about twisted thinkers going from darkness to dawn. It shows how they can conduct responsible relationships in this world. In other words, the twisted thinker must change on the inside first, in the place of man's darkness—spiritual, relational, moral, rational. No deep or consistent change is possible until light enters the darkness of their thinking and goes straight to the bottom, where we see the embodiment of evil mentioned in the previous chapter.

Ultimately, the light of Jesus Christ can make it possible for anyone to live responsibly, forever. In Him we can breathe and be revitalized. However, this can't be done successfully without Him, especially when eternity is the issue. With Jesus as the model, what will it mean for a twisted thinker to go from their dark mind to the dawn of responsible, loving relationships. And what will it mean for you if you want to help?

Two things. First, they must be willing to go all the way into the abyss to defuse the bomb. Second, a light separate from them must penetrate their darkness, because they can't do it on their own.

Although Jesus, like no one else, gets to the place of total darkness where man can be redeemed, we can be part of that process for anyone practicing twisted thinking. This means we can be a light that willingly enters the darkness of their thinking to help give them a chance to breathe and become what He would have them be.

STARs CONCLUSION

If you identify yourself as a twisted thinker, my desire is that you're now experiencing a sense of hope by committing to going into the darkness and finding that becoming a STAR is possible. Before I finish, however, I would like to add a few last thoughts to encourage you as you move toward deep personal change. These thoughts are also intended for anyone else who wants to get involved in the transformation process.

1. Twisted thinking must be understood before it can be changed. I'm the one writing this book but I'm still learning about it. Yet I believe the basics are all here for you to grasp. Hang in there!

2. We need to distinguish between activating a twisted thinking pattern and its consequences from those of actually *being* a twisted thinker. No one on planet earth can escape triggering any one of these patterns, but not everyone is a twisted thinker committed to an irresponsible lifestyle. Either way, though, twisted thinking results in damage to relationships. This work is intended to help identify twisted thinkers, but it also explains how to address a particular pattern you may be struggling with even if you're not actually committed to twisted thinking. Hang in there!
3. Measuring repentance focuses more on changing twisted thinking first, then on changing behavior, although it's possible that both could be happening simultaneously. Even if changing the thinking isn't happening first I don't want you to believe there's anything wrong in working with twisted thinkers to change their behavior. But they will have to enter the darkness of twisted thinking to achieve deep changes that will actually last. Unless the intent of the heart of the twisted thinker has been changed, they won't become a STAR and their conscience won't be recovered. But if you're a twisted thinker who has started the process . . . hang in there!

    I believe Christians everywhere need to put an emphasis on measuring repentance—whether someone is changing or not—by holding twisted thinkers accountable for how they think. If we help build into their accountability structure a means for measuring that, it will go a long way toward telling if, in fact, they are repenting. Christian organizations struggling with having been burned by twisted thinkers will make better decisions regarding the healing of a twisted thinker before rushing in prematurely to say it has happened when it hasn't. Be patient and hang in there with them, because it will take some time for the transformation to happen. Even then, it doesn't stop until we get to heaven. Yes it's truly possible that trust can be rebuilt.
4. Whether a person is a twisted thinker or guilty of activating a twisted thinking error, they must be dealt with out of respect and redemptive love. Otherwise this book will only serve as a tool to process and manage them. It would be possessive thinking if that were the case. So, I want to encourage you to examine and assess your own heart's attitude if you decide to be a light in their darkness.

5. Throughout the book you've probably noticed how important words are when holding a person accountable for twisted thinking. They're a major key to knowing if the twisted thinker's direction is changing. Just one word can change the whole direction of where a person is going. Listening carefully for the word that reveals the motivation behind their conversation—sometimes unconsciously—will turn on more lights.

Words are powerful. After the Samaritan woman told the people in her town what Jesus had said to her, John 4:41 records these words: "And because of his words many more became believers." His words were powerful not only because He knew how to apply the appropriate ones to a given moment, and not only because He knew the needs of others, but because He spoke from the heart. People who met Him knew He was the real deal, because His words revealed it.

The difference between His convictions and those of any twisted thinker is one of production. Psalm 119:130 makes that clear: "The entrance of your words gives light; it gives understanding to the simple."

The goal of a twisted thinker is to use words for maintaining the comfort of their own dark side. Let me encourage you not to be afraid to question their use of words when those words reveal that they're heading in the wrong direction.

When we use words with twisted thinkers, in turn, we should use them as tools of redemption, pointing the twisted thinker in responsible directions in which their conscience can be recovered and they can be connected to God and to you. It's miraculous when that happens.

> Delight yourself in the LORD and he will give you the desires of your heart. Commit your way to the LORD; trust in him and he will do this: He will make your righteousness shine like the dawn, the justice of your cause like the noonday sun. (Psalms 37:4-6)

Appendix A

TWISTED THINKING DEFINITIONS

Closed Thinking
a. I am not receptive (tunnel vision—the only way is how I see things).
b. I am not self critical (emotionally vacant—I don't care how I hurt others).
c. I am not disclosing information (deliberately vague—I won't give details).
d. I'm good at pointing out and talking about the faults of others. e. I lie by omission

Martyred Thinking
a. I view myself as a victim when I'm held accountable.
b. I blame social conditions, my family, the past, and other people for what I do.

Inflated Thinking
a. I view myself only as a good person to avoid responsibility for offenses.
b. I fail to acknowledge my own destructive behavior.
c. I build myself up at the expense of others.

Stubborn Thinking
a. I won't make any effort to do things I find boring or disagreeable.
b. When I say "I can't" I'm really saying "I won't."

Reckless Thinking
a. I think living in a responsible way is unexciting and unsatisfying.
b. I have no sense of obligation but I'll get you to obligate yourself to me.
c. I'm not interested in being responsible unless I get an immediate payoff.

Impatient Thinking
a. I do not use the past as a learning tool when it gets in the way of my plans.
b. I expect others to act immediately when I demand it.
c. I make decisions based on assumptions, not the facts.

Fearful Thinking
a. I have irrational fears but refuse to admit them.
b. I have a fundamental fear of injury or death when I'm not in control.
c. I have a profound fear of being put down.
d. When I'm held accountable I feel lousy and experience a "Zero State."

Manipulative Thinking
a. I have a compelling need to be in control of others and every situation.
b. I use manipulation and deceit to get into and take control of situations.
c. I refuse to be a dependent person unless I can take advantage of it.

Arrogant Thinking
a. I think I'm different and better than others.
b. I expect out of others what I fail to deliver.
c. I'm super-optimistic because it cuts my fear of failure.
d. I will quit at the first sign of what I consider failure.

Possessive Thinking
a. I perceive all things and people as objects that belong to me.
b. I have no concept of the "ownership rights" of others.
c. I will use sex for power and control and not intimacy.

Appendix B

GOING FOR THE BIG E!

The ultimate goal of any twisted thinker's irresponsible fantasy is to pursue an unadulterated "*Big E*"—the *Excitement of the Forbidden*.

This term came out of Drs. Samenow and Yochelson's work with the criminal population in America. They discovered that every criminal they interviewed had the same goal of pursuing any brand of excitement that was forbidden. It's the proverbial drug of choice because forbidden excitement can be achieved anytime and anywhere. It's a rush! Their studies support what Augustine had already stated in *Confessions*.

I believe both examples support what the Bible calls "the cravings of sinful man, the lust of his eyes and the boasting of what he has and does" (I John 2:16). So, whether it's criminal behavior, an addictive issue, or being habitually irresponsible, excitement of the forbidden is the pursuit and that's why it's called the *Big E*.

At the same time there's nothing wrong with legitimate forms of excitement. After moving to Wisconsin in 1987 I've became a Green Bay Packers fan. In Sturgeon Bay, Wisconsin, there's a man in the church I once pastored who loves the Chicago Bears. Between us there's a lot of excitement when the Bears and Packers meet—it's about enjoying competition between friends. No one is trying to control the other, but there is excitement.

Yet the *Big E*'s promise of power and control is illegitimate because it always hurts someone or something. When someone chases it they will twist the relationship, even when other people are ignorant of what they're doing.

Something sick happens to a person when irresponsible fantasies are indulged. The Bible calls it a "searing of mind" in which tunnel vision keeps the person from thinking about what the consequences might be. Unfortunately, in searching for explanations, well-meaning people often ask questions that could alter the mug shot and hinder healing. Typical questions imply that low self-esteem or family dysfunctions are behind the twisted thinker's irresponsible behavior.

Appendix C

PULLING EVERYTHING TOGETHER

This book has put the emphasis on recognizing and transforming twisted thinking, but if you are not a twisted thinker then the book offers a way to love the twisted thinker better. In this appendix I want to provide a practical application of the bookend principles in Romans 1:18-32, for you to do just that.

Chart—Applying the Bookend Principles in Romans 1:18-32

The chart below gives a bird's eye view of how twisted thinking operates and affects the rest of the world. You'll find that closed thinking isn't mentioned because it's already linked to every other thinking error. My hope is that you will be able to understand more fully not only the need to transform twisted thinking, but also how to begin the process.

> The wrath of God is being revealed from heaven against all the godlessness and wickedness of men who suppress the truth by their wickedness, and since what may be known about God is plain to them, because God has made it plain to them. (vs. 18, 19)

Bookend Principles: Men are unreceptive; not tolerating the disagreeable/truth; pursuing *Big E*s or wickedness because responsible living is unexciting and unsatisfying, so they ignore facts and make decisions based on assumptions. The cluster is Closed—Stubborn-Reckless-Impatient Thinking.

> For since the creation of the world God's invisible qualities—his eternal power and divine nature—have been clearly seen, being understood from what has been made, so that men are without excuse. (vs. 20)

For although they knew God, they neither glorified him as God nor gave thanks to him, but their thinking became futile and their foolish hearts were darkened. Although they claimed to be wise, they became fools and exchanged the glory of the immortal God for images made to look like mortal man and birds and animals and reptiles. (vs. 21-23)

Bookend Principles: Men not being self critical; thinking they are different and better than God/others; perceiving all things and people as objects that belong to them and then having a compelling need to be in control of them and every situation. The cluster is Closed—Manipulative-Arrogant-Possessive Thinking.

Therefore God gave them over in the sinful desires of their hearts to sexual impurity for the degrading of their bodies with one another." vs. 24 (Consequences for practicing Closed and Stubborn in thinking) "They exchanged the truth of God for a lie, and worshiped and served created things rather than the Creator—who is forever praised. (vs. 25)

Bookend Principles: Men not being receptive by faulting truth for a lie; not wanting to be held accountable; not using the past as a learning tool because what they know about God gets in the way of their plans, and then deciding to manipulate their worship to stay in control of agendas. The cluster is Closed—Impatient-Zero-Manipulative Thinking.

Because of this, God gave them over to shameful lusts. Even their women exchanged natural relations for unnatural ones. (vs. 26) (Consequences for practicing Closed and Possessive Thinking)

"In the same way the men also abandoned natural relations with women and were inflamed with lust for one another. Men committed indecent acts with other men, and received in themselves the due penalty for their perversion. (vs. 27) (Consequences for practicing Closed and Possessive Thinking)

Furthermore, since they did not think it worthwhile to retain the knowledge of God, he gave them over to a depraved mind, to do what ought not to be done. They have become filled with every kind of wickedness, evil, greed and depravity. (vs. 28) (Consequences for practicing Closed—Zero-Manipulative-Arrogant thinking)

They are full of envy, murder, strife, deceit and malice. They are gossips, slanderers, God-haters, insolent, arrogant and boastful; they invent ways of doing evil; they disobey their parents; they are senseless, faithless, heartless, ruthless. Although they know God's righteous decree that those who do such things deserve death, they not only continue to do these very things but also approve of those who practice them. (vs. 29-32)

Chart: Example of bookend principles regarding some sins mentioned in verses 29-32, showing how they will be attached to a thinking error. Remember, all other thinking errors act in concert with closed thinking. Closed thinking is corrected when the twisted thinker is open to the challenge of obvious lies or apparent contradictions. We'll see the person being self-critical and telling the truth. So, at the very least, the cluster will involve the correctives for closed thinking in concert with the correctives of another thinking error (dominant or less dominant) for each sin mentioned.

Chart: Example of bookend principles regarding some sins mentioned in verses 29–32, showing how they will be attached to a thinking error. Remember, all other thinking errors act in concert with closed thinking. Closed thinking is corrected when the twisted thinker is open to the challenge of obvious lies or apparent contradictions. We'll see the person being self-critical and telling the truth. So, at the very least, the cluster will involve the correctives for closed thinking in concert with the correctives of another thinking error (dominant or less dominant) for each sin mentioned.

Sins	Twisted Thinking	Corrections
Envy	Possessive	Discover consequences for acts of ownership. See people with names and not as objects. Realize people have rights.
Murder	Manipulative	Develop empathy for others/victims.
	Arrogant	Understand that their fantasies and schemes are used to maintain a false, possessive sense of uniqueness. Develop ability to ask for help. Realize people have rights.
	Possessive	Same as corrections for Envy
Strife	Martyred	Must accept their part in creating the situation; recognize choices; recognize they are the victimizers and not the victims.
	Inflated	Make balance sheet to show good deeds don't make up for bad behavior.
Deceit	Stubborn	Identify and challenge excuses to avoid effort.
	Impatient	Examine and develop responsible goals. Make decisions based on facts and not assumptions.
	Manipulative	Must realize the way in which their quest for power is conducted and the purposes it serves. Develop empathy and understand the effect their power thrusts have on others.
Malice	Inflated	Develop a ripple effect chart to see who has been hurt.
	Fearful	Get facts and realize that feelings need not determine behavior.
	Manipulative	Same as corrections for deceit
	Possessive	Realize people have rights. Point out double standards.
Gossips	Inflated	Same as corrections for Malice and Strife
	Reckless	Distinguish between activities that are of genuine interest and those that are for point scoring, refraining from the latter.
	Arrogant	Same as corrections for Murder
	Possessive	Same as corrections for Envy, Murder, and Malice

For other sins mentioned in Romans 1:29-32, you can use the definitions for each thinking error mentioned in chapter two, the correctives already mentioned in the chart above, and the exposure of each error mentioned in each chapter dedicated to that error. If you have grasped the macro concept you should be able to do this. Give it a try and then talk it out with others, as you develop a strategy for correcting either your own thinking errors or those of others who are twisted thinkers.

Appendix D

DISCUSSION STUDY GUIDE

Chapter 1: The Same Mud

1. Lickety-split—Could you give a concrete example of the Lickety-split pattern and how it works?
2. Reflecting back on earlier years, can you recall and share times when you might have unknowingly played the game of Lickety-split?
3. Would you give an example of what Jesus said amounted to washing the outside of a cup to avoid the hard work of going to the unseen world of our hearts and minds?
4. Many Christians have grown up believing that once converted we "automatically" became "new creatures." Why or why not is this belief supported by reality?

Chapter 2: Becoming a STAR

1. In the paradise moment with Adam and Eve, the author presents questions that he said Eve would have to ask Adam. What kinds of questions would a practicing twisted thinker avoid? What questions could be self serving?
2. Can you recall a specific time when God seemed utterly invisible and you opted for tangible relief rather than using the toolbox that the author has suggested?
3. Is real and lasting change possible, apart from God? Would this process for change work for anyone who says a person can't really know if God exists? If no, why? If yes, why?
4. The author talks about feeling a sense of shame while imagining his mug shot was being taken. Although the scriptures takes a spiritual mug shot of every person, do you think most people approach Scripture while open to the impact of sin? Why or why not?

5. How can selective reading of scripture allow us to bypass the consequences of sin in our hearts when we are pursuing grace and comfort?

Chapter 3: The Transformation Process

1. As you work through the thinking pattern evaluation, did you discover things about yourself of which you were previously unaware? What were they?
2. In applying the bookend principles to twisted thinking patterns, the author stated that they are useful because there's no pressure to be exactly "right," or to make sure no mistakes are made when holding a twisted thinker accountable. How does this help you?

Chapter 4: Closed Thinking

1. The author makes a distinction between walls and boundaries. What are you hearing him say?
2. Being non-receptive plays a big part in closed thinking. Can this pattern be played out in religious cultures? If so, how? If not, why?
3. Does becoming emotionally numb happen slowly for the twisted thinker? Is it a choice at the beginning?
4. How does keeping secrets hurt family relationships?
5. The author says, "It's possible to be honest and not be open but it's impossible to be open without being honest." Do you agree? Why or why not?
6. The most "open" moment in history involved Jesus on the cross. Why was that not a weak moment even though it might have appeared to be?
7. How can our understanding of the Cross help us when we look and feel vulnerable, while being open to others?
8. What do you think is the difference between being closed and having closed thinking?

Chapter 5: Martyred Thinking

1. Can you recall a situation in which you confronted someone's thinking or behavior, and they initiated a lickety-split by shifting blame to someone else? What happened to that relationship as a result?
2. Have you ever heard someone say" "I'm not asking you to forgive me—I just want you to know I'm sorry?" What's going on with the offender in an exchange like that?
3. Can you recall times when lapsing into martyred thinking might have gotten you off the hook and disconnected?
4. What do you understand the writer is saying when he says that martyred thinking is the springboard into irresponsible behavior?
5. Although the author gives several illustrations of irresponsible behavior, would you share from your own experiences in life in which you have witnessed it?

Chapter 6: Inflated Thinking

1. Everything hangs on a person's definition of goodness. How does the biblical principle that "Any good behavior used to establish goodness" begin to deflate inflated thinking? (???)
2. People can be shocked by twisted goodness. The author gave an equation to understand how that shock develops, using the concept of going below the street. How does indulging in unseen, irresponsible fantasies play into inflated thinking?
3. How do you think it can help to realize that the concept of time and space is irrelevant to whether good behavior is seen as a genuine change for any practicing twisted thinker? (???)
4. How can inflated thinking hinder the development of empathy?
5. Why is having empathy necessary for deep change to take place with anyone practicing twisted thinking?

Chapter 7: Stubborn Thinking

1. Have you ever been confused by someone's immature behavior, even though they might have been mature in other areas of their life?
2. The author talks about several shackles of immaturity, by which stubborn thinking is reinforced, such as short cuts, lack of endurance, being connected only to self, and having grandiose standards. What is the author saying when he mentions the concept of energy vs. effort and how it plays into the above?
3. Sometimes it seems that consequences work in reverse, causing further anger and bitterness. Is it possible that this reaction can be avoided? Do you think it should be avoided at any cost? Why or why not?
4. How can developing a contract for change help the twisted thinker?

Chapter 8: Reckless Thinking

1. Sharon H. Ridge stated that before forgiveness can find its way back into the lexicon of liberation it must be linked to justice. How can God fit into the picture if an offender hasn't been brought to justice?
2. Do you think the concept of measuring one's twisted thinking is valid as an aid in determining if change is really happening for the twisted thinker? Why or why not?
3. What do you think the author means by suggesting that most twisted thinkers believe they are "nobody's sucker?"
4. How does "point scoring" hurt the process of change for any twisted thinker?
5. You've come a long way in this book—as the author says, "below the street." Are you prepared to go further? What are you hoping for?

Chapter 9: Impatient Thinking

1. In a twisted thinker's disregard for the future they might say, "This time it's going to be different." In what way does this comment

reflect infantile thinking? What can be the value of going back into a twisted thinker's past and examining unresolved behaviors?
2. The author said that Saul used the expressions "I thought" and "I felt compelled." How often have you heard someone say "I couldn't help myself" as a way of excusing their own "uncontrollable" behavior?
3. How does making assumptions hurt in building relationships?
4. Do you think it's possible for God's Spirit to transform twisted thinking without help from responsible people or others who've demonstrated the change it takes to become a STAR?

Chapter 10: Fearful Thinking

1. In this chapter the author invited you to stop and deeply reflect on the object of your hope. Does that hope put you on the road to becoming a STAR?
2. Do you think it's possible to seize the moment, devoid of hope, while still opening up the pathway to the big "E?"
3. Has you ever struggled in a relationship with a person who cut you off by becoming a "rock?" What effect did that person have on others?
4. When we hurt others, how easy is it to experience inflated thinking instead of self disgust? How important is it to embrace self disgust in the way the author explained that whole concept?
5. As you study the cycle of fearful (zero) thinking, what concrete examples for each box can you share?
6. Would you state an imaginary or real fear and then use the S.O.L.V.E. format to evaluate that fear?

Chapter 11: Manipulative Thinking

1. How can we avoid the folly of "acting or sounding spiritual" to impress others? Isn't legalism a classic example of biblical power illegitimately applied, with devastating results?
2. Think of situations where you've used a power thrust on someone. Or, when they've used on you. What's your favorite power thrust?

3. What does it mean for you to be powerful in relationships?
4. If a twisted thinker is "closed," could confrontation of an overt power thrust result in a change of style from "force-flash" to "sneak-slick?" If so, how much do we need to be cautious about early assumptions of constructive change to the twisted thinker?

Chapter 12: Arrogant Thinking

1. How does the concept of "never arriving" help in correcting arrogant thinking?
2. What is the difference between self-esteem and self-respect? How can someone with low self-respect have a high level of self-esteem? If they have low self-respect are they more likely to have low self-esteem?
3. What are some things about each person in your group that demonstrate the concept that we're all made of the same mud?

Chapter 13: Possessive Thinking

1. Are the author's comments about levels and shades of evil similar to the concept of a seared conscience?
2. Isn't the multilevel effect of evil a major flaw with a "situational ethics thinking" in which good and bad is all relevant and people can set their own boundaries apart from God?
3. Do you believe that twisted thinking accounts for the increase in incidents of sexual abuse and rape in our society?
4. Does the ownership attitude reveal a lack of empathy?
5. Since possessive thinking is a critical part of twisted thinking, it seems really important to understand how it ties into double standards. Can you give more examples?
6. In using the format of Romans 1:29-32, work through the other sins mentioned and follow the pattern of the chart to see the thinking errors and correctives to that sin issue.

Chapter 14: From Darkness to Dawn

1. What is the difference between healthy skepticism and unhealthy cynicism?
2. When the author talks about real change, what do you understand him to be saying?
3. Give an example of how one "word" can reveal motivation?
4. How scary is the concept of finding light (the Light of Jesus) in the place of darkness for you? Do you think it's worth the leap?

Appendix E

STAR ENERGIZER EVALUATION

If you would like a fuller and more complete **Evaluation of Twisted Thinking Patterns** mentioned in chapter 3, the online STAR Energizer Evaluation, created by Jerry Price, located on *www.starenergizer.com* is designed to take you further.

THE STAR ENERGIZER

The STAR Energizer stimulates people to discover who they are so they can flourish and be successful. It is neither a personality inventory nor a psychological evaluation but rather an assessment tool measuring our emotional response to the way we think about being successful.

When someone interested in relationships wants to produce at higher level corporately, personally, or spiritually, the STAR Energizer targets the place where success begins—IN THE MIND. It encourages successful thinking to promote responsible decision making. When we understand how we're thinking, we can better see where we're all headed on any life stage.

THE VALUE OF USING THE STAR ENERGIZER

Our thinking processes are a lot like getting to the summit of a mountain. Some paths can take us off course, limiting our ability to get to the top and enjoy the best view possible. By pointing toward preferred thinking patterns and success builders or relational achievement skills used to reach life's mountain tops, the STAR Energizer operates like a Global Positioning System to guide us on a track of personal growth. It also provides firsthand knowledge of unsuccessful thinking patterns and success blockers taking us off course. There are times when tough calls and transitions must be made to be responsible and successful. The Energizer's value is in increasing your confidence and competence to make those calls and thrive.

You may go to *www.starenergizer.com* to get additional questions answered and see testimonials of those who have completed the evaluation.

www.ingramcontent.com/pod-product-compliance
Lightning Source LLC
LaVergne TN
LVHW041540070426
835507LV00011B/842